GLOBAL MANGA

For Laura

Global Manga

"Japanese" Comics without Japan?

Edited by

CASEY BRIENZA
City University London, UK

ASHGATE

© Casey Brienza and the contributors 2015

All rights reserved. No part of this publication may be reproduced, stored in a retrieval system or transmitted in any form or by any means, electronic, mechanical, photocopying, recording or otherwise without the prior permission of the publisher.

Casey Brienza has asserted her right under the Copyright, Designs and Patents Act, 1988, to be identified as the editor of this work.

Published by
Ashgate Publishing Limited
Wey Court East
Union Road
Farnham
Surrey, GU9 7PT
England

Ashgate Publishing Company
110 Cherry Street
Suite 3-1
Burlington, VT 05401-3818
USA

www.ashgate.com

British Library Cataloguing in Publication Data
A catalogue record for this book is available from the British Library.

The Library of Congress has cataloged the printed edition as follows:
Brienza, Casey.
 Global Manga : "Japanese" comics without Japan? / by Casey Brienza.
   pages cm
 Includes bibliographical references and index.
   ISBN 978-1-4724-3543-9 (hardback)—ISBN 978-1-4724-3544-6 (ebook)—ISBN 978-1-4724-3545-3 (epub) 1. Comic books, strips, etc.—History and criticism. 2. Graphic novels—History and criticism. I. Title.
 PN6710.B69 2015
 741.5'9—dc23
                                                                                             2014046295

ISBN: 9781472435439 (hbk)
ISBN: 9781472435446 (ebk – PDF)
ISBN: 9781472435453 (ebk – ePUB)

Printed in the United Kingdom by Henry Ling Limited, at the Dorset Press, Dorchester, DT1 1HD

Contents

List of Figures *vii*
Notes on Contributors *ix*
Acknowledgments *xiii*
Glossary *xv*

Introduction: Manga without Japan? 1
Casey Brienza

1 The Western *Sailor Moon* Generation: North American Women and Feminine-Friendly Global Manga 23
  Magda Erik-Soussi

2 The Manga Style in Brazil 45
  Roberto Elísio dos Santos, Waldomiro Vergueiro, and Victor Wanderley Corrêa

3 *Scott Pilgrim* vs. *MANGAMAN*: Two Approaches to the Negotiation of Cultural Difference 55
  Aaron Pedinotti

4 Euromanga: Hybrid Styles and Stories in Transcultural Manga Production 75
  Nicolle Lamerichs

5 "Manga is Not Pizza": The Performance of Ethno-racial Authenticity and the Politics of American Anime and Manga Fandom in Svetlana Chmakova's *Dramacon* 95
  Casey Brienza

6 On Everyday Life: Frédéric Boilet and the Nouvelle Manga Movement 115
  Tiago Canário

7	An American Manga Artist's Journey Down a Road Less Drawn *David Blanchard*	133
8	Sporting the Gothic Look: Refashioning the Gothic Mode in German Manga Trends *Antonija Cavcic*	147
9	Constructing the Mangaverse: Narrative Patterns in Marvel's Appropriation of Manga Products *Manuel Hernández-Pérez*	167
10	Pinoy Manga in Philippine *Komiks* *Karl Ian Uy Cheng Chua and Kristine Michelle Santos*	185

Index   *201*

List of Figures

1.1	*Sparkler Monthly* online digital magazine, published by Chromatic Press. Cover illustration by rem	42
3.1	The first appearance of the Katayanagi twins. From *Scott Pilgrim vs. the Universe* (2009)	62
4.1	*Oost West* (2009). Cover illustration by Marissa Delbressine	82
4.2	Minzpyjama, "Octavian," *Lemon Law*, Volume 5 (2012, 124)	87
4.3	Anne Delseit and Sai Nan, "China Blue," *Lemon Law*, Volume 4 (2011, 37)	88
7.1	*Hitokiri Volume 1*, by David Blanchard	136
9.1	The Hulk's transcreation in Mangaverse makes an explicit reference to *tokusatsu* cinema products such as the film *Godzilla* (1954). From *Mangaverse: Eternity Twilight* (2002) © Marvel	178
9.2	Hank Pym's transcreation in Mangaverse resembles the most iconic of Akira Toriyama's characters Goku, from *Dragon Ball* (1984–95). From *Mangaverse: Eternity Twilight* (2002) © Marvel	180
10.1	Elmer Damaso, "One Day Isang Diwa," *Culture Crash*, Volume 1, Issue #6 (2001)	191
10.2	Enjelicious, "Looking for a Better Boyfriend," *Oh No! Manga* (April 2012)	196

Notes on Contributors

David Blanchard has over 13 years of experience in the global manga field. While still a student he founded his own independent studio and publishing house, Perfect Commando Productions, which over the years he has built up from an amateur operation into a business with international distribution and sales. Self-published titles include *Hitokiri* (2010) and *Éirinn Go Brách* (2013).

Casey Brienza is a sociologist specializing in the study of the culture industries and transnational cultural production. Over the past several years, her research has progressed along two parallel streams. The first of these is an investigation of the social organization and transnational influence of the culture industries, using manga publishing in the United States as a case study. The second stream is related to the digital technologies of publishing and reading which have emerged at the beginning of the twenty-first century. She joined City University London's Department of Culture and Creative Industries as Lecturer in Publishing and Digital Media in March 2013.

Tiago Canário is a Brazilian journalist with a master's degree in Communication and Contemporary Culture, focused on analysis of media products and languages. Currently, he is based in Busan, South Korea, as part of the Korean Government Scholarship Program, to do PhD research in Visual Culture. His academic interests are cinema, criticism, and graphic narrative issues related to everyday life experiences. He is part of two research groups, the Grupo de Pesquisa Recepção e Crítica da Imagem (GRIM) and the Laboratório de Análise Fílmica (Nanook), both of them in the Universidade Federal da Bahia (Ufba), Brazil.

Antonija Cavcic is a PhD candidate at Murdoch University who has lived and worked extensively in Japan. Her research interests lie in Japanese boys' love manga (BL) fandom and doujinshi practices, as well as Asian queer studies.

Karl Ian Uy Cheng Chua received his PhD from Hitotsubashi University, Tokyo in 2010. He is an Assistant Professor at the Department of History and Japanese Studies Program, Ateneo de Manila University, Philippines. He has published articles in *Philippines Studies* and book chapters in *Japan and Southeast Asia: Continuity and Change in Modern Times* (Ateneo de Manila University Press),

Controversial History Education in Asian Contexts (Routledge), and *Imagining Japan in Post-war East Asia* (Routledge).

Roberto Elísio dos Santos has a PhD in Communication, is a professor of the Postgraduate Program of Universidade Municipal de São Caetano do Sul (USCS), Brazil, vice coordinator of Comics Observatory of Universidade de São Paulo (USP), and author of several books about comics.

Magda Erik-Soussi has worked as a freelance writer and editor in the manga industry since 1999 and is credited in approximately 150 volumes of manga and prose under the pen name Lianne Sentar. She has an MSc in Chemistry from Saint Joseph College, CT and has worked as a public health researcher in biochemistry for five years. She is one of the founders of Chromatic Press.

Manuel Hernández-Pérez is a lecturer in the Catholic University of Valencia San Vicente Mártir where he teaches seminars about the relationships between psychology and media production. In 2013, he completed all postdoctoral lecturing qualifications for Information Management at the University of Murcia with the presentation of his doctoral thesis, *Cross-Media Narrative in the Context of the Japanese Entertainment Industry: Manga, Anime, and Videogames*. He has also been visiting researcher in the Université Libre de Bruxelles and the University of Edinburgh, where he has conducted research about narrative, psychology and media reception.

Nicolle Lamerichs is a lecturer and researcher at Maastricht University's Department of Literature and Arts. Nicolle has published articles in edited collections and in peer-reviewed journals such as *Transformative Works and Cultures*. She hosts workshops and panels at fan conventions to present her findings and chairs the Dutch feminist fan convention YaYCon. She is also a guest writer for popular magazines such as *Aniway* and professional blogs such as *Crossmedialog*.

Aaron Pedinotti is a doctoral student in New York University's Department of Media, Culture and Communication. His dissertation, which concerns the ontology and political implications of multi-model fictional worlds, is influenced by recent developments in continental philosophy, including Speculative Realism and the non-philosophy of Francois Laruelle, as well as by phenomenology and the Frankfurt School. He has published work in the peer-reviewed journal *Communication + 1* and in the inaugural volume of *O-Zone: A Journal of Object Oriented Studies*.

NOTES ON CONTRIBUTORS

Kristine Michelle Santos is currently a postgraduate student in the School of Humanities and Social Inquiry at the University of Wollongong. Her current areas of study are gender, girls' culture, popular culture, and Japanese studies. Her dissertation looks at the rich history of Japanese girls' culture and their involvement in fan activities, particularly in the production of fan works such as doujinshi.

Waldomiro Vergueiro is Professor in Communication Sciences at the Escola de Comunicações e Artes of Universidade de São Paulo, Brazil. He is the founder and coordinator of the Comics Observatory of the Universidade de São Paulo, the most important research center on comics in Latin America, and the author of several books about comics.

Victor Wanderley Corrêa has a master's degree in Communication in the Postgraduate Program of Universidade Municipal de São Caetano do Sul (USCS), Brazil.

Acknowledgments

"All artistic work, like all human activity, involves the joint activity of a number, often a large number, of people," and edited collections are hardly any exception to Howard Becker's classic sociological insight from *Art Worlds*. I owe a debt of gratitude to the many individuals and institutions that have supported this research on global manga.

First thanks must go to John Thompson, who expressed enthusiasm for my work in its earliest stages, only a few weeks after I'd started an MA program at NYU, and eventually agreed to take me on as his PhD student supervisee in Cambridge. This book may be thought of as an outgrowth of—and logical next step from—my doctoral thesis. None of it would have been possible without you.

It is true, though, that research can feel like traveling down a very lonely road. What ever would I have done without my fellow Cambridge "survivors" Ozan Aşık, Charlie Barlow, Nick Boston, Rosamund Conroy, Beth Grace, Jonathan Ong, Tomas Undurraga, Peter Walsh, Monica Wirz, Dominic Yeo, and the rest of the PPSIS PhD students to share it?

I am also profoundly grateful to Trinity College, Cambridge and the Alumnae Association of Mount Holyoke College for their generous financing of my studies and fieldwork and to the Department of Sociology at Rutgers University for hosting me as a Visiting Scholar in the 2010–11 academic year. In particular, I'd like to thank Karen Cerulo, Paul McLean, and Ann Mische for their hospitality.

The planning for this collection began shortly after I joined the Department of Culture and Creative Industries at City University London. Sincerest thanks to my new departmental colleagues Debbie Dickinson, Cecilia Dinardi, Ana Gaio, Rosalind Gill, Jo Littler, Andy Pratt, and Marisol Sandoval for their welcoming support and friendship throughout a period of painful professional uncertainty and transition. Toby Miller and Dave O'Brien, who have since left us to take up posts elsewhere, also have my gratitude. In addition, I have benefited from exchanges with Rachel Cohen, Sam Friedman, David Haynes, Malcolm James, Dan Mercea, Ernesto Priego, Lyn Robinson, and Chris Rojek. Above all, however, is the profound debt I owe to Keith Simpson, who pushed himself past his own reasonable limits during the final weeks and months so that I too might hope to exceed mine.

Neil Jordan of Ashgate has been a big supporter of sociological perspectives on comics and manga. He first approached me ahead of the annual conference of the British Sociological Association back in 2011, and his unwavering faith in the value of such perspectives—even in the face of my many, albeit inevitable, inconstancies—is in itself invaluable. I also really appreciate the comments on this proposal provided by Jaqueline Berndt and Toni Johnson-Woods, both of whom cheerfully parted the veil of anonymous peer review so that I might get to know them. The final manuscript strives to incorporate their helpful feedback.

Comics scholars in the United Kingdom are easily among the most collegial academic communities in the world. Thank you to Martin Barker, Will Grady, Paul Gravett, Simon Grennan, Ian Hague, Paddy Johnston, Sarah Lightman, Anna Madill, Nina Mickwitz, Chris Murray, Joan Ormond, Julia Round, Roger Sabin, Dan Smith, Nicola Streeten, Tony Venezia, Paul Williams, and Sarah Zaidan for being a home away from home.

Many thanks as well to Daniel Allington, Glynn Anderson, Melissa Aronczyk, Robert Baensch, Anne Barron, Ele Belfiore, Rod Benson, Gurminder Bhambra, Debbie Borisoff, Eve Bottando, Mary Churchill, Clayton Childress, Maureen Donovan, Shai Dromi, Brooke Duffy, Shinsuke Eguchi, Christian Fuchs, Ian Gadd, Katrina Gulliver, Maggie Hames, John Holmwood, Ron Jacobs, Susan Jacobson, Ben Kafka, Jean Khalfa, Mikhail Koulikov, John Laprise, Xinghua Li, Zhan Li, Andrew Lindner, Janet Lorenzen, Neda Maghbouleh, Marianne Martens, Laura Miller, Dhiraj Murthy, Bobby Nayyar, Naoko Nemoto, Gary O'Brien, Fusami Ogi, Gloria Oh, Penn Pantumsinchai, Devon Powers, Jillian Powers, Andrea Press, Matthias Revers, Danielle Rich, Adrienne Shaw, Aram Sinnreich, Bev Skeggs, Deirdre Sumpter, Mary Taylor, Eleanor Townsley, S. Courtney Walton, Junhow Wei, Yoke-Sum Wong, Guobin Yang, Shujiro Yazawa, Elizabeth Young, Nancy Yuen, and Lin Zhang for having shared in this long and circuitous journey. There are surely others whom I've forgotten; even if you are not on this page, rest assured that your names are, each and every one of them, inscribed on my heart.

My family is deserving of an extra-special mention for their years of tolerance of my unorthodox career path. We take a long time to become who we are.

Last but certainly not least, I wish to extend a gigantic thank you to the 12 contributors to this collection. As intellectuals and industry practitioners, you are at the cutting edge of one of the most exciting new areas of inquiry in the study of global and transnational cultures. I am delighted and honored to have had the opportunity to collaborate with all of you in the production of *Global Manga*. Any errors which remain are, of course, my own.

Glossary

Anime (Japanese) — Short for "animation." Japanese animation
Bande dessinée/BD (French) — Franco-Belgian comic books
Boys' love/BL (Japanese) — Genre of manga focusing on male/male homoerotic romance for women
Circle (Japanese) — Doujinshi publishing group, which may consist of one, two, or more individuals
Cosplay (Japanese) — Short for "costume play." Fan practice of dressing up as and role-playing favorite characters
Doujinshi (Japanese) — Literally "same-person-publication." Self-published materials, often comics
Dz-manga (Algerian) — Global manga from Algeria
Fansub (English) — Pirated episodes of anime subtitled by fans
Fujoshi (Japanese) — Literally "rotten girl." A fangirl, particularly focused on BL and yaoi
Gekiga (Japanese) — Literally "dramatic pictures." Japanese comics for adult men, published primarily in the 1950s to 1970s. Coined by Yoshihiro Tatsumi
Gothic Lolita (Japanese) — A style of fashion, predominantly for women, incorporating both Gothic and ornate, Victorian elements
Josei (Japanese) — Genre of manga for women
Kaiju (Japanese) — A genre (usually live-action film) featuring monsters
Kodomo (Japanese) — Genre of manga for young children
Komiks (Filipino) — Comics from the Philippines
Ladies (Japanese) — Genre of manga for women, often assumed to be more focused on sexualized romance themes than josei
Lolicon (Japanese) — Short for "Lolita Complex." A genre, usually for men, featuring underage girls in sexual situations
Mangaka (Japanese) — Manga artist
Manhua (Chinese) — Comics from China, Hong Kong

Manhwa (Korean)	Comics from Korea
Mecha (Japanese)	Short for "mechanical." A genre featuring giant robots
Moé (Japanese)	Short for "moeru [to bud; to burn]." Refers to super-cute character designs (and properties which feature them), typically intended for male otaku
Nouvelle Manga (French)	Literally "New Manga." Term for a genre of comics focused on everyday life. Coined by Frédéric Boilet
Otaku (Japanese)	Literally "your household." An obsessed fan, stereotypically male and socially awkward
Scanlation (English)	Pirated digital copies of manga pages translated by fans
Seinen (Japanese)	Genre of manga for young men
Shotacon (Japanese)	Short for "Shotarou Complex." A genre, either for men or for women, featuring underage boys in sexual situations
Shoujo (Japanese)	Genre of manga for girls
Shounen (Japanese)	Genre of manga for boys
Shounen ai (Japanese)	Subgenre of shoujo manga from the 1970s featuring schoolboys in tragic, homoerotic relationships
Tankoubon (Japanese)	Collected editions of manga
Yaoi (Japanese)	Short for "yama nashi, ochi nashi, imi nashi [no peak, no denouement, no meaning]." Male/male homoerotic fiction. Typically refers to fanfiction in Japan but may be used in place of BL elsewhere
Yonkoma (Japanese)	Literally "four panels." Four-panel comic strips
Yuri (Japanese)	Literally "lily." Genre of lesbian manga, either for men or for women

Introduction
Manga without Japan?

Casey Brienza

The germ of the idea for the book you are now holding in your hands took root at precisely the point my fieldwork in the American manga publishing industry had reached its conclusion. This was in the early autumn of 2011, and the industry was just beginning to emerge from the wreckage of the financial crisis. North American sales, which peaked at an estimate $210 million in 2007, had since dropped by half, to $105 million, according to the independent research firm ICv2. More than a half-dozen publishing houses, including Tokyopop, the Los Angeles-based independent that had kicked off the manga boom a decade ago, did not survive. The publishing arms of anime companies ADV and Bandai were also gone. So were the US subsidiaries of Japanese companies such as Aurora Publishing and Broccoli. CMX, the manga imprint of DC Comics, was abruptly shuttered. And even Go! Comi, another West Coast indie press specializing in shoujo manga, had left the scene. The largest players left standing included Viz Media and Kodansha Comics, which together represented the American activities of Japan's three largest manga publishers, Shueisha, Shogakukan, and Kodansha, and Yen Press, the main manga and graphic novel imprint of Hachette USA. Of the remaining independents, the largest was Digital Manga, which from the earliest days of its founding had become known for publishing boys' love manga.

Yet despite a field newly cleared of quite a lot of the competition, my informants were anything but optimistic. Some were worried that the bestselling Japanese properties like *Fruits Basket* and *Naruto* of the first decade of the twenty-first century were an artefact of history and that, creatively, Japan was tapped out for new material. Of course, this is a subjective assessment, endlessly debatable, but in a way it can also become a self-fulfilling prophecy. And arguably more important, in any case, were the ways in which they were reluctantly starting the process of coming to grips with new anxieties about their future in the wider trade publishing industry. The Amazon Kindle, which first debuted in 2007, had turned e-books for the very first time into a market category to be reckoned with, and manga publishers were scrambling to find new models of publishing and distribution to help them cope with this new digital environment—and the ways in which a vast ocean of online piracy which predated the manga boom and had only swelled in tandem with it would be likely to challenge them in new ways. How does one sell manga as e-books when they are all already available for free as scanlations?

The answer to this question seemed, in a fundamental way, so obvious that it might be all too easily overlooked: Sometimes the most rational response to radical new uncertainties is to go right back to the basics. And this is precisely what the American manga publishing industry seems to have decided—each company on its own terms—to do. Why wait impatiently for the next big hit from Japan? Why bother trying to compete with "free"? Sometimes it really is just easier to do it yourself and commission and make your own. By now, an entire generation of young Americans had come of age on a diet of Japanese manga, and some craved an opportunity to make their own. From conception to finish, no one from Japan even need be involved. By the end of 2011, all of the US manga publishers left standing, with the exception of Kodansha Comics,[1] had either published—or were planning to publish—original manga. Tokyopop, which had famously pioneered so-called Original English-Language (or OEL) manga, would, in its own way, live on through the promulgation of this practice and the newfound creative opportunities for its already experienced and market-tested artists who had published with them.

Furthermore, from my perspective as a sociologist keen to map out this transnational field of cultural production, the push toward original manga was particularly notable. It would, as a matter of fact, have been notable on its own terms, even if my informants had not chosen to highlight it in their interactions with me. But in actuality, some of them *had* highlighted it in their interactions with me, and those who did were often among the most experienced and well-regarded professionals in their field. In one particularly poignant moment, for example, a manga editor who had invited me into her home pulled a book proudly off the bookcase in her living room and said, "This was one of my proudest moments." The volume in question was the Japanese-language edition of an original American title, one of the first original manga that this woman, the series' editor, had ever worked on in her career. Though already several years old, her copy's dust jacket had not yet lost that distinctive, hot-off-the-press shine; this book had only rarely been exposed to the open air, and it was clearly very precious. Yet until that moment, I had not known that this original manga first commissioned and published in the United States had also been

---

1 In terms of publishing titles licensed from Japan, the Kodansha Comics imprint was the successor to Random House's Del Rey Manga, which had previously published several original manga, including the Eisner Award-winning *Yōkaiden* by Nina Matsumoto. Del Rey continues to publish works in this vein, most notably manga based upon Dean Koontz's Odd Thomas series of young adult novels, illustrated by Queenie Chan.

INTRODUCTION

released in Japan; I'd had no idea that this book I was holding in my hands even existed in the first place.

That brief moment, flipping reverently through a comic book taken down from its place of pride in this woman's apartment, was telling. Many of the Japanese titles she had edited had been bestsellers in the United States for her company. This original manga had, in fact, been a bestseller too—important evidence to all in the field that "manga" which had not come from Japan had the potential to be profitable. Indeed, her work had been instrumental in supporting her company's entire publishing program, and her professional reputation in the field had been built upon this record of success. Yet that was not the part of her career she wished to highlight. Instead, this editor wanted to show me physical evidence of the directionality of the transnational field being put in reverse, an instance where the American was made to become Japanese.

Only a few weeks after that interaction, I returned to Cambridge and began to write up my research. It, along with many other encounters with this editor's colleagues throughout the field, became the basis for my decision to conceptualize transnational cultural production as "domestication." Thus, when a Japanese manga is published in English in the United States, it may be said to have become "domesticated." The *Oxford English Dictionary* provides the following four-part definition for the verb, "to domesticate":

1. *trans.* a. To make, or settle as, a member of a household; to cause to be at home; to naturalize.
    b. *transf.* and *Figure* To make to be or to feel 'at home'; to familiarize.
2. To make domestic; to attach to home and its duties.
3. To accustom (an animal) to live under the care and near the habitations of man; to tame or bring under control; *transf.* to civilize.
4. *intr.* (for *refl.*) To live familiarly or at home (*with*); to take up one's abode. *Obs.*

This definition points to the term's many advantages as a make-ready yet precise concept capturing a greater range of social activity than more limited terminology such as "translation," "adaptation," "intermediation," or "localization." As a verb, domestication may signify both action and ongoing state of being, which allows me to discuss it in terms of both the production of new social practice and its maintenance across time and space. It is also transitive, which means that one can domesticate as well as be domesticated, and the sense in which humans exert their will on plants and other animals in order to domesticate them for specific instrumental ends allows me to think about asymmetrical configurations of power, the manifestations of deliberate force, and the desire to control. This is a causative construction (i.e. made to domesticate or made to be domesticated). Naturally, it may also be used reflexively (i.e. domesticating oneself). And crucially, domestication, unlike localization, need not be a unidirectional process. One can be simultaneously domesticating the object, oneself, *and* the nation of origin. Lastly—but certainly not least, in my view—the word is aesthetically and intuitively pleasing; domestication is linked to the home, and publishing companies are often referred to as "publishing houses" or, colloquially, just "houses." The home, furthermore, is stereotypically thought of as being the domain of women, and manga as a category of books has become feminized in terms of its content, as well as its target readership and production (Brienza 2011; Prough 2011).

In any case, this is not the place to fully develop domestication as a theoretical concept, but for my purposes here the most important thing to note is that original manga as a sociological and cultural phenomenon was, in my view, inexorably linked to the domestication of Japanese manga in the United States. Nor was it, fundamentally, historically-specific or in any other manner unique to this particular transnational field. If my findings were correct, then the domestication of manga would always inevitably lead to the production of original manga which did not involve the direct creative or financial input of anybody Japanese.

Defining Global Manga

And this does indeed appear to be the case. Yet there has been, to date, a relative dearth of research on this topic. Perhaps that is because even manga fans often have trouble taking these works seriously; some would dismiss it as "fake manga," as pale imitations of their Japanese counterparts, unworthy of attention from readers, let alone researchers. In fact, there is no one universally agreed upon name for these works; appellations applied in the English language alone include OEL manga, world manga, Amerimanga, and international manga. Following earlier writing on Felipe Smith's *MBQ* and *Peepo Choo* (Brienza 2013), however, I have settled on the term "global manga" as the most flexible and semiotically open possibility. By global manga, I am emphatically *not* referring to Japanese manga published in translation or manga which has been physically exported from Japan.[2] I am referring, rather, to the published sequential art products of a sometimes globalized, sometimes transnational, sometimes hyperlocal world in which something its producers and consumers might call "manga" can be produced without any direct creative input at all from Japan.

---

2 The phrase "global manga" has previously been used elsewhere to signify both the globalization and cultural flow of Japanese manga (e.g. Bouissou 2008) as well as international scholarship on Japanese manga (e.g. Berndt 2010, 2011). Neither of these senses are primarily intended here.

INTRODUCTION

Superficially speaking, this definition of global manga seems straightforward enough. But what do I really mean by "without any direct creative input"? By this I intend to distinguish between the symbolic and stylistic appropriation, borrowing, and/or reinterpretation, both intentional and unintentional, which occur when- and wherever there is creative production, and *actual* economic and/or labor inputs into that production. This distinction is particularly important in light of academic and policy debates about the role of popular culture in other spheres of public life, such as the economy and politics. The Japanese government's response to Douglas McGray's article on "Japan's Gross National Cool" for *Foreign Policy* and its subsequent promotion abroad of cultural goods such as manga, anime, music, and fashion, has been much discussed in the literature (e.g. Brienza 2014; Otmazgin 2012; Sugiura 2008; Valaskivi 2013). Unfortunately, it is extremely difficult to trace a direct, empirical line connecting cultural appeal to tangible benefit for Japan or the Japanese; soft power is impossible to measure definitively, and certainly McGray's view that Japanese cultural appeal abroad must be coupled with an infusion of sympathetic foreign talent into Japan's domestic labor force has, given resistance to any immigration reform in the face of slow-motion demographic disaster, been conveniently lost in translation. One may therefore understand global manga as a medium which has incorporated requisite cultural meanings and practices from Japanese manga but does not otherwise require any Japanese individual or collective entity in a material, productive capacity. Global manga may well be evidence of Japan's Gross National Cool, if that is to be accepted as a valid unit of analysis, but it is not obviously contributing directly to Japan's GDP.

Of course, as Felipe Smith's career in manga would indicate, there are boundary cases. A rigorous reading of my definition would mean that *MBQ*, first published by Tokyopop, counts as a global manga, whereas *Peepo Choo*, first published by Kodansha, does not. Indeed, one might argue, Smith, who emigrated from the United States to Japan in order to produce *Peepo Choo*, exists as a living, breathing example of what McGray really intended for the future of the Japanese cultural economy when he wrote "Japan's Gross National Cool." Smith does continue to be, however, an exception to the rule; the proportion of non-Japanese manga artists breaking into the Japanese industry remains vanishingly small, and most of those are from South Korea. Perhaps the most prominent Koreans are the writer/artist team In-wan Youn and Kyung-il Yang, best known for *Shin Angyou Onshi* [Blade of the Phantom Master] and *Defense Devil*, both published by Shogakukan. Youn and Yang have also had success in Korean manhwa publishing. Another Korean artist writing under the pen name Boichi, like Smith, relocated to Japan in order to work on the ongoing manga series *Sun-Ken Rock*.

Slightly more common are Japanese artists finding career opportunities in manga and other related fields of graphic design outside of Japan. However, it is quite rare, though not entirely unheard of, for such artists to publish properly "original" work in countries such as the United States and France. More often, they are illustrating scripts by non-Japanese writers; a particularly prominent example is the *Princess Ai* series, which is written by Tokyopop founder Stu Levy (under the pen name DJ Milky) and illustrated by Misaho Kujiradou. The first three volumes of *Princess Ai* were published simultaneously in Japan and North America, and in Japan chapters were serialized in Shinshokan's manga magazine *Wings*. Another example is Chuck Austen's *Boys of Summer*, illustrated by Hiroki Otsuka and published by Tokyopop. Whether or not these boundary cases "count" as global manga I would leave to each reader's own discretion, but my personal inclination would be to say that they count. Regardless, for analytical purposes it is worth noting that much of the material published by American companies constitutes work for hire, with the Japanese artist ranking very much as the junior partner in the endeavor, and given the preoccupation with debates about soft power and who stands to benefit as a consequence of these transnational organizational processes and cultural flows, this is not, in my view, an insignificant factor. This is, rather, what domestication is all about.

What Is "Manga"?

Before proceeding further with any in-depth description and analysis of global manga proper, however, it is important to establish an understanding of what precisely is meant by the word "manga." This must be addressed in some detail. The word originates from the Japanese compound reading of the two Chinese characters 漫画, meaning "random" or "irresponsible" and "picture," respectively. While the earliest recorded usage of the word dates back to the 1770s, it did not acquire its modern sense until the early part of the 1900s with Japan's exposure to and emulation of Western forms of cartoon art (Shimizu 1991). Today, "manga" may be written in any of the four scripts (hiragana, katakana, kanji, or romaji) of modern Japanese and commonly refers to any sort of comic book or strip, or printed cartoon.

Manga is big business in its country of origin. Approximately one out of every four books now sold in Japan is a volume of manga (Pink 2007), and this enduring popularity with audiences of all ages and both genders traces its history[3] back to the period immediately following the second World War. A cheap medium of entertainment sold primarily to children became a site of visual and narrative experimentation by manga artists such as Osamu Tezuka as well as an outlet for anti-establishment social and political commentary in the mid-1900s. The market continued to expand throughout the postwar years,

---

3   For an in-depth treatment of the history of manga in Japan, see Isao Shimizu (1991) or Frederik L. Schodt (1983).

and by the late twentieth century, manga had become thoroughly mainstream, a medium of communication and expression available everywhere and about, potentially, anything (Kinsella 2000).

Despite this diversity, some gross generalizations about content can be made. An astute observer entering the manga section of a Japanese bookstore will notice that all of the books are arranged first by the gender and age of the target audience, then by publisher, then by imprint, and finally alphabetized by author surname and title. This arrangement represents the ranked priorities of manga publishing in Japan, and the gendering of manga genres is central. While there certainly are, say, horror manga, action adventure manga, and mystery manga, these content-based genres are not as important as those which explicitly identify the gender and age of the target audience. The latter include shounen (for boys), shoujo (for girls), seinen (for men), kodomo (for very young children of both genders), and josei or ladies (for women). Some genres, even when implying a unity of content, are implicitly gendered; the most important examples in this vein include boys' love (for women) and moé (for men).

When used by English language speakers, the word "manga" typically refers to "story manga," a format telling a continuous story over a large number of pages and often serialized.[4] It also connotes certain stereotypes about specific types of narrative and artistic content such as character designs with big eyes, graphic, sexualized violence, and/or science fiction and fantasy themes. In practice, however, the bestselling titles in the United States and, indeed, around the world, nearly always conform to one of more of these aforementioned stereotypical characteristics. Even so, the American manga industry itself defines manga rather differently. On one level, a "manga" is any comic first published in Japan, irrespective of format or genre, but on another level it can be, quite simply, anything a publisher says it is. The industry definition of manga, as has been elsewhere argued (Brienza 2009; Brienza 2011), evolved to have less to do with visual style or content or country of origin and more about the presentation of the book as a mass-produced commercial object and the intended target audience. In the most extreme cases, manga is simply a comic book of a particular trim size and price point that girls and women would be expected to read. Whether or not

---

4 Some English speakers in the United Kingdom also use the word "manga" to refer to animated cartoons for television, video, or film from Japan. The confusion originates from a marketing campaign in the 1980s by the anime company Manga Entertainment to rebrand what the Japanese call "anime" as "manga," which was deemed easier to pronounce. As this usage is no longer common in Japanese or accepted in other parts of the English-speaking world, I use "manga" exclusively for the printed medium.

it is from Japan is of secondary importance.[5] If this sounds vague that is because, quite simply, it is, and a rigorous, universally agreed upon definition does not exist among industry professionals themselves, and it is within precisely this sort of space of definitional ambiguity that what I have termed "global manga" begins to take root as a categorical cultural product in its own right.

Locating the Cultural Production of Global Manga

If global manga is to be defined as the "the published sequential art products of a sometimes globalized, sometimes transnational, sometimes hyperlocal world in which something its producers and consumers call 'manga' can be produced without any direct creative input at all from Japan," then there is a complex methodological question which arises from this definition: Where is the cultural production of global manga located? On one level, it makes sense to think about global manga in terms of its nation or region of origin. Indeed, in my own research, I refer to the American manga publishing industry as a transnational field of cultural production—and unlike other fields of trade publishing in the United States which might properly be thought of as "Anglo-American" (see Thompson 2010), manga, I would argue, is genuinely centered on and oriented toward the US and to a lesser extent Canada, with Australia, New Zealand, and the United Kingdom as, for virtually all practical purposes, secondary export markets. And so, for the purposes of *Global Manga* as well, that is the conceptualization used throughout.[6] This section provides an overview of global manga in 1) Asia, 2) the Americas, 3) Europe, and 4) Africa and the Middle East, respectively.

Asia

Intra-Asian cultural flows do not necessarily operate according to the same logic as cultural flows between other regions (Iwabuchi 2002), so it surely comes

---

5   See Brienza (2014) for a discussion of the origin and development of "original manga" and Brienza (2013), along with Chapters 1, 3, 5, and 7 of this volume, for in-depth analysis of representative examples of this medium.

6   This categorization is purely a pragmatic one; it is not theoretically or empirically supported and therefore must not be accepted uncritically. As noted in my definition, global manga can be a "global," "transnational," or even "hyperlocal" product. Take, for example, the *Twilight* graphic novels released by Yen Press. Based upon young adult novels by an American author and published by Hachette USA, the graphic novels are illustrated by a Korean artist who uses visual conventions from Japanese manga. On this basis, these books are clearly global manga, but are they American, Korean, both, or neither?

as no surprise that the history of global manga production in Asia is by far the longest and richest of any region. This is particularly the case in countries such as Taiwan and Korea, where there are enduring cultural connections to Japan, due to Japan's colonial ambitions in the region prior to World War II. The manga publishing industries in these two countries date to the 1950s with unauthorized releases of Japanese titles and, over time, developed into locally produced original titles. Although relatively little has been written on the phenomenon in Taiwan,[7] the scholarly literature on Korean comics, called *manhwa*, has recently become particularly rich and well-developed. Chie Yamanaka (2006; 2013) has written some of the most important historical overviews of this field, focusing both on Korea's long and quite sophisticated industrial production of unauthorized Japanese manga and the preoccupation, in light of the growing number of Korean-produced titles, with identifying *manhwa*'s national distinctiveness. Otherwise, with the exception of one study of *gekiga*-like *manhwa* from the 1970s (Leem 2011), most of the work on contemporary Korean comics has focused on *sunjeong* [girls] titles (e.g. Choo 2010; Noh 2004; Yoo 2012; Yoon 2002). The 27-volume *sunjeong manhwa* series *Goong* [Castle] by So-Hee Park, which ran from 2002 to 2012, has attracted particular interest, perhaps because of the political implications of its alternate-universe setting where there is still, in the contemporary period, a Korean royal family and because it has been translated for publication in both Japan (by Shinshokan) and the United States (by Yen Press). As Kukhee Choo (2010, 6.13) observes, *Goong* "provokes nationalism among Korean readers and ambivalence among Japanese readers, and functions as a political text within both cultures."

There is a long and important tradition of *manhua* in Hong Kong, with action and martial arts-themed stories dominating the industry in the 1980s and early 1990s. Wai-ming Ng (2003) argues that there are Japanese elements in the history, art, and industry of these *manhua*. Comics for girls were far rarer, and with the exception of the now-nostalgic *Ms. 13-Dot*, Wendy Siuyi Wong (2010) claims that material locally produced in Hong Kong is too weak to compete with ubiquitous Chinese-language translations of Japanese manga. Other parts of mainland China, in contrast, have gotten into manga much more recently, post-economic liberalization. As in other regions, the subject of boys' love in China has thus far garnered the most attention (Chao 2013; Xu and Yang 2013). Yanrui Xu and Ling Yang (2013) argue that BL with father-son incest themes are a particular feature of the genre in China because, under Confucianism,

---

7 A few exceptions include Chen and Hsu (2013), Lent (1999, 2010a), and Tseng and Tsai (2010). The first two volumes of a Taiwanese manga series by Yu-Chin Lin were published in English translation by DramaQueen in 2006 as *Vision of the Other Side*. These are now out of print.

family structure sits at the core of the organization of power in society and is therefore subject to eroticization.

The countries of Southeast Asia, including Indonesia, Malaysia, the Philippines, and Singapore, have their own vibrant cultures of global manga. Ng (2000) argues that Southeast Asia came into contact with Japanese manga not directly but rather through the mediation of Hong Kong and Taiwan; this mirrors Koichi Iwabuchi's (2004)' argument that Japanese culture industries require American partners in order to disseminate popular culture to other Western countries. As such, global manga does not have as long a history in these Asian countries as others. Yet there is nevertheless considerable productivity. The Malaysian Benny Wong, for example, won an International Manga Award for *Le.Gardenie* (Tai 2007). And Indonesia, despite the religious conservatism of Islam, has a thriving amateur BL subculture (Abraham 2010). Chapter 10 of this book provides fascinating insight into the relationship between global manga in the Philippines, called Pinoy manga, and the country's tradition in *komiks*. Apart from infrequent interventions such as these, however, global manga from Southeast Asia continues to be under-researched.

The Americas

Brazil is home to the largest Japanese ethnic community outside Japan in the world, and, according to the chapter on "The Manga Style in Brazil" contributed by Roberto Elísio dos Santos, Waldomiro Vergueiro, and Victor Wanderley Corrêa, that country's tradition in global manga dates to the 1960s—almost as old, in other words, as the modern manga publishing industry in Japan itself. Other Latin American countries, most notably Peru and Argentina, also have significant populations descended from Japanese immigrants. However, research on comics in any style or tradition in Latin America continue to be rare even in the twenty-first century (Lent 2010b), and there are undoubtedly fascinating studies yet to be conducted and articles yet to be written on Latin American manga.

An overview of the North American global manga (sometimes also known as OEL manga or Amerimanga) scene is provided in Chapter 5, so I will not rehearse that here. Published scholarship on the topic is, however, quite limited, in spite of the continued political, cultural, and linguistic dominance of the United States. Exceptions include Dru Pagliassotti (2009), who has written about the production of "GloBL" manga, and my previously published chapter about Felipe Smith for the anthology *Black Comics* (Brienza 2013). Therefore, *Global Manga* ought to make a significant contribution to the understanding of original manga in North America through its close readings of *Scott Pilgrim* and *MANGAMAN* in Chapter 3, *Dramcon* in Chapter 5, and Marvel's Mangaverse in Chapter 9. The richly described first-person accounts from two founders of global manga indie presses, Chromatic Press in Chapter 1 and Perfect Commando Productions in Chapter 7, will likewise surely be invaluable.

It is worth noting that Australia and New Zealand, though technically in the Asian-Pacific region, may be seen as an extension of the production and consumption of global manga in North America, due to the dominance of the English language there. The same, to a lesser degree, might be said of South Africa. Indeed, the professional OEL manga artists from Australia identified and discussed by Jason Bainbridge and Craig Norris (2010), Queenie Chan (*The Dreaming*) and Madeline Rosca (*Hollow Fields*), were in fact published by North American manga houses, Tokyopop/Del Rey Manga and Seven Seas, respectively.

Europe

Increased rationalization of territorial rights to Japanese manga translated into any one language has increased integration among all of the English-speaking countries. This means, in practice, that the manga made available for sale in the United Kingdom are the same books that have been produced, primarily, for an American readership, and since in many respects Anglo-American trade book publishing can be conceptualized as a single field (see Thompson 2010), the amount of distinctly European global manga commercially published in English is limited.[8] One notable exception to this, however, is SelfMadeHero's Manga Shakespeare series, which pairs abridged dialogue from original plays with contemporary visual style. Publisher Emma Hayley (2010, 270) explains how, by 2005 "there was a growing number of young artists in the UK who considered themselves to be mangaka. Some ten years ago this pool of talent would not have existed in the UK ..." She got in contact with the British doujinshi circle Sweatdrop Studios, invited them to pitch ideas, and eventually signed Sonia Leong for "Romeo and Juliet" and Emma Vieceli for "Hamlet." Manga based upon 14 plays were ultimately published between 2007 and 2009.

Within Continental Europe, France, Italy, and Germany have the largest markets for manga (Bouissou et al. 2010). Italy's has the longest history and, therefore, probably the longest history of locally-produced manga, starting in the 1990s (Pellitteri 2006). But that of France, specifically, is now larger in absolute terms even than the United States, so it should come as no surprise that France and the French-language comics industry is one of the most noteworthy sources of global manga—and in particular, so-called Nouvelle Manga. In Chapter 6, Tiago Canário provides an in-depth treatment of Frédéric

---

8 On the other hand, as Lamerichs observes in Chapter 4, amateur European manga artists will often publish in English in order to increase the potential size of their readership.

Boilet's New Wave-inspired and internationally ambitious movement, and the subject has, perhaps because of the magnitude of its auteuristic pretensions, attracted the attention of other scholars as well (Ahmed 2011; Vollmar 2007). Yet in many respects, the movement has less in common with manga than with French cinema and the avant-garde.

Of the three biggest markets for manga in Europe, Germany, despite—or perhaps *because of*—its lack of tradition in indigenous comics publishing—arguably has the richest and most interesting field of locally-produced original manga today. Paul M. Malone (2009; 2010; 2011; 2013) has written extensively about global manga in Germany. Interestingly, he asserts that most important artists are women and are often first- or second-generation immigrants of Eastern European or Asian descent (Malone 2011). For example, Christina Plaka (*Yonen Buzz*) is Greek; Judith Park (*Y Square*) is South Korean.[9] As a consequence of this female-dominated production, shoujo and boys' love manga, both professional and amateur, predominate (Malone 2009; 2010; 2013); in fact, "the German comics industry is currently dependent specifically upon *shōjo* [sic] manga, whether imported or home-grown, to a degree virtually unique in the West" (Malone 2010, 25). This vibrancy allows creators to appropriate, repurpose, and otherwise interact with themes and tropes common to Japanese manga, such as "the Gothic mode," as discussed by Antonija Cavcic in Chapter 8; yuri, as discussed by Nicolle Lamerichs in Chapter 4; and even hot-button legal issues and taboos such as shotacon (Malone 2013).

In comparison to what has been written on France and Germany, scholarship on global manga in other European countries remains underdeveloped. However, as Lamerichs demonstrates in her chapter on Euromanga, there is niche production in the Netherlands, and this undoubtedly happens in many European countries as well.

Africa and the Middle East

Of all of the regions of the world, global manga in Africa and the Middle East are probably the least well-studied. As elsewhere, news reports suggest that interest in manga is led by young women; the Dubai branch of the Japanese bookstore chain Kinokuniya, for example, reports that approximately 500 copies of English-language manga are sold there each week and that shoujo manga are especially popular (Sakurai 2013). The first ever global manga published in the United Arab Emirates, however, draws upon the conventions of shounen manga. Written in classical Arabic and published by PageFlip Publishing, an indie press founded by the Emerati Qais Sedki, *Gold Ring* features a 15-year-old

---

9   Both of these German global manga artists have had their works published in English translation. See Chapters 4 and 8 for more information about German manga.

Emirati falconer named Sultan (Good 2009). But because it is illustrated by the Japanese female artistic duo known as Akira Himekawa, it might, as discussed above, be considered a boundary case.

A notable exception to the dearth of global manga scholarship focused on this region is the work of Alexandra Gueydan-Turek (2013; 2014), who has written on Algerian manga. Algeria, with its historic links to France, has had above-average levels of access to Franco-Belgian *bande dessinée* as well as French-translated Japanese manga. Its own locally produced global manga, which Gueydan-Turek terms "Dz-manga," may be seen as a postcolonial alternative to Western-inspired aesthetic forms (Gueydan-Turek 2013). By adopting creative practices associated with Japan, young people can distance themselves from French culture and the attendant postcolonial baggage. Yet despite the production of both shounen and shoujo Dz-manga, the medium does not, at least as of yet, appear to be challenging Algerian gender roles: In particular, it "offers relatively little transformational ability to female artists and readers who might hope to find an alternative space in print. Despite the unique platform that girls' manga provides in Algeria, its practitioners appear unable to escape dominant gender narratives" (Gueydan-Turek 2014, 110). Moreover, "disparities between Dz-*shōnen* [sic] and Dz-*shōjo* [sic] manga replicate the unequal relationships between the sexes that persist in daily life" (Gueydan-Turek 2014, 110–11). Instead, "Algerian manga seems to have reached critical and popular acclaim because it provides its readers with the comfort and amusement of exploring fantasy characters who are much like themselves" (Gueydan-Turek 2014, 111).

But is "Global Manga" *Really* Manga...?!

Clearly, then, there are comics with no direct links to Japanese individuals or industry being produced and consumed all over the world that at least some producers and consumers would elect to call manga. But if it cannot be said to be labor by Japanese hands or supported by Japanese institution or investments, is this global manga *really* manga, and if so, what makes it manga and why? The 10 chapters in this collection all evince, either explicitly or implicitly, intense preoccupation with this exact issue. In Chapter 5, I examine in detail the debates about the definition of manga which emerge around the topic of OEL titles like Svetlana Chmakova's *Dramacon* on an online anime discussion forum. The various definitions, all of them controversial, mooted there are also reflected in various forms throughout the rest of the contributions to this collection.

The most common understanding of what manga is relates to manga as "style." Chapters 2 and 4 even deploy the word outright in their titles! However, each contributor formulates what is distinctive about manga's stylistic content in a myriad of nuanced ways—as the use of specific sets of aesthetic, narrative, and/or paratextual conventions, for example, or following Neil Cohn (2010), use of a distinctive visual language. Manuel Hernández-Pérez, for example, demonstrates how Marvel's Mangaverse appropriates character designs from famous Japanese franchises and applies them to various well-established superheroes from its own comics franchises. Elísio dos Santos and his co-authors, meanwhile, point out that global manga in Brazil is, at times, explicitly labeled as being presented *"[e]m estilo mangá"* [in the manga style]. However, if this stylistic appropriation is perceived to be too slavish, allegations of low quality, base imitation, and/or outright fakery soon follow. David Blanchard reports in his autobiographical contribution of having been the target of precisely those sorts of attacks, and this is probably a universal phenomenon in every field of global manga production.

Accusations of imitation are undoubtedly linked to another, often complementary understanding of what manga really is—a marketing function. Enduring ideological tensions between art and commerce are likely to be contributing factors, but what is really striking in some of the chapters are the richly detailed accounts of how something termed "manga" can actually be a big selling point for comics publishers. Obviously, this does not always work to the publishing house's advantage, as Marvel's case makes abundantly clear, but failure is by no means universal. Artists ranging from the Brazilian Mauricio de Sousa (*Monica's Gang*), as shown in Chapter 2, to the Canadian Bryan Lee O'Malley (*Scott Pilgrim*), as shown in Chapter 3, have deployed the manga label as a strategy to sustain their own commercial success and cultural relevance. On the other side of the divide between art and commerce, as shown in Chapter 6, the artists such as Frédéric Boilet coined the term "Nouvelle Manga" in part in order to promote their own works and creative philosophy, as well as provide a coherent backstory for what they would like to be seen as a global movement in comics creation. But perhaps most compelling of all is Magda Erik-Soussi's account, in the chapter which opens this book, of manga as the quintessential "female gaze" medium for North American women of a particular generation and that therefore producing one's own global manga is a self-affirming, even feminist, act.

Indeed, Erik-Soussi's position on global manga is especially notable for its politics of gender identity. A similar political valence for manga is evident in many of the other chapters, and taken together with previously published research, it would be hard not to conclude that manga's appeal to female artists and readers found in geographically non-contiguous regions is anything but a coincidence. Women were at the forefront of the popularization of Japanese culture in the West in the nineteenth century (Yoshihara 2003), and they continue to be at the forefront of this active transportation of cultural products and practices around the world in the contemporary period. Although some scholars (e.g. Gueydan-Turek 2014) are skeptical of global manga's transformative potential, series like *Sailor Moon*, genres like boys' love, and Japanese manga artists like CLAMP do appear to be providing some young people—women especially—with inspiration and role models, both human and fictional, unavailable to them in their own countries' popular culture. Indeed, the subaltern status of pioneering shoujo manga artists in Japan and the sorts of content, such as Cavcic's "Gothic mode," in which they specialize appear to be resonating outside of Japan with constituencies of young women negotiating feelings of marginality and inequality at home. Under such an epistemological regime, global manga is manga simply because it cannot be, by these people's own local understandings of the word, comics. Or *komiks*. Or *bande dessinée*.

Equally fascinating, and connected to the above, are the diverse and often controversial ways in which global manga is deployed to intervene in discourses of ethnic, racial, and national identities. In some cases, these are tied up in imperialist or immigrant histories with Japan; Pinoy manga in the Philippines is an excellent example of the former. The nationalist promotion of Korean manhwa is another. Aaron Pedinotti's chapter on *Scott Pilgrim* and *MANGAMAN*, on the other hand, shows that there is a range of personal views of ethnic cultural exchange through manga, and that racial hierarchies in the West are not yet a thing of the past—indeed, some of the productive assumptions and realities related to race and power depicted throughout this collection are problematic and quite unsettling. Lastly, Nicolle Lamerichs' account of the Dutch manga *Oost West* shows how, as for Erik-Soussi's Western *Sailor Moon* Generation, global manga production can be as much about interrogating one's own national identity and culture as it is about interrogating another's.

Future Directions

As a matter of fact, I would go so far as to argue that these debates about whether or not global manga is really manga completely miss the larger point—that global manga exists and that there are a range of sociological meanings and practices associated with it which, to date, have been grievously underexplored. As long as the field is distracted by this or that contested definition of "manga," a range of far more important areas of academic inquiry are being ignored. So if something called "manga" can be published that is not in any strict sense Japanese, here are just a few of the questions which may be asked: What do these fields of cultural production look like? Why and under what sorts of conditions do they arise and flourish? Who gets to decide what counts as "manga," and who benefits from that decision? What are global manga's implications for contemporary economies of cultural and creative labor? And finally—perhaps most important of all—what does it mean, therefore, for manga to be "authentically" Japanese and what, precisely, is at stake?

The time is ripe, in my view, to change the terms of the debate and explore new and different avenues of inquiry. Of course, it would not be feasible to enumerate the full range of potential future directions here. However, I would like to highlight one particular area in which I am confident *Global Manga* excels: The marriage of autobiographical accounts from industry insiders to the latest in scholarly insights. For ethical reasons, I cannot disclose the name of that manga editor with whom I had the privilege of a one-on-one show and tell, and to protect my informants—some of whom might, in the worst-case scenario, face retribution from their employers for speaking to me—there are practical limits on the level of detail I can provide about any of our interactions. No such prohibition is necessary in the cases of Blanchard and Erik-Soussi, two independent global manga creators and publishers, for they have told their stories in their own voices, and they write with tremendous courage. They and their works are no longer mere objects of academic study; instead, they rank as equals in this collection to the researchers who would ordinarily treat them as data and participate fully in the production of new scholarly knowledge about that which they are, as practitioners, most expert.

And what, one might ask, can be learned from them? Well, as already discussed, the importance—obsession, even—with what to call what they do is shared, as is the cultural significance of Japanese manga for young people, especially young women, outside of Japan. It is also easy to see from their accounts, for example, how readers, fans, and consumers of cultural products come to rationalize wanting to produce their own and then proceed to do exactly that. And the issues raised in the previous section about inequalities and identities related to gender, ethnicity, nation, and so forth just barely scratch the surface.

But there is one further topic that ought to be central to any substantive social inquiry into global manga, and that topic is failure. In Chapter 5, Blanchard recounts tale after tale of failure—the silent rejection of his pitch to Images Comics, a collaborative project conceptualized but never gotten off the ground, a bid to license manga right to popular property that just reads like a nightmarish run-around. Few cultural producers are so candid about their failures, and most of the other chapters' contributors would rather elide the failures and write about global manga's successes. Nonetheless, failure is a fact of life in the industry, and many, if not most, initiatives do fail. Canário implies that the Nouvelle Manga Movement was more flash in the pan than sustainable enterprise in Chapter 7. Every historical account of comics and manga publishing is littered with cases of discontinued series and failed publishing houses. Even Tokyopop, founded in the late 1990s as Mixx Entertainment, briefly overtook Viz in 2002 to become the largest manga publisher in the United States, as well as a pioneer of OEL manga, went out of business a decade later. It is, in my view, testimony to the cultural significance of global flows of Japanese popular culture that global manga producers have tried, try, try, and try yet again to domesticate this medium and make it succeed.

In any case, this book does not presume to provide definitive answers to any of the questions posed above, or any others, for that matter, but it does aim to take seriously the political economies, worlds of work, and range of productive meanings and practices associated with these Japanese comics outside Japan—throughout the Americas, Europe, and Asia. And to this end, I have assembled an international and interdisciplinary cohort of researchers and practitioners on the cutting edge of an emerging creative field who, together, paint a richly detailed picture of many of the complexities and controversies of global manga. Their collective labor is the fruit borne of that germ of an idea from several years ago. Join me now in savoring the harvest. Turn the page.

References

Ahmed, Maaheen. 2010. "Reading (and Looking at) *Mariko Parade*—A Methodological Suggestion for Understanding Contemporary Graphic Narratives." *Global Manga Studies* 2: 119–33.

Bainbridge, Jason and Craig Norris. 2010. "Hybrid Manga: Implications for the Global Knowledge Economy." In *Manga: An Anthology of Global and Cultural Perspectives*, edited by Toni Johnson-Woods, 235–52. New York: Continuum.

Berndt, Jaqueline, ed. 2010. *Global Manga Studies Volume 1: Comics Worlds and the World of Comics: Towards Scholarship on a Global Scale*. Kyoto: Kyoto Seika University International Manga Research Center.

Berndt, Jaqueline, ed. 2011. *Global Manga Studies Volume 2: Intercultural Crossovers, Transcultural Flows: Manga/Comics*. Kyoto: Kyoto Seika University International Manga Research Center.

Bouissou, Jean-Marie. 2008. "Global Manga. Perché il Fumettto Giapponese è Divenuto un Prodotto Culturale Mondiale [Global Manga: Why Japanese Comics Have Become a Worldwide Cultural Product." In *Il Drago e la Saetta. Modelli, Strategie e Identità dell'Immaginario Giapponese* [The Dragon and the Dazzle: Models, Strategies, and Identities of Japanese Imagination], edited by Marco Pelliteri, 493–507. Latina, Italy: Tunué.

Bouissou, Jean-Marie, Marco Pellitteri, Bernd Dolle-Weinkauff, and Ariane Beldi. 2010. "Manga in Europe: A Short Study of Market and Fandom." In *Manga: An Anthology of Global and Cultural Perspectives*, edited by Toni Johnson-Woods, 253–66. New York: Continuum.

Brienza, Casey. 2009. "Paratexts in Translation: Reinterpreting 'Manga' for the United States." *The International Journal of the Book* 6 (2): 13–20.

Brienza, Casey. 2011. "Manga Is for Girls: American Publishing Houses and the Localization of Japanese Comic Books." *Logos: The Journal of the World Publishing Community* 22 (4): 41–53. doi:10.1163/095796512X625445.

Brienza, Casey. 2013. "Beyond B&W? The Global Manga of Felipe Smith." *Black Comics: Politics of Race and Representation*, edited by Sheena C. Howard and Ronald L. Jackson II, 79–94. London: Bloomsbury.

Brienza, Casey. 2014. "Did Manga Conquer America? Implications for the Cultural Policy of 'Cool Japan.'" *International Journal of Cultural Policy* 20 (4): 383–98. doi:10.1080/10286632.2013.856893.

Chao, Tien-yi. 2013. "Features of Hybridization in In These Words." *Journal of Graphic Novels & Comics* 4 (1): 9–29. doi:10.1080/21504857.2012.757247.

Chen, Yi-ching, and Stacy Hsu. 2013. "Taiwan's Comic Artists Edge out Japanese Rivals." *Taipei Times*. December 24. http://www.taipeitimes.com/News/taiwan/archives/2013/12/24/2003579709.

Choo, Kukhee. 2010. "Consuming Japan: Early Korean Girls Comic Book Artists' Resistance and Empowerment.'" In *Complicated Currents: Media Flows, Soft Power and East Asia*, edited by Daniel Black, Stephen Epstein, and Alison Tokita, 6.1–6.16. Victoria: Monash University ePress. http://books.publishing.monash.edu/apps/bookworm/view/Complicated+Currents/122/xhtml/chapter6.html.

Cohn, Neil. 2010. "Japanese Visual Language: The Structure of Manga." In *Manga: An Anthology of Global and Cultural Perspectives*, edited by Toni Johnson-Woods, 187–203. New York: Continuum.

Good, Oliver. 2009. "Gold Ring: The UAE's First Manga." *The National*. July 20. http://www.thenational.ae/arts-culture/art/gold-ring-the-uaes-first-manga.

Gueydan-Turek, Alexandra. 2013. "The Rise of Dz-Manga in Algeria: Glocalization and the Emergence of a New Transnational Voice." *Journal of Graphic Novels & Comics* 4 (1): 161–78. doi:10.1080/21504857.2013.784203.

Gueydan-Turek, Alexandra. 2014. "Cute Girls, Tough Boys: Performing Gender in Algerian Manga." *European Comic Art* 7 (1): 85–111. doi:10.3167/eca.2014.070105.

Hayley, Emma. 2010. "Manga Shakespeare." In *Manga: An Anthology of Global and Cultural Perspectives*, edited by Toni Johnson-Woods, 267–80. New York: Continuum.

Iwabuchi, Koichi. 2002. *Recentering Globalization: Popular Culture and Japanese Transnationalism*. Durham, NC: Duke University Press.

Iwabuchi, Koichi. 2004. "How 'Japanese' is Pokémon?" In *Pikachu's Global Adventure: The Rise and Fall of Pokémon*, edited by Joseph Tobin, 53–79. Durham, NC: Duke University Press.

Kinsella, Sharon. 2000. *Adult Manga: Culture and Power in Contemporary Japanese Society*. Honolulu: University of Hawai'i Press.

Lent, John A. 1999. "Local Comic Books and the Curse of Manga in Hong Kong, South Korea and Taiwan." *Asian Journal of Communication* 9 (1): 108–28. doi:10.1080/01292989909359617.

Lent, John A. 2010a. "Manga in East Asia." In *Manga: An Anthology of Global and Cultural Perspectives*, edited by Toni Johnson-Woods, 297–314. New York: Continuum.

Lent, John A. 2010b. "The Winding, Pot-Holed Road of Comic Art Scholarship." *Studies in Comics* 1 (1): 7–33. doi:10.1386/stic.1.1.7/1.

Malone, Paul M. 2009. "Home-grown Shōjo Manga and the Rise of Boys' Love among Germany's 'Forty-Niners.'" *Intersections: Gender and Sexuality in Asia and the Pacific* 20. http://intersections.anu.edu.au/issue20/malone.htm.

Malone, Paul M. 2010. "From BRAVO to Animexx.de to Export: Capitalizing on German Boys' Love Fandom, Culturally, Socially and Economically." In *Boys' Love Manga: Essays on the Sexual Ambiguity and Cross-Cultural Fandom of the Genre*, edited by Antonia Levi, Mark McHarry, and Dru Pagliassotti, 23–43. Jefferson, NC: McFarland & Co.

Malone, Paul M. 2011. "Transcultural Hybridization in Home-Grown German Manga," *Global Manga Studies* 2: 49–60.

Malone, Paul M. 2013. "Transplanted Boys' Love Conventions and Anti-'Shota' Polemics in German Manga: Fahr Sindram's 'Losing Neverland.'" *Transformative Works and Cultures 12*. http://journal.transformativeworks.org/index.php/twc/article/view/434/395.

Ng, Wai-ming. 2000. "A Comparative Study of Japanese Comics in Southeast Asia and East Asia." *International Journal of Comic Art* 2 (1): 45–56.

Ng, Wai-ming. 2003. "Japanese Elements in Hong Kong Comics: History, Art and Industry." *International Journal of Comic Art* 5 (2): 184–93.

Noh, Sueen. 2004. "The Gendered Comics Market in Korea: An Overview of Korean Girls' Comics, Soonjung Manhwa." *International Journal of Comic Art* 6 (1): 281–98.

Otmazgin, Nissim Kadosh. 2012. "Geopolitics and Soft Power: Japan's Cultural Policy and Cultural Diplomacy in Asia." *Asia-Pacific Review* 19 (1): 37–61. doi:10.1080/13439006.2012.678629.

Pagliassotti, Dru. 2009. "GloBLisation and Hybridisation: Publishers' Strategies for Bringing Boys' Love to the United States." *Intersections: Gender and Sexuality in Asia and the Pacific* 20. http://intersections.anu.edu.au/issue20/pagliassotti.htm.

Pellitteri, Marco. 2006. "Manga in Italy: History of a Powerful Cultural Hybridization." *International Journal of Comic Art* 8 (2): 56–76.

Pink, Daniel H. 2007. "Japan, Ink: Inside the Manga Industrial Complex." *Wired*. October 22. http://www.wired.com/techbiz/media/magazine/15–11/ff_manga?currentPage=all.

Prough, Jennifer S. 2011. *Straight from the Heart: Gender, Intimacy, and the Cultural Production of Shojo Manga*. Honolulu: University of Hawai'i Press.

Sakurai, Takamasa. 2013. "Middle East Embraces Japanese Culture through Manga." *The Star Online*. January 25. http://www.thestar.com.my/story/?file=%2F2013%2F1%2F25%2Flifeliving%2F12598460&sec=lifeliving.

Schodt, Frederik L. 1983. *Manga! Manga!: The World of Japanese Comics*. New York: Kodansha International.

Shimizu, Isao. 1991. *Manga No Rekishi* [The History of Manga]. Tokyo: Iwanami Shoten.

Sugiura, Tsutomu. 2008. "Japan's Creative Industries: Culture as a Source of Soft Power in the Industrial Sector." In *Soft Power Superpowers: Cultural and National Assets of Japan and the United States*, edited by Yasushi Watanabe, David L. McConnell, and Joseph S. Nye, 128–53. Armonk, NY: M.E. Sharpe.

Tai, Elizabeth. 2007. "Doing Malaysia Proud." *The Star Online*. July 8. http://www.thestar.com.my/story/?file=%2F2007%2F7%2F8%2Flifebookshelf%2F18237148&sec=lifebookshelf.

Thompson, John B. 2010. *Merchants of Culture: The Publishing Business in the Twenty-First Century*. Cambridge: Polity.

Tseng, Chi-Shoung, and Chin Chia Tsai. 2010. "The Exclusion and Inclusion of Japanese Manga in Taiwan: A Historic Narratology of Culture Image Expression." *The Global Studies Journal* 3 (1): 183–202.

Valaskivi, Katja. 2013. "A Brand New Future? Cool Japan and the Social Imaginary of the Branded Nation." *Japan Forum* 25 (4): 485–504. doi:10.1080/09555803.2012.756538.

Vollmar, Rob. 2007. "Frédéric Boilet and the Nouvelle Manga Revolution." *World Literature Today* 81 (2): 34–41.

Wong, Wendy Siuyi. 2010. "Drawing the Ideal Woman: Ms. Lee Wai-Chung and Her *Ms. 13-Dot*." *Global Manga Studies* 1: 177–84.

Xu, Yanrui, and Ling Yang. 2013. "Forbidden Love: Incest, Generational Conflict, and the Erotics of Power in Chinese BL Fiction." *Journal of Graphic Novels & Comics* 4 (1): 30–43. doi:10.1080/21504857.2013.771378.

Yamanaka, Chie. 2006. "Domesticating Manga? National Identity in Korean Comics Culture." In *Reading Manga: Local and Global Perceptions of Japanese Comics*, edited by Jaqueline Berndt and Steffi Richter, 193–204. Leipzig: Leipziger Universitätsverlag.

Yamanaka, Chie. 2013. "*Manhwa* in Korea: (Re-)Nationalizing Comics Culture." In *Manga's Cultural Crossroads*, edited by Jaqueline Berndt and Bettina Kümmerling-Meibauer, 85–99. London: Routledge.

Yoo, Soo-Kyung. 2012. "On Differences between Japanese and Korean Comics for Female Readers: Comparing 'Boys Over Flowers' to 'Goong.'" In *Manhwa, Manga, Manhua: East Asian Comics Studies*, edited by Jaqueline Berndt, 43–64. Leipzig: Leipziger Universitätsverlag.

Yoon, Yeowon. 2002. "A Study of the Development of Sunjong Manhwa by Hwang Mina, Kim Hyerin and Choi In-Sun." MA Thesis, Vancouver: University of British Columbia. http://circle.ubc.ca/handle/2429/12302.

Yoshihara, Mari. 2003. *Embracing the East: White Women and American Orientalism*. Oxford: Oxford University Press.

Chapter 1
The Western *Sailor Moon* Generation: North American Women and Feminine-Friendly Global Manga

Magda Erik-Soussi

Like many editors in the manga industry, I didn't start working in manga "because I needed a job." Manga was my obsession. Fiction was *always* my obsession, and there happened to be a "job" version of it that could (sometimes) pay my rent. As a child, instead of joining a sports team or taking piano lessons, I read voraciously and conquered video games; by the time I was a teenager, I'd discovered manga and anime and was writing hundreds of pages of fanfiction in my free hours after school. By 17, I'd been hired by my favorite manga company to write children's books based on a franchise I was obsessed with, and the job led to more writing and editing work on manga, light novels, and an anime magazine. In my 15 years in the industry, I've worked on 150 books of manga and prose as a freelancer for four companies and recently started my own publishing house to publish global manga and light novels for women.

But if manga hadn't been my career, it still would have been my life. Like many "geeks" in America and Canada, my obsession with fiction started young. Very young. It was an integral part of who I was, and my fiery passion for manga specifically was sparked by a single anime that shaped me during a key developmental period of my life (and the development of a lifelong creativity). I know I'm not alone in this; since the average geek dedicates so much of her life and passion to fiction, it's only natural that fiction would also shape her. And that the *nature* of the fiction could insult or empower her.

For the purposes of this chapter, I'll define "geek" as someone with obsessive or nearly obsessive interest in fiction with a fantasy/science fiction bent. It's a nebulous term to begin with, and until recently, it carried a strong negative stigma (and still does, in many circles). But in 2014, the term is paraded by "geek" communities as a reclaimed symbol of identity, and is often used as a filter for friends and relationships the way "outdoorsy" is in more traditional single ads (in fact, a number of dating sites like Geek 2 Geek [http://www.gk2gk.com]

boast that they're specifically a dating hub for geeks to find other geeks to love). I'm going to use the traditional stereotype of the last 40 years for this chapter: the person who spends her life indoors, playing video games, reading comics and novels, and spending her weekends playing *Dungeons and Dragons*.

The interests of a lifelong geek start presenting from an early age: she prefers reading to playing outside, video games instead of parties, crayons instead of makeup. There's a leaning toward fantasy worlds—she escapes into them and often creates or expands them. Once she's old enough to start pursuing her preferred media, she chooses fantasy novels, comic books, video games, and anime. I subscribe to the notion that "there's one in every family," because it seems that whenever I speak to Baby Boomers about my job, they exclaim, "Oh! My son/niece/neighbor loves that Japanese stuff," referencing only the manga/anime facet of geekdom (which is only one piece of a variety of overlapping interests).

It's this ingestion and creation of fantasy escapism in a child's formative years that I want to focus on, especially how it intersects with girls' formation of identity, sexuality, and creativity through adolescence. Geek-leaning girls who grew up in the 1970s and 1980s—the latter half of Generation X—grew up with King Arthur and the destructive women in his life who didn't follow honor codes (Guinevere and Morgan le Fay), with J.R.R. Tolkien and his dearth of female characters, with the *Dungeons and Dragons* mentality (first published in 1977) of male power fantasies of scantily clad, muscled women relegated to "back row" combat (archery or magic) or riding huge mystical beasts between their bare thighs. For girls growing in the 1980s to the 1990s—the first half of the Millennials—there were more "female-oriented" options: He-Man had his power equivalent in She-Ra, *Jem* and *My Little Pony* had women-dominated casts and strong elements of magic or science fiction, and in general, girls interested in fantasy worlds were recognized as a market separate from boys. There was stigma, of course; fantasy media targeted for "all audiences" invariably had a male lead, and in a lot of geek circles, including my own, "girl fantasies" were othered, and male fantasies were aspirational.

But Millennials also got something else: the "magical girl" anime *Sailor Moon*. Although anime and manga had been translated into English before, the selections were limited, strongly modified for a Western audience, and often targeted at children or boys (such as the series *Voltron*). *Sailor Moon* was based off the manga of the same name, created by a woman (Naoko Takeuchi), and run in a magazine aimed at elementary and middle-school aged girls in Japan (*Nakayoshi*). Even with a majority-male animation staff and the modifications eventually made for a Western audience, *Sailor Moon* still channeled the then 20-year movement of shoujo manga in Japan, of women writing emotive, dramatic, unapologetically feminine fantasy works for other women. It was coded differently from Western "girl" fantasy—it wasn't drowning in the color pink, it wasn't a spin-off of a show for boys, it didn't solely focus on fashion and make-up yet somehow erase the sexuality and identity inherent in dress-up games. And even when DiC Entertainment applied a significant degree of Western sanitation to *Sailor Moon* (e.g. gender-flipping a gay character to make him a straight woman, marketing the show and its merchandise for children), it resonated with a huge variety of viewers: children and teenagers and adults of all gender identities.

And that audience grew. Although *Sailor Moon* struggled during its original run on television, it was eventually brought back in the face of outcries from its cultish fanbase. When the manga for *Sailor Moon*—black and white and wildly different from traditional American superhero or kids' comics—was first translated into English by Tokyopop (then Mixx Entertainment) in 1997, it was so financially successful that it solidified Tokyopop as a company, allowing them to go forward and help shape the North American manga market and release more titles for girls (Lillian Diaz-Przybyl, former Senior Editor of Tokyopop, email message to author, December 19, 2013). After going out of print for 5+ years due to licensing issues, the manga was reprinted in English by Kodansha Comics USA in 2011; despite the instability of the North American manga market at that point and its general wariness of "classic" manga and reprints, as per the company's own announcement, the first volume (of 12) sold out of its first print run of 50,000 copies in only four weeks (*Kodansha Comics* 2011). For comparison, in the days of the North American manga boom (mid noughts), a first print run for a Tokyopop manga only needed to sell from 20,000 to 25,000 copies to be considered a success, and by 2010, half that number (Lillian Diaz-Przybyl, former Senior Editor of Tokyopop, email message to author, December 19, 2013). A new *Sailor Moon* anime (*Pretty Guardian Sailor Moon Crystal*) will debut in a few months, more than 15 years after the original anime first debuted, live-streamed from Japan and with subtitles in ten languages to meet the massive worldwide demand. *Sailor Moon* left (and still maintains) an indelible mark on the science fiction/fantasy/"geek" industry in North America, and it helped usher in a new era of success for translated anime and manga, opening the floodgates to a vastly expanded library of titles, including shoujo manga (largely unknown to North America before *Sailor Moon*).

But in my mind, one of the most profound effects *Sailor Moon* and subsequent shoujo manga had on the North American geek industry/community wasn't financial. It was psychological. *Sailor Moon* had a distinctly "Female Gaze"; it was created with the expectation that the audience would be mostly female or specifically seeking a female perspective. For this reason, it became a gateway for new feminine power fantasies for Western geeks—something more provocative than the pink, sanitized offerings of the West, yet something more juvenile than the Female Gaze media in North America for adults (e.g. romance novels and "chick flicks"). In the way that She-Ra was the power equivalent of He-Man, Sailor Moon was the power equivalent to Western superheroes, yet she was introduced to North America not as a spin-off or sidekick; Sailor Moon began and ended with herself. And contrary to the very masculine power fantasies thrust on "powerful" female characters in Western fantasy, *Sailor Moon*'s feminine core was raw and honest, putting focus on the huge, mostly female cast's struggles with morality, friendship, jealousy, sexuality, vulnerability, and desire to protect loved ones. It resonated with women and touched audience members of all gender identities who longed for a new power fantasy that left traditional male-slanted issues far behind.

I was born in 1982 and thus am one of the oldest Millennials to have grown up with *Sailor Moon*. I was 13 years old when it began its first run on American television in 1995, and it plays a large part of how I grew to accept feminine media and the femininity in myself. I can also link it very directly—and very literally—to empowering me into a career of creating and publishing manga and related fantasies by and for other women. I have many peers in the North American manga industry, both creators and editors, who are women born within five years of me who grew up loving *Sailor Moon*. It was a gateway into manga, shoujo, and feminine power fantasies that truly resonated with us.

I think *Sailor Moon* is the reason the North American manga market, including its global manga, has so many women in positions of creative and editorial power. When Marvel and especially DC Comics are constantly under fire for being run "like a boy's club" and not giving enough screen time (and care) to female characters (Abad-Santos 2003), manga has excellent diversity of gender representation on a creative and editorial level; niche genres from Japan targeted at women (including boys' love) hold a firm market share in North America; and unapologetically shoujo or Female Gaze series, including *Fruits Basket*, are openly celebrated as huge hits. And of the new global manga being produced, much of it too is being made by and for women.

The beginning of the North American manga boom was tied closely to the timing and success of *Sailor Moon*. By linking that expression of female power so tightly to the growth of the market, the acceptance and even celebration of the feminine is more entrenched in the manga market than in much of the existing North American science fiction/fantasy industry (comic books, video games, fantasy novels). And since manga and anime overlap with so much of these geek industries now, by extension, *Sailor Moon* ushered in a new wave of recognition of feminine power by geek industries, communities, and, yes, individual geeks themselves. As is evidenced by the success of the supernatural *Twilight* and the post-apocalyptic/science fiction *Hunger Games* franchises, feminine perspectives and values are growing in traditionally masculine fantasy spaces.

The generation raised on *Sailor Moon* is playing an important role in shaping the next generation of geek media and the people who both create and consume it. The rise of feminine-friendly global manga, mostly created by women themselves, is already a clear result of that. Female Gaze global manga has had lasting success, and the demand for it only seems to be growing, concurrent with the demand for fem-catering media in general. My publishing house, Chromatic Press, runs open comics submissions for global manga and specifically requests Female Gaze. We're literally reviewing the work of the *Sailor Moon* generation and the younger Millennials they in turn helped influence, and the quality, passion, and drive is humbling.

I consider my personal experience as a Western geek who was introduced to *Sailor Moon* around puberty and later joined the manga industry as a creator, editor, and eventual publisher of global manga as a very literal example of this phenomenon. In order to better describe this experience, I offer an industry retrospective through the lens of my life.

Embracing the Feminine through *Sailor Moon*: Individual

For the purposes of this chapter, I'll define "popcorn" media as stories marketed as fun and disposable, even if they're also "smart." They reflect and enforce popular culture; they are marketed heavily, merchandised, and sold in mainstream retail outlets when they're popular enough. Much of the geeky media described heretofore—and the media that still dominates many geek circles in terms of popularity—can be described as "popcorn."

In North American media, there has long existed an outlet for popcorn feminine media more advanced than the gendered media for young girls and tweens: romance novels and "chick flicks" (a label often attached to romantic comedy films, or really, most lighthearted romance/dramas with a female lead). Both sizeable and stable genres within the book and film industry, respectively, they both expand on girl and tween media by introducing "adult" themes like sexuality and politics (workplace or otherwise) into fiction targeted to women. However, where girl and tween media often focus on empowering—literally or figuratively—their characters in order to provide positive role models for young viewers, romance novels and chick flicks oftentimes take a step *back* from this and strip some of that power from their female characters. I think this is a standard for a number of reasons:

1. This "more adult" media is intended to be realistic, and thus it represents patriarchal structures and its female characters' place within it.
2. Western expressions of feminine sexuality, even with female creators or a well-researched female audience, is often mired in a culture of sexual shame and guilt.
3. Fantasy and science fiction are small subsections of romance novels and chick flicks (until recently), eliminating the easier, more established (and even juvenile) trope of giving female characters supernatural powers to elevate them to "powerful."

4. More systemic media sexism leaks in without specific child and young adult "watchdogs" (parents, teachers, etc.) to combat them.
5. Many romance novels and chick flicks are billed as escapist fantasies for women who desire an aggressive man/overpowered woman paradigm that lies under the surface of the patriarchy but is overtly discouraged in feminist spheres (this includes the genre of "bodice-rippers").
6. More adult popcorn media traditionally rely on sex, shock value, or "low art" tactics in order to increase sales and thus rely on existing "taboo" issues that are rarely progressive on a societal level; they embrace the lowest common denominator idea of "cheap media" that is often specifically contrary to empowering children and tween media.

Interestingly, this trend toward power degradation can be seen in Japan, too, as josei manga and ladies' comics—Female Gaze for an audience older than the traditional audience of shoujo manga—are often about women struggling to find balance in a sexist system, not rising above it to find success and power. These manga also rarely ignore or subvert the patriarchal system entirely, while the entire shoujo subgenre "magical girls" (which includes *Sailor Moon*) is often dedicated to that, primarily associating superpowers with being or becoming feminine.

Of course, this isn't to say that the North American media market is incapable of selling an empowered view of sexuality to a teenage or adult audience; indeed, the young adult literature market, meant for tweens and teens but often enjoyed by adults, has a long tradition of raw but empowering stories about coming of age, sexuality, and gender. Many girls in my generation grew up with Judy Blume. But these books—and they often remain exclusively as prose, unless they're adapted into another medium that may or may not be faithful to the themes of the source material—are often created for and marketed to young girls as something explicitly empowering. They're often endorsed by schools and parents, which somewhat groups them in with children's materials. Popcorn media, including *Sailor Moon*, has a more subtle effect on the female adolescent psyche, since it's marketed directly to her as "fun" and "desirable." Like the effect of rail-thin models in popular culture on a young woman's body image despite body-positivity passed down to her by, for example, teachers, popcorn media does not require any stamp of approval to exert its influence.

In any case, part of the appeal of importing shoujo and *Sailor Moon* specifically is that, unlike popcorn media for girls and tweens in the West, even shoujo for young girls addresses romance novel and chick flick themes such as sexuality, desire, identity in a broader social context, and jealousy. Paired with the more empowering themes of media for young girls, *Sailor Moon* and many other shoujo provide a provocative look into feminine power. This melting pot of themes "for children" and "for teens/adults" feels almost revolutionary in the West—a package of the childlike with the adult, an especially good fit for girls developing through early adolescence and inherent issues of identity and sexuality.

Before I discovered *Sailor Moon*, I was wary of media that felt "too feminine," as I felt it talked down to me and I couldn't relate to the seemingly selfish desires of the female characters (overly focused on their appearance, an obsession with boys, and friendship that boiled down to the simple "power of heart" mentality). I longed for media and personal expression that had been coded to me as masculine: courage, heroism, valor, victory. In addition, I think like many young girls in male-dominated spaces (including geek spaces), there was an underlying fear that masculinity was aspirational and femininity degrading. It felt easier, "safer," to identify with male characters, even if I was presented with truly strong female characters. Indeed, when I was 12 or 13 years old and was first discovering the female power fantasies written by Tamora Pierce, I distinctly remembering thinking her headstrong and sex-positive female lead Alanna was arrogant and uncomfortably promiscuous. (The character had a total of three sexual partners in her lifetime.) I sincerely doubt the same characteristics would have had me judging a male character so strongly, despite my personal gender identity as a woman. The internalization of sexism is a powerful negative force.

Sailor Moon was explicitly feminine yet originated from a different culture's expression of feminine power, so it looked and felt different; it didn't carry the same politics or stigma as Western feminine media. It was also immediately more sexual, with girls in miniskirts, high heels. There was also a widespread perception at the time that Japanese anime was mostly adult fare: "Those Japanese cartoons have sex in them!" (This was largely fear-mongering but also true to an extent, due to the more adult anime that had been marketed in the West.) I remember catching glimpses of *Sailor Moon* commercials on television—it immediately struck me as foreign, and a little bizarre, but the girls in colorful costumes intrigued me, despite my wariness of "girl's stuff." At the same time, the anime *Project A-Ko* was being advertised in America, and it similarly had powerful girls in school uniforms. I snuck glances through a comics version in the drug store, almost embarrassed I would be caught looking at these powerful girls and their bare legs.

But what surprised me—and ultimately caused me to start watching the show—was that so many of my female peers in the eighth grade were already watching *Sailor Moon*. And it wasn't just the expected fans, i.e. kids who grew up with anime in another language or geeks who sought fantasy in all forms—it was a wide sampling of girls, including the popular and the sexually experienced who were usually talking about parties or boys instead of cartoons. I was floored by the fact that these trend-setting girls were willing to openly enjoy a girly cartoon when we were just a year shy of high school.

It wasn't long before I was engrossed in the show myself. *Sailor Moon* presented all the geeky trappings I wanted (magic, superpowers) along with continuity between episodes, rare in Western cartoons but a staple of anime, which built a robust fantasy world for me to escape into. The cast was dominated by female characters who were larger than life and yet flawed in a very raw, compelling way, and superficial feminine touches—an elegant talking cat, compacts turned into superhero talismans—tickled my fancy without overwhelming me with too much femininity at once. Perhaps most compelling was the love story: Sailor Moon and her love interest, fellow superhero Tuxedo Mask, were simultaneously reincarnations of royals in love from a doomed fantasy kingdom, ordinary students who bickered whenever they saw each other, and superheroes who were sometimes allies, sometimes enemies. It was like a deluxe Love Story Sundae of distinct but complementary tastes, and I adored every single one, to say nothing of the combination. The fact that the love story successfully drove much of action-packed plotline intrigued me, especially considering Tuxedo Mask was presented to the audience as an object of desire. He was capable yet vulnerable, masculine yet pretty, accessible yet adult. This wasn't a muscled barbarian or a knight with a chiseled jaw like I was used to; this was basically an underwear model who fought evil in a tuxedo, and although he was a chest for Sailor Moon to cry on, he was also a puppet for the evil queen antagonist, and it wasn't unusual for him to be tied up or fallen to his knees before his love or the evil queen alike. The way the main love interest/male lead could alternate between extremely powerful and extremely vulnerable, especially with a strong, sexualized undercurrent throughout, was something I'd never seen before.

Even if I found it difficult to relate to the female characters themselves—and I did, to an extent, as I was so used to relating to male characters—I related to the show *itself* and the things it valued. I related to that Female Gaze. I wanted the power of the girls and the chance to be brave and heroic, but I also wanted Tuxedo Mask, and the ability to both save him and be vulnerable around him. *Sailor Moon* combined the aspects of power I had always coded as masculine with the power of female desire—in this case, heterosexual (although *Sailor Moon* also had an abundance of queer and transgender themes, which I'll go into later)—and yet also allowed Sailor Moon to fail, bicker with her colleagues, grow jealous of her friends, and cry her eyes out. It had school lunches and fireballs and dark kingdoms and passionate kisses. It had everything. It taught me to want things I didn't know I wanted because I'd never seen them packaged that way before, and I'd never been catered to in such a way by my fantasy media.

It affected me in an extremely personal way. When I saw what I *thought* was the final episode, I cried my eyes out because I thought it was over. I was ashamed of how fully I'd embraced it. My time of free desire and power was over, and I had to return to my life before it—a geeky girl who liked the "right" kind of Western fantasy, the sterile and skewed masculine kind, despite the fact that I'd seen a burst of color and free-spirited femininity that I could never forget.

But after the weekend, the next season started. And the lid on my boxed femininity stayed open.

Embracing the Feminine through *Sailor Moon*: Socialization and Creativity

In the same way that the popularity of *Sailor Moon* across various cliques got me interested in it, the social aspect of *Sailor Moon* only deepened my obsession. The fad status of the show wore off quickly, but the fans who remained banded together. We talked about the show constantly. We learned to draw the characters in art class, play the songs in the show on our instruments during orchestra break. In this way, we were "traditional" geeks, obsessed with a fictional world to the detriment of socialization outside of it. In fact, I bonded so deeply with certain friends over *Sailor Moon* that my friends who *weren't* avid *Sailor Moon* fans, even if they shared other interests with me, became peripheral acquaintances for times when I could take a break from my obsession (which weren't all that frequent). My social life was skewed and insular, even if it was active and far-reaching. I later learned the term for this shared obsession: fandom.

One of the most positive aspects of fandom—to counter, perhaps, the negatives that come with particularly obsessive fandom, in my case—is the collective creativity. Escaping into fantasy is cathartic, but there's a limit to the catharsis if it ends with the source material and discussion of it. Using *Sailor Moon* as a subject and a muse, my friends and I learned how to draw and paint. I was hungry for new material, and my re-creations helped sate my desire for something truly new.

In Japan, there's an entire, booming industry for fandom in a gray area of copyright law called doujinshi. Amateurs and even professionals (usually under pseudonyms) will write and draw these self-published comics and prose fiction of existing characters and spread them to fellow fans, sometimes for a tidy profit. Although the English-language doujinshi industry barely existed in the 1990s (and is still very small today), English-language fanfiction, the prose equivalent, was already very popular by the time I got online in 1996 and only grew with time into a *huge* component of English-speaking fandom today. In 2012, for example, a popular piece of fanfiction based on *The Hunger Games* received almost two million hits (Alter 2012). And infamously, the tremendously successful novel *50 Shades of Grey* was originally written and distributed as free *Twilight* fanfiction.

Fandom, as a community around the adoration and exploration of media, is a powerful catalyst for general creativity, and leads to original content (more on that later). The infrastructure, e.g. archives through which to post fanfiction, and existing readership introduce the average fanfic writer to an immediate community of fellow writers and readers. It succeeds as a giant, international writers' group, with a number of factors that increase interactivity:

1. Face-to-face meet-ups of online fanfiction communities are rare, so feedback and responses aren't limited to geography or time zones.
2. For many, the greater sense of anonymity online allows them to be more honest.
3. Since the fandom shares the same source material, the writers are usually working in a similar genre/for a similar audience and thus immediately have a connection to other writers.
4. The fanfiction readership—fans of the source material who are hungry for more—introduces the writer to an immediate, diverse audience, which, once again, often shares some degree of taste with the writer, because of the source material that originally brought them together.

In the way that *Sailor Moon* brought me into a community of other girls who watched the show, *Sailor Moon* fanfiction brought me into a much bigger community that specifically celebrated creativity. It renewed my obsession, and it wasn't long before I was writing my own. I had dabbled in creative writing before, but fanfiction turned me into a writer, and taught me about deadlines, reaching an audience, and the line to walk between gratification and self-indulgence. I had countless readers, feedback, and encouragement to do more. In my first year of writing fanfiction, when I was 15 years old, I religiously released weekly chapters, resulting in hundreds of pages of material. The fanfiction community further fueled my desire to create.

The value of fandom socialization—empowering in some ways, isolationist in others—takes on a new element in specifically creative fandom communities like a fanfiction circle. By writing, my personal views were being exposed in my creative works, and I was suddenly forced to face my personal beliefs—which included, for a time, homophobia—by the diverse, critical audience of the source material. As an adult, I can appreciate the variety and normalization of queer themes in *Sailor Moon*, especially within the Female Gaze—the exploration of sexual relationships between the female characters is subtle but powerful; gay villains are still evil, even if their love is sympathetic; one of the lesbian Sailor Scouts wears a male school uniform to school; Sailor Scouts in the final season literally have male bodies until they transform, at which point their bodies "turn" female and gain magic. In fact, it's through these queer themes that *Sailor Moon* attains much of its female power dynamic—being a Sailor Scout (and wearing the overtly feminine uniform) is associated with powers and justice, and one must be a woman to wear it, regardless of the Scout's identity in her/his civilian life. There are certainly *Sailor Moon* fans who explored queer issues in their own lives through these themes in *Sailor Moon* (Chambers 2013). In my case, joining the *Sailor Moon* fanfiction community forced me to address my own homophobia and become a more inclusive writer, since my audience, given source material that had clear, positive representation of certain queer issues, explored and championed the themes in its fandom community.

After developing an audience in the *Sailor Moon* fanfiction world, I reached out to my readers about writing original fiction. They were extremely supportive. I went on to self-publish two original books between the ages of 16 and 18, which I sold through my *Sailor Moon* fansite. I received checks in the mail with inspiring letters from North America, Europe, and Southeast Asia; I made pen pals and received fan work, including illustrations and a MIDI-composed song, for my original work. Although *Sailor Moon* had served as a way to bring my audience and me together, we were bonding through *creativity*, and the positive feedback loop was spawning more creative works—this time, original content. As I would later learn, this jump from fandom to original work—and the blurred line between the two, as many original content creators still participate in fandom "on the side"—is a common one, especially in the age of the internet, and in a community inspired by Japan and its doujinshi market.

I joined the professional manga industry in 1999, when I was 17 years old. The English-language publisher of the *Sailor Moon* manga (Mixx Entertainment/Tokyopop) was planning to publish children's novelizations of the series. Filled with the confidence inspired by my success in *Sailor Moon* fanfiction and the size of our online community, I wrote Mixx a passionate, defensive email about how "this was a job for a fanfiction writer," should they be willing to acknowledge us. I was later hired for the job, with little more than my fanfiction backlist and one of my self-published novels as my relevant experience.

Stu Levy, head of the company, was excited to promote me as a young woman writing a series for young girls. When the novelizations were complete, he moved me into adapting translated manga and light novels. I stayed with Tokyopop as a freelancer until they closed their North American doors in 2011, making me one of the oldest freelancers in the North American manga industry. Throughout my entire career, and to this day, I receive fan mail for those novelizations, confessions from people, mostly women, who followed my work for years, and tales of excitement when people first discovered that someone my age could have a professional writing job—especially since I moved from amateur fanfiction to, essentially, professional fanfiction. Young writers constantly reached out to me for advice on writing, even sometimes claiming that they learned how to improve their craft by reading my work.

Sailor Moon and its community empowered me to create; my status as a young woman who "understood" *Sailor Moon* empowered me in the eyes of Stu Levy, since *Sailor Moon* was so financially successful for him; and my example inspired *others* to create. As *Sailor Moon* was one of the first big hits for the current North

American manga/anime industry—especially on the manga side, as very few manga were translated into English before *Sailor Moon*—this essential tie to the feminine, feminine power fantasies, and female creators was integrated into the North American manga industry and fandom from very early on.

When Mixx/Tokyopop began their Rising Stars of Manga contest in 2002,[1] this feminine influence in the Western manga industry started to show itself in original Western manga.

The Rise of Shoujo Manga: Translated and Global

In the mid to late 1990s, the translated manga industry in the West was still reasonably small. The few companies that translated manga—especially Viz Media—published a variety of titles in a multitude of genres, but many fell into obscurity. (This included some short shoujo titles by foundational shoujo creator Moto Hagio, and *Banana Fish*, widely considered in Japan to be one of the most beloved shoujo series ever written but which never managed to become popular in English.) The "big" titles in the 1990s—*Dragon Ball* (Viz), *Ranma ½* (Viz), *Oh My Goddess* (Dark Horse), *No Need for Tenchi* (Viz), and *Pokemon* (Viz)— despite finding popularity with female readers, were mostly shounen and seinen manga, i.e. originally written for boys and young men. The anime industry was more developed and arguably had even more of a masculine influence; *Neon Genesis Evangelion* and *Cowboy Bebop* had a distinctly Male Gaze, and even a series like *Slayers*, which had a female lead, was still not shoujo.

But shoujo representation still left its mark. *Sailor Moon* was a definite hit, and two fantasy manga series—*Magic Knight Rayearth* (Tokyopop) and *X/1999* (Viz)—were high-profile and successful enough that they ushered in a wave of future manga and anime hits (including shoujo and josei titles) for their all-female creation team, CLAMP. Once the high-powered shoujo fantasy *Fushigi Yûgi* started finding success as both an anime (Media Blasters) and a manga (Viz) in the late 1990s, shoujo power fantasies had carved out a niche in this burgeoning industry.

The next wave of shoujo manga—the very late 1990s through to the middle of the first decade of the twenty-first century—expanded on the concept of Japanese Female Gaze in softer, quieter tones; high school romance stories and low-powered fantasies that explored feminine issues outside of saving the world. Titles like *Mars* (Tokyopop) and *Peach Girl* (Tokyopop) paved the way for romance giants like *Boys Over Flowers* (Viz), the rightfully controversial *Hot Gimmick* (Viz), and the hugely successful *Fruits Basket* (Tokyopop), which had two

---

1 Editor's Note: See Chapter 5 for more information about Tokyopop's Rising Stars of Manga contests.

million copies in print with the release of the fifteenth volume in a 23-volume series (Tokyopop 2006).[2] This market share for the Female Gaze also expanded to boys' love, the male-male romantic genre in Japan for women, which was so successful that it became a major focus and cash-earner for Digital Manga Publishing (DMP), one of the oldest exclusively manga translation publishers to still exist. Eventually even manga giant Viz Media founded its own boys' love imprint, SuBLime.

By 2005 or so, shoujo was a huge component of the manga market, partially due to the developing industry standard to bypass monthly "floppy" comics periodicals in the style of superhero comics and skip right to releasing full trade paperback graphic novels, which were carried in bookstores. More girls went to bookstores than to comics shops, and thus shoujo was reaching its target audience. In addition, shoujo titles were popular with even grizzled comics veterans (male, female, or otherwise) due to their fresh perspective and subject matter. *The Comics Journal*, recently criticized for a history of ignoring women and their influence in comics (MacDonald 2013), even released an entire issue dedicated to the discussion of shoujo and women reading comics in 2005.

Around the same time, the North American manga industry started experimenting heavily with original English-language manga, later called OEL or global manga. Although manga-inspired comics had certainly been released in North America before this point, including *Ninja High School* (Antarctic Press), *Gold Digger* (Antarctic Press), *Cathedral Child* (Cyberosia Publishing), and the licensed English-language doujinshi *Dirty Pair* (Studio Proteus/Eclipse Comics), bigger manga and comics publishers began to enter the arena. Notably, Marvel reimagined many of its existing superheroes—including Spider-Man and the Fantastic Four—in a limited series of manga-inspired interpretations, known collectively as the Marvel Mangaverse.[3] Indeed, several of the writers and artists working on this collection were actually from the aforementioned titles, including Ben Dunn of *Ninja High School*, Adam Warren of *Dirty Pair*, and Lea Hernandez of *Cathedral Child*. And Tokyopop, a manga giant at the time, began a talent search contest known as the Rising Stars of Manga, which led to the company's multi-year initiative to develop global manga in English. Due to a wide variety of factors, Tokyopop's overall global manga initiative struggled to find an audience and attain financial success, and after Tokyopop ceased publishing books in English in 2011, many global manga, including unfinished series, were trapped in out-of-print, rights limbo, souring creators, publishers, and readers on global manga. Future publishers, including Hachette USA imprint Yen Press, were more conservative in their attempts at global

---

2 In the interest of full disclosure, I adapted the manga scripts for *Fruits Basket* beginning with volume 15.

3 Editor's Note: See Chapter 9 for more information about Marvel's Mangaverse.

manga, especially as the North American manga industry struggled through the Great Recession.

But interestingly, female creators were a large percentage of global manga creators, and global shoujo titles were some of the more successful. Two of the biggest Tokyopop global manga titles, *Dramacon* and *Bizenghast*, were distinctly shoujo, with female creators. *Dramacon* creator Svetlana Chmakova[4] went on to publish another original shoujo series with Yen Press (*Nightschool*) before publishing the manga version of a James Patterson young adult novel series (*Witch & Wizard*). Amy Reeder, who published a shoujo title with Tokyopop (*Fool's Gold*), later worked as an artist at DC Comics, including on the series *Batwoman*. Becky Cloonan, already an accomplished comics artist before she came to Tokyopop, nonetheless published a volume of her first self-written adventure manga *East Coast Rising* with Tokyopop, and now self-publishes Eisner Award-winning comics and works for a variety of major comics publishers, including DC Comics, where she was the first woman to draw the main *Batman* title (see Beck 2013).

Of the manga companies who still exist in the North American market, Yen Press is the most aggressive in their global manga publishing program, although the majority of their global manga titles are manga adaptations of bestselling prose novels published by Hachette. In addition to choosing many female-oriented prose novels to adapt into manga, including *Parasol Protectorate/SOULLESS*, *Beautiful Creatures*, and the massively popular *Twilight*, many of these manga artists are women, including a number of women in North America—Svetlana Chmakova, rem, and Cassandra Jean, just to name a few. And of the women mentioned, most were born in 1977 or later, making them no more than teenagers when *Sailor Moon* began airing on American television. Like me, they were part of the Western *Sailor Moon* Generation.

I think this connection is no coincidence. In the wake of *Sailor Moon* and the rise of manga in North America, a generation of girls were exposed to the profound, consistent feminine influence in manga—including a deluge of Japanese female creators, a feminine-positive fandom, and related fandom creativity. While comics giants Marvel and DC have consistently struggled to hire more women and write more "female-friendly" series in the wake of controversy, the foundation of manga in the West was already more egalitarian with regard to gender. Much of manga editorial in the industry is female. Many of the creators are female. And so much of the content unabashedly caters to the Female Gaze. The feminine is valued in North American manga.

---

4   Editor's Note: See Chapter 5 for more information about *Dramacon* and global manga creator Svetlana Chmakova.

Digital Publishing: Manga, Global Manga, and Webcomics

Naturally, I was depressed when Tokyopop closed its English-language publishing house in 2011. Tokyopop was my employer and had always been one of the more experimental manga companies; it had always valued shoujo for its success, and in a search for the "next best thing" had been willing to publish a variety of quirky shoujo to see what would strike a chord with readers. This was also following the closing of many other small publishers and imprints, including CMX, the branch of DC Comics that was dedicated to off-beat and classic shoujo titles, and Aurora Publishing, a subsidiary of a Japanese josei publisher that published shoujo, josei, and boys' love in English. I was tired of both working on and reading what counted as "safe" shoujo at that point: high school romances, simplistic fantasies or period pieces, and fetishy, superficial material that relied on shock value to impress. In many ways, the manga industry had fallen back on the Japanese equivalent of romance novels and chick flicks. Although I still appreciated the more explicit feminine power fantasies in the vein of *Sailor Moon*, the truly inventive, exploratory shoujo that the Western market had imported—titles like *Planet Ladder* (Tokyopop), *Cipher* (CMX), and *Basara* (Viz)—had poor or mediocre sales and thus were largely abandoned in the Great Recession.

As a member of the Western *Sailor Moon* Generation, I longed for something more in the shoujo vein, to once again sate my hunger for a new exploration of the feminine. And in the same cycle that had driven me to *Sailor Moon* fandom, I started to wonder if I perhaps shouldn't depend on the source material for everything, if perhaps relying on Japan was too unpredictable, considering the state of the American manga industry. Global manga had brought some genuinely interesting new ideas to shoujo, and it spoke to *me*, as a Westerner, because of the influence of its Western origins. I still adored Japanese manga and the unique insight it carried, but global manga, with its hybrid, transnational mix of influences, could expand shoujo into new, exciting possibilities. I shared Tokyopop's excitement for it and felt that I'd learned from Tokyopop's missteps.

The problem with global manga, apparently, was that the traditional North American manga publishing houses were wary of investing in it. After all, it was expensive, working directly with creators was unpredictable, and global manga had already struggled (and largely failed) to find a reliable audience in the West. Since the translated manga industry—which had a much more predictable, reliable consumer base, even shaky as *that* was—was already becoming more conservative, it was *especially* unlikely that global manga would be the place for shoujo to move outside of its "safe zone."

However, there was a new publishing route on the rise: digital self-publishing on the internet. Just like how I began self-publishing fanfiction and eventually a few original novels online in the 1990s, the digital space had swelled for independent comics creators looking for their own niche audience. They did not need a traditional publishing house to give them access to readers. The success stories, like *Penny Arcade*, a three-panel comic strip about video games that grew into a multimedia pop-culture empire, and *Megatokyo*, a four-panel Male Gaze comic that swiftly morphed into a global manga with "punch lines" on every page, both normalized reading independent comics online and empowered new creators to self-publish online.

Long-form global manga attempted a new model. The creator would publish one to three pages per week online, with no thought for punch lines or short-form "pay-offs," to slowly unravel the material originally limited to graphic novels. Considering how global manga had bypassed monthly serialization altogether and jumped straight into full graphic novel releases, severely slowing down the publication in this manner seemed counter-intuitive. But with no publishers or advances to support them, that release format was most comfortable for creators. It enabled them to sustain a comics production schedule while keeping their day job, and the piecemeal releases helped them slowly build a readership over a longer period of time. Money could be earned through PayPal "donation" buttons, online ad revenue on the website, merchandise made (but not licensed) through third-party printing companies, and self-published graphic novels once there was enough material to compile.

Over time, some of these global manga were very successful—in a financial sense, and/or in a developmental sense for published creators. In Female Gaze manga specifically, erotic boys' love titles *Starfighter* and *Teahouse* had large followings and a number of self-published paperbacks. *Demonology 101*, a global manga by Faith Erin Hicks, was an early step in Hicks' eventual career as a successful independent comics artist and Eisner Award nominee. Jen Lee Quick, one of Tokyopop's former global manga creators, started the online-exclusive *Witch's Quarry* manga after her Tokyopop series *Off*Beat* was left unfinished and trapped in rights limbo.

When the crowdfunding platform Kickstarter launched in 2009, providing an easy framework for readers to fundraise independent artistic projects, the financing for these comics both expanded and became extremely visible. Readers, it appeared, were happy to pledge money for independent digital content, whether or not it was already available free to read online. Some of the early success stories included E.K. Weaver's *The Less Than Epic Adventures of TJ and Amal*, a manga and boys' love friendly free webcomic that raised almost $15,000 in its quest for $4,500 to self-publish a first collected volume, and C. Spike Trotman's *Smut Peddler*, an anthology of out-of-print (originally published by Saucy Goose Press) and new feminine-friendly erotic comics, which raised over $83,000 on a $20,000 goal. At the time of this writing in the spring of 2014, the aforementioned *Starfighter* had managed to raise $143,000+ (of a $70,000 goal) through Kickstarter to fund a visual novel video game related to the comic, and the all-new *Smut Peddler 2014* had raised a shocking $185,000+ (of a $20,000 goal). Comics for women can clearly generate money!

It was this new digital marketplace that caught my eye for the future of global manga publishing. The translated manga industry had already begun releasing digital versions of their print manga to combat scanlations, pirated, fan-translated scans of Japanese books; Digital Manga Publishing had begun a new system of exclusively digital releases and sales, promising Japanese licensors and editorial staff royalties off the back end instead of payment up front (Beasi 2010); and digital distributors like Comixology and the Amazon Kindle had provided a visible platform for all comics, including manga and global manga. *Self-published* global manga even had access to some of these systems, including the swiftly expanding global manga publisher/community Mangamagazine.net (now Inkblazers), a crowd-sourcing system that allowed creators to keep all rights to their work yet split a $20,000 monthly pot among the most popular series, funded by subscriptions, print book sales, and the like. The flexibility of the digital space also allowed for multimedia publishing with relative ease. This revitalized a practice that had been largely abandoned in manga and global manga publishing in favor of graphic novels, that of serialization.

Digital publishing and self-publishing allowed for an explosion of visible global manga talent—creators from all over the world who could succeed in genres, formats, and styles that traditional global manga publishers would never have released in the print market. One of the most obvious success stories is that of Andrew Hussie's *Homestuck*, a sprawling epic of comics and multimedia that became a massive fiction empire online; his Kickstarter for a video game sequel to his story raised almost $2.5 million. This lack of a publishing house "gatekeeper" opened up a sort of Wild West for global manga, allowing a revitalization of creativity and a romantic sense of "anyone, anywhere, has the potential to be successful here." I can't overstate how important that facet of digital publishing has been for the collective creativity behind global manga.

But I also saw a lack of strong leadership in *polishing* new global manga, an arguably essential step in establishing a stable, long-term market. Publishers like Tokyopop and Yen Press had strong editorial teams, but the creative guidance and curatorial functions of the traditional editorial hand were dwindling online, mostly due to self-publishing becoming "the new normal" for digital publishing. Many of the aforementioned digital publishers were either re-releasing self-published manga or providing an open platform for creators to submit their own work with little editorial guidance. For all the benefits and opportunities that self-publishing online provided, it also resulted in a huge, intimidating sea of global manga very difficult to wade through, especially for those used to the traditional manga market and the filters inherent in a submissions and acquisitions process. And the digital business model, unfortunately, put virtually all work and risk on the shoulders of the creators—very few publishers or distributors offered advances, and of the few, such as Inkblazers, that offered direct pay for content, the pay generally came as the result of an established readership and popularity, which the creator usually had to cultivate on her own ... often through releasing hundreds of free pages online and somehow rising to the top of the massive self-publishing market. Digital publishers and distributors were mostly piggybacking on the already established success of self-published global manga and helping creators monetize it, not polish it.

Although I loved all the opportunities of self-publishing and saw no fault in companies helping highly motivated creators make money from their hard work and taking a cut themselves, I also wanted more options for *content-developing* publishers in the digital market. Like the traditional print publishing houses, I wanted digital publishers that offered advances, editorial support, and a curatorial hand. I wanted a digital version of "making it" or "being discovered" that traditional publishers had once offered to creators. There was certainly space for such publishers, and they didn't need to conflict with the self-published market—indeed, they could *complement* it, offering a different experience and support system for undiscovered *and* successful self-published talent alike.

Moreover, I wanted a focus on feminine-friendly content and opportunities for the Western *Sailor Moon* Generation and the younger readers/creators raised under their influence. So many manga industry editors were women within or peer to the Western *Sailor Moon* Generation; it was time for them to start *leading* those companies and not just doing the work on the ground. Global manga creators working in shoujo—again, many raised in a Western market with *Sailor Moon*—had been at the center of much of the past success in the print market for global manga, so why not focus on those creators and their content? I don't think these creators and editors were succeeding in the comics industry *despite* being women or writing Female Gaze media. I think they were succeeding *because* of who they were and what they wrote. They were reaching an audience that hungered for them.

I wanted an outpost of old-fashioned manga publishing in the digital sphere for global manga creators, as an opportunity distinct from, though not entirely unconnected to, the rise in digital self-publishing. And I hoped to specifically tailor it, both on the creative level and the consumer level, to the generation of feminine power that had risen up under *Sailor Moon*.

Chromatic Press and the Future of Female Gaze Global Manga

So, on the basis of discussions which began in 2012, I gathered three colleagues and started Chromatic Press, an independent digital publishing house of English-language global manga and prose with manga-style illustrations (as well as audio dramas, my other love from Japan). It included Lillian Diaz-Przybyl, one of my former editors at Tokyopop who shared many of my opinions on media; Rebecca Scoble, my longtime writing and editing partner who worked as a consultant to libraries building manga collections; and Jill Astley, a prominent member of the English-language fandom for Japanese Female Gaze video games. We all liked similar media, and in the case of everyone except Jill Astley (born in 1977), we were all born in 1982 and grew up with the same media and publishing influences. We knew what we wanted, and we wanted to start commissioning and publishing it ourselves. We already had a long list of English-language creators—mostly women, mostly writing shoujo—whom we wanted to approach, including former global manga creators who had worked for Tokyopop.

The decision to be a primarily Female Gaze publisher was something we all implicitly agreed on, since we specifically wanted to publish the media we and our ilk wanted to read—but we hesitated to make that desire explicit. We were happy to say we wanted to be an inclusive, progressive publisher for socially responsible works, but we weren't sure we wanted to alienate readers who would turn away at something so overtly feminine ... since, despite manga being a feminine-positive space, few manga companies had aligned themselves with a gender-leaning mission statement. We all identified as female, we all wanted to read Female Gaze work, and we wanted to hire mostly female Female Gaze creators, yet we weren't sure we wanted that to be on our banner! There were a number of reasons for this, including our desire to keep our audience as wide as possible, but I can't deny that a factor in this was our fear of being so overtly feminine. We had company discussions about using the color pink very, very sparingly due to the politics of pink and femininity in the West, once again unearthing my fears of the dreaded "othering" and lack of critical acclaim of feminine works I had felt before *Sailor Moon*.

In the eleventh hour, we decided to embrace our Female Gaze outlook, making it explicit in the wording of our goals and in the design our logo, which features a feminine silhouette on a laptop. I'm very glad we did, because the reaction was overwhelmingly positive. In 2013, when we officially announced ourselves as a company, manga critics, comics journalists, and fans flooded us with support. One manga journalist and designer, Lissa Pattillo, redesigned our corporate website pro bono and sent it to us as a gift; we later hired her for design work, and now she's a share-holding member of the company and head of our website. I received an email from a female editor who used to intern at Marvel who was willing to work for us without pay, simply because we were the kind of company she had "always wanted to work in." She's currently a freelancer for us—and paid.

And the creators started to come. Overwhelming female, they flooded us with excited inquiries and pitches for global manga and manga-inspired prose. Influential global manga creators we loved, including Becky Cloonan and Lea

Figure 1.1   *Sparkler Monthly* online digital magazine, published by Chromatic Press. Cover illustration by rem

Hernandez, started speaking positively about us in public spaces. When we ran our first publisher's table at the Toronto Comic Arts Festival a few months later, we made contact with a lot of independent comics artists and writers. The average male creator (with a few exceptions) nodded politely when I told him about our company—but many of the women lit up when they saw my company name tag, exclaiming, "I've heard of you—I think I might pitch!" We were being spread in feminine communities, and they were excited. Global manga titles currently on our list and serialized in our digital magazine *Sparkler Monthly* include *Dire Hearts* by Christy Lijewski, *Windrose* by Studio Kôsen, and *Off*Beat* and *Gatesmith*, both by Jen Lee Quick. We have also published several short stories.

Indeed, at the Toronto Comic Arts Festival in May 2014, the following year, I moderated a panel about the Female Gaze market. When I mentioned the "*Sailor Moon* Generation," the term immediately caught on with global manga creators and manga bloggers, even with nothing more than a few minutes to summarize what I meant by it. I therefore have every reason to believe that *Sailor Moon*'s influence is well understood in the global manga community, both implicitly and explicitly.

And despite some lingering discomfort with our overtly feminine tone in the tradition of Japanese shoujo—one of our creators asked if we really wanted to discuss "glitter" so much on our company Twitter—our audience is largely embracing it, as evidenced by excited tweets when they receive Chromatic Press packages in the mail covered with star stickers. And we definitely have men in our audience, pitching to us, joining forum discussions, and buying our products.

Chromatic Press closed our first completely open round of submissions, where anyone from anywhere could pitch a creative project to our company, in the fall of 2013. After responding to the very last prose submission with a decision—it was a decent Female Gaze work about identity that I ultimately rejected, although I sent along some positive feedback and advice on how to restructure and resubmit—the writer included this note on the bottom of her response:

> ... once upon a time when I was in seventh grade and liked anime and didn't go to the same church as everyone else and therefore had *very* few friends, I was really getting into *Sailor Moon* and I started reading those *Sailor Moon* light novels that Tokyopop was putting out. Being voracious in my quest for *Sailor Moon* things and very thorough, I ended up reading your author biography at the back of the book and then visiting your website (which I remember included writing advice). I thought you were about the coolest person I had ever heard of. Just by writing *fanfiction* you got *noticed* as a writer *and then you got to write* Sailor Moon *OMG that's like THE ULTIMATE COOL JOB.* Which is just to say ... I think it's really exciting to be corresponding with you right now on a writer-to-

writer level (!!). (Margaret Brandl, email message to author, Nov 20, 2013; used with permission.)

To me, Margaret's email elegantly summarizes the impact of *Sailor Moon* on a new generation of global creators who have begun to embrace the feminine. *Sailor Moon* inspired a cycle of feminine power and creativity in my own life. And if that cycle is broader than me—and I believe it is, from what I've seen—then that's a cycle I'm happy to perpetuate.

References

Abad-Santos, Alexander. 2003. "Meet the Women Who Are Changing Marvel and Comics." *The Wire*, October 14. Accessed December 12, 2013. http://www.thewire.com/entertainment/2013/10/meet-women-wholl-change-marvel-and-comics/70484.

Alter, Alexandra. 2012. "The Weird World of Fan Fiction." *The Wall Street Journal*, June 14. http://online.wsj.com/news/articles/SB10001424052702303734204577464411825970488.

Beasi, Melinda. 2010. "Digital Manga Guild: Revolution or Folly?" *Manga Bookshelf*, November 1. http://mangabookshelf.com/9930/digital-manga-guild-revolution-or-folly.

Beck, Laura. 2013. "Meet the First Lady to Draw Batman Since His Inception in 1939." *Jezebel*, February 8. http://jezebel.com/5982669/meet-the-first-lady-to-draw-batman-since-his-inception-in-1939.

Chambers, Becky. 2013. "Sailor Jupiter, Gender Expression and Me." *The Toast*, October 11. http://the-toast.net/2013/10/11/sailor-jupiter-gender-expression.

Kodansha Comics. 2011. "Sailor Moon Volume 1 Goes Back for Second Print Four Weeks after Release." http://kodanshacomics.com/sailor-moon-volume-1-goes-back-for-second-print-four-weeks-after-release.

MacDonald, Heidi. 2013. "So What Does a Gal Have to Do to Get into The Comics Journal Anyway?" *The Beat*, November 5. http://comicsbeat.com/so-what-does-a-gal-have-to-do-to-get-into-the-comics-journal-anyway.

Tokyopop. 2006. "FRUITS BASKET Hits 2 Million." *The Beat*, December 6. http://comicsbeat.com/fruits-basket-hits-2-million.

Chapter 2
The Manga Style in Brazil

Roberto Elísio dos Santos, Waldomiro Vergueiro,
and Victor Wanderley Corrêa

The first Japanese immigrants arrived in Brazil in 1908. They and their descendants have long maintained strong ties to Japanese culture, even during the Second World War. According to Pacievitch (2008, 12), there are currently 1.5 million Japanese and Japanese-Brazilians in permanent residence within the territory of Brazil; the country has had the largest Japanese ethnic population outside Japan in the world since the 1930s.

The Japanese presence in Brazil has positively influenced different national and cultural characteristics, including the arts and publications such as comics, which have come to incorporate elements of Japanese manga. Found on newsstands and bookstores all over the country in vast numbers and a wide variety of monthly, weekly, and special issues, the history of manga in Brazil is divided into two distinct eras, each of which reflects the characteristics of Brazilian society, the country, the local comics publishing industry, and the consumption of cultural material in Brazil.

The first era began in the 1960s, when Japanese-Brazilian comics artists like Minami Keizi and Claudio Seto started to produce graphic narratives that followed the artistic style of manga, while adding Brazilian themes and situations to their stories. Around these artists, the comics publishing house Edrel was established, which published comedy, erotica, science fiction, and action-adventure tales (with Asian themes). The stories produced by the country's Japanese-Brazilians appealed to a niche audience that knew and was used to reading the manga medium originating from Japan.

The second period of manga in Brazil began in the late 1980s, with the opening of trade with Japan, changes in the comic book market, and the television broadcast of Japanese animation, or anime, especially the successful series *Cavaleiros do Zodíaco* [Knights of the Zodiac], or *Saint Seiya*, which was very popular among Brazilian adolescents. This second period differed from the first as it was more innovative and reached all audiences—not only Japanese-Brazilians—and expanded the range of manga publications available, thereby changing the format and the aesthetics of all comics in Brazil.

Manga and Adult Comics in Brazil

According to Nagado (2005, 53), Brazil was "the first country to produce local manga outside of Japan (around 1962, thanks to Japanese-Brazilian artists)." It is possible that this statement is not true but rather the product of excessive nationalism. However, true or not, it is important to emphasize that, at the beginning of the 1960s, Brazilian artists such as Minami Keizi, Claudio Seto, and Julio Shimamoto were producing comics that were very similar to Japanese manga. As Japanese-Brazilians, these artists grew up immersed in Japanese culture and in close contact with the manga that their parents and grandparents received from their native country, which were used to maintain knowledge of the Japanese language and way of life. It is possible, then, that emulating the manga style of drawing and narrating was almost second nature for these artists and served as both a tribute to their cultural roots and as a strategy to establish a particular way of producing comics, a means by which to diversify their stories from the North American comics that dominated the Brazilian market in that period.

Minami Keizi, perhaps the most important of these Brazilian artists of Japanese descent, was born in 1945. Living 450 kilometers from the city of São Paulo, now Brazil's largest metropolis and the capital of the State of São Paulo, he spent great part of his youth drawing comics for his own and his family's pleasure. But he soon began submitting stories to Brazilian publications, and some of them were accepted and published. Encouraged by one of his publishers, he studied drawing via correspondence from the Escola Pan-Americana de Arte [Pan-American School of Art] and moved to São Paulo, then becoming known as the "fastest growing city in the world" and "the locomotive of Brazil." The metropole would eventually prove to be a source of tremendous professional opportunity for him.

However, Keizi faced many difficulties at the beginning of his career as a comics artist. His style of drawing, which was strongly influenced by manga, was largely ignored by publishers. After several rejections, in 1966, he finally succeeded in publishing *As Aventuras de Tupãzinho* [The Adventures of Tupãzinho], a comics series which had as its protagonist a Brazilian character Keizi had created back in 1962, in the newspaper *Diário Popular* [People's Daily]. This can be seen as an example of the incorporation of local, indigenous cultural tradition into manga. (Tupã is a native deity who created the world by blowing the earth.) However, to meet the newspaper's demands, Keizi had to erase most of the character's manga features, thereby making him a kind of copy of the North American comics character Hot Stuff, known in Brazil as Brasinha. Nevertheless, the comic strip's publication in the newspaper made it possible for the character to obtain some recognition among readers and succeeded in opening a few doors for the author. One year later, in 1967,

Tupãzinho starred in his own comic book, published by Pan Juvenil Company. On this occasion, elements of Keizi's manga style were reintroduced into the stories, thus bringing it closer to Japanese products in visual design.

By combining the money he received for his work as a comics artist and the profits he obtained from selling books by mail, Keizi prospered. He succeeded in launching his own publishing company, Edrel, after three years of living in São Paulo. Edrel began its commercial life by exploring illustrated gag comedy and erotic photographs of young women in titles like *Garotas & Piadas* [Girls & Jokes], *As Mais Quentes Piadas* [The Hottest Jokes], and *Calmante* [Tranquilizer]. This content represented the best means for Edrel's survival, as there was huge interest in these kinds of publications at the time in Brazil. The erotic aspect of his most successful publications convinced Keizi Minami that he should choose the adult reader as the target audience of his publishing company. Following this reasoning, he soon began to prioritize the publication of comic books with a strong erotic component. As he was well acquainted with the eroticism present in Japanese manga, it was natural that he turned his focus to this style of drawing when he launched his most famous comic book, *Estórias Adultas—Gibi Moderno* [Adult Stories—Modern Comic Book].

This kind of comic was already present in his company's portfolio, in the work of the artist Fernando Ikoma, who had joined the company early on. His first published story for Edrel had been *As Aventuras de Playboy* [The Adventures of Playboy], a 50-page narrative in a visual language of comics that was strongly influenced by manga. *Estórias Adultas* included Ikoma characters such as the "superhero" Fikon, named after the first letters of the author's name, and The Coward, focused on the abolition of violence. Ikoma also produced stories for other Edrel titles, like the science fiction *A Espiã de Vênus* [The Spy from Venus] and the humorous horror comic *A Turma da Tumba* [The Tomb's Gang], which took place in a cemetery.

The most prolific Japanese-Brazilian artist to publish comics with Edrel was Claudio Seto, who created the erotic detective series *Karate*, which was inspired by martial arts films. He had an inexhaustible source of ideas and drew comics in different genres. In his many years of working for Edrel, he produced a huge variety of stories, from samurai adventures to psychological dramas, Westerns to espionage, which transformed him, according to Gonçalo Júnior (2010, 151) into "the most original and important comic book author in Brazil."

Another of Edrel's artists of Japanese descent who could not disguise the influence he had taken from manga was Paulo Fukue. Working alongside his brother Mario Fukue, he was an expert in science fiction stories, sometimes flirting with the experimental, as in *Volar*, which involved an interplanetary vampire, and *Orius*, set on a sinister planet.

Faced with the demands of censorship during the period of Brazilian military dictatorship, which lasted from 1964 to 1985, Edrel was closed in

1972 due to economic problems and disagreements among its partners. After its closing, some of its artists went on to work for Grafipar Publishing. This company was founded in 1978 in the city of Curitiba, in the state of Paraná in the south of Brazil, and its aim was similar to Edrel's—to publish adult comics in Brazil. Claudio Seto was particularly active in this new publishing house as well, reviving many of his characters there, including Maria Erótica, a complex girl dealing with sexual repression. He also created the cowgirl Katy Apache (a character subsequently drawn by many artists) for Grafipar.

Yet another important artist of Japanese descent, Julio Shimamoto, worked for Grafipar. Shimamoto was already a veteran artist in the comics field when the company was established; however, at Grafipar he was able to explore at length his relationship with the manga style, using it in a great number of his narratives, especially those related to samurai.

Manga's Influence upon the Brazilian Publishing Industry in the 1980s and 1990s

When the military dictatorship faded at the beginning of the 1980s, censorship of the media also ended. This new situation made it possible, among other initiatives, to publish different kinds of comic books. Along with mainstream material, underground comics—both Brazilian and American—were made available to the public. But the economic crisis that hardened at end of the decade hampered the growth of the publishing industry.

In relation to manga, the remarkable fact at that time was the creation of the Associação Brasileira de Desenhistas de Mangá e Ilustrações [Brazilian Association of Manga and Illustration Artists], or "Abrademi" for short, in 1984. Francisco Sato (2005, 62) notes that during this period "most of the participants were of Japanese descent who grew up reading manga in Japanese and had acquired knowledge of the design of manga." He also emphasizes that today an association like Abrademi "brings together TV animation and games fans, and not only manga or comics fans."

Some Brazilian publishing houses tried to release Japanese original manga titles, including *Lone Wolf and Cub*, *Akira*, *Crying Freeman*, *Mai, the Psychic Girl*, and *The Legend of Kamui*, in Portuguese at the end of the 1980s. But the really big boost to the popularization of manga in Brazil occurred at the beginning of the 1990s, when Brazilian television began to broadcast anime series like *Cavaleiros do Zodíaco* [Knights of the Zodiac] and *Sailor Moon*, which attracted a teen audience.

Sandra Monte (2010, 54–5) points out that Brazilian television started to show *Cavaleiros do Zodíaco* at a time that was marked by shows increasingly targeted towards a young audience, such as programming on MTV and the US cartoon *The Simpsons*. She also notes that the narrative structure of this anime is similar to soap operas shown in Brazil, a televisual format already very familiar to the public:

> In other words, as a soap opera, *Cavaleiros do Zodíaco* was a cartoon that always made the viewer follow the cartoon in order to know the outcome, similar to the practice of watching soap operas, which for decades has been a programming model implemented on our television. (Monte 2010, 54)

Sonya B. Luyten (2000) says that during the 1990s the public came into increasing contact with Japanese media products; manga became better known in the West to a larger audience because anime began to be broadcast on television and movie screens worldwide, supported by a powerful dissemination machine. Thus, manga began "to be translated, especially into English and French, and from there to other Western languages" (Luyten 2000, 225).

In the wake of the success of these animated television series, the magazine *Herói* [Hero] was launched by two small Brazilian publishers, Acme (later renamed Conrad) and Sampa. The company published articles, news, and criticism on a large range of pop culture products (films, comics, television series, etc.), but mainly focused on manga and anime. Soon, other titles joined *Herói*, like *Heróis do Futuro* [Heroes of the Future] and *Anime-Do*, for instance, providing readers with information about the kind of entertainment they liked: interviews with Brazilian voice actors and comics writers and artists, profiles of characters, news reports on upcoming films, and so on.

Taking advantage of the growing popularity of Japanese pop culture products among the Brazilian public, some publishers decided to release new manga titles. This, in turn, inspired a new generation of young Brazilian artists to start to produce comics influenced by manga aesthetics.[1] These artists included Marcelo Cassaro, Erika Awano, Alexandre Nagado, Eduardo Francisco, Fábio Yabu, Rodrigo Reis, and Lydia Megumi, among others, who developed their own distinctive art styles and helped to disseminate titles like *Holy Avenger*, the webcomic *Combo Rangers*, and the graphic novel anthology *Manga Tropical*.

Combo Rangers: One of the First Brazilian Webcomics

Combo Rangers, created by Fábio Yabu in 1998, began as a parody of live-action fighting team series, such as *Power Rangers*. Produced directly for the internet, it

---

1 João H. Lopes (2010) identifies some elements of the manga style as follows: simplification by suppression of traits; differentiated use of letters, onomatopoeia, and balloons; peculiar drawing of the hair and eyes; deformation; etc.

paid homage to other media products favored by the target reader through the use of intertextuality and humor. With a personal approach, these comics were updated weekly, and additional content was posted daily. The public simply needed to access the website to read the stories free of charge.

These comics relied on the use of computer graphics to expand the screen, so that the characters could cross the panel. Sounds were added to the images, which subsequently incorporated a version of Flash for animation used at moments of the plot when the heroes transformed. These tools permitted this webcomic to go beyond the possibilities of physical print-based comics, and readers reacted positively to this new digital media narrative.

The interactivity enabled by the internet allowed continuous contact between the creator and the consumer and, even in its early days, changed the relationship between the sender and the receiver of a message. Yabu, moreover, took full advantage of this opportunity with his comics by starting one of the first national independent productions on the internet and using techniques freed from the limitations of physical pages that had previously been unthinkable. Yabu also used colloquial phrases, which were akin to simple, everyday conversation, combined with textual features common to the internet chat slang of that period.

After two successful years, *Combo Rangers* changed its profile, becoming more explicitly oriented toward the consumer market. The characters started to appear in advertisements in various media, like radio and television, and on various branded products aimed at children, such as notebooks, lunchboxes, stickers, t-shirts, and miniature action figures.

But the feature that had led originally to the webcomic's success also made the public reject the published version of *Combo Rangers*. The two-dimensional comics had no sound or movement, and the interaction between artist and audience was limited. Furthermore, the colors of the computer graphics had to be reduced when printed due to the available palettes of that period. In competition with its own online material, the production costs involved in the conversion of digital stories for the print process doomed the publication to failure.

The first printed version, consisting of 12 issues, published by Editora JBC and distributed to newsstands, did not reach expected sales. The second version, by a larger publisher, Panini, won greater acceptance, mainly due to its nationwide distribution, affordability, and lack of competition from the digital version. JBC published a new edition in 2013, *Combo Rangers—Somos Heróis* [Combo Rangers—We Are Heroes], which was sold in comics shops. In the printed editions, it is possible to note the evolution of Yabu's artistic style as well as his plots, which progressed from narratives for children to ones for slightly older, teenage readers, and involved a reduction of satire but without losing its original charm. In these comics, the relationships between the major characters is one important theme explored by the author.

Holy Avenger: From RPG to Comics

Inspired by the role-playing game *Dungeons and Dragons*, *Holy Avenger* is an fantasy-adventure tale. Written by Marcelo Cassaro with art by Erica Awano, this title was the first Brazilian manga-style comic to reach 30,000 copies sold monthly. The story originated from games written for the *Dragão Brasil* [Dragon Brazil] magazine, which was targeted at RPG fans. Therefore, *Holy Avenger* "incorporated themes based on roleplaying games, video games and Japanese animations, adapting the Japanese storytelling and visual narrative to the national language" (Corrêa 2013, 84). In all, 40 issues of *Holy Avenger* were published from 1995 to 2004, plus some miniseries. Readers were teenagers who not only bought the magazines but also went to conventions and supported the authors. Valéria Bari (2011, 241) suggests that:

> In a country like Brazil, where the interests of youth are linked to consumerism and the increasingly public, more simplistic and binding performances of instant fame, seeing a teen movement aroused by reading a fictional work draws the attention of Brazilian adults interested in a vision of a positive future.

As a fantasy story, *Holy Avenger* is set on an unknown continent, Arton, where the savage and uninhabited land of Galrásia is located. Conflict begins when a young girl named Lisandra, who was conceived mysteriously in Galrásia, arrives in the city of Valkaria searching for the famous thief Sandro Galtran. Together, Lisandra and Sandro head off in pursuit of the Virtue Rubies linked to the Nature Goddess, who gives the girl powers that transform her into a druid.

All issues included a two-page spread with a map to show the locations of the fictional land in which the story takes place and a line that indicates the journey of the characters. Also included were a summary of the previous issues' events and profiles of the main characters, describing their characteristics and motivations. This format is used regularly in almost all manga titles, mainly in shounen manga magazines produced for young boys. Following the conventions of many Japanese manga, the first three pages of each chapter of *Holy Avenger* were in color and the rest of the edition was printed in black and white. Each issue contained 32 pages, and on page 24 there was a preview of the next issue.

This comic also shared other similarities with Japanese manga. The language consisted of simple and common words, the layout of the pages allowed for a quick read—accentuated by the constant presence of speed lines, onomatopoeic words (i.e. sound effects) which were highlighted with artistic letters, and speech balloons which were less rounded than usual (Corrêa 2013, 91). The use of intertextual references was another distinctive element of the narrative of *Holy Avenger*. Allusions to manga and anime characters from Japanese properties were common throughout, as well as references to anime music sung by the characters and the video games and RPGs that served as the bases for structuring the narrative.

However, in spite of this fantasy setting, the plots and the characters managed to speak to the real-life challenges faced by young Brazilians. Thus, according to Braga (2011, 192–3):

> First, one can consider that the production of *Holy Avenger* was due simply to an attempt to attract readers passionate about manga, in order to capture a market niche already thematically consolidated. Second, a manifestation of ... the mode of national artistic production ... Third, an expression of the cultural survival of society.

Brazilian Manga Trends in the Twenty-First Century

Mangá Tropical (2002), a compilation that brings together a group of Brazilian artists who create comics in the manga style, collects together different stories that deal with everyday issues faced by their young Brazilian characters. The stories cover topics such as urban violence, romance, and problems at school, and some stories are located in São Paulo, the largest city in Brazil. Other attempts to create Brazilian comics in the manga style include the titles *Mangá Brasil* [Manga Brazil], *Mangá X*, and *Ação Magazine* [Action Magazine]. These publications opened up new space for both veteran and new Brazilian comics artists, but none were particularly successful, mainly because they were edited by small presses.

In 2008, Mauricio de Sousa, the most popular comics artist in Brazil, launched the monthly magazine *Turma da Mônica Jovem* [Monica Teen], which uses a manga style (Corrêa 2013, 72). This title sells over a million copies per issue, and by favoring the publication of independent material, altered the public perception of Brazilian comics and won new readers, mainly women, from all over the country. One of the most prominent characteristics of Mauricio de Sousa's comics is the use of intertextuality. Parodies of children's classic literature, movies, superhero comics, and TV serials, among other media products, and the transformation of the comic's own text into concrete objects (balloons, panel frames, etc.) are common features of this artist's narratives.

Mauricio de Sousa's *Monica's Gang*, similar Charles Schulz's *Peanuts*, is based on a cohort of small children who live and play in the neighborhood Lemon Tree Villa. The author created *Turma da Mônica Jovem* to compete with the Japanese manga published in Brazil—the design of the comic appropriates the aesthetics of manga.[2] There is even a crossover with Osamu Tezuka's characters

---

2 The front cover of *Turma da Mônica Jovem* magazine explicitly includes the phrase, "*Em estilo mangá*" [In the manga style].

(such Tetsuwan Atom, Kimba, and Princess Sapphire) in issues 43 and 44. Most of the plots depict scenarios of romance and jealousy, and intrigues within a high school setting, but there are also adventure narratives that follow RPG and video game-like structures. Thus, it is at the crossroads between shoujo and shounen manga and clearly intended to attract both male and female readers.

Recently, Mauricio de Sousa transformed another of his child characters into a teenager and launched the magazine *Chico Bento Moço* [Young Chico Bento], whose protagonist is a teenage hillbilly who goes to a big city to study. The plots focus on the character's inability to live in a modern society, which is different and far away from the small town where he grew up. Like *Monica Teen*, this publication uses a manga style.

Final Considerations

From *As Aventuras de Tupãzinho* to *Chico Bento Moço*, many influences have led to the production of so-called Brazilian manga. In the beginning, only Japanese-Brazilians were familiar with the characteristics of the manga's visual language and style and could understand its uniqueness as a sequential art. But with the growing circulation of manga around the world, its presence increased in Brazil as well. The existence of a great number of readers with Japanese heritage in Brazil is frequently mentioned in order to explain the popularity of manga in this country; however, the reality, we would assert, is not so simple. The reason for the success of manga in Brazil, and Brazilian artists' intentions to produce comics that emulate it, can, in our view, be found in the characteristics of the medium itself. More than other comics industries, Japanese manga has been able to successfully generate and sustain stories directed towards specific segments of the public, especially adolescents and young adults. Genres appealing to these demographics are not something that Brazilian readers could find in their own domestic comics market. Thus, many readers migrated from the North American comics to manga, feeling that the latter could provide them with a better source of entertainment, along with a better reflection of the concerns of people of their age and sharing their way of life. Brazilian comics artists, in turn, recognized that migration and are now using specific, manga-inspired creative strategies to maximize its commercial potential. Yet in the end, it is possible that the creation of Brazilian comics with manga-like stylistic features is just a way of meeting the challenge of an invasion of "alien" comics in order to guarantee the survival of a "native" comics industry.

References

Bari, Valéria. 2011. "A Ressignificação dos Conflitos Civilizatórios em *Holy Avenger* [A Reinterpretation of Civilizational Conflicts in *Holy Avenger*]." In *A História em Quadrinhos no Brasil: Análise, Evolução e Mercado* [The Comic Strip in Brazil: Analysis, Evolution, and Market], edited by Waldomiro Vergueiro, and Roberto E. dos Santos, 241–7. São Paulo: Laços.

Braga, Amaro. 2011. *Desvendando o Mangá Nacional: Reprodução e Hibridização dos Quadrinhos* [Unraveling the National Manga: Reproduction and Hybridization of Comics]. Maceió: Edufal.

Corrêa, Victor W. 2013. "A Inovação do Moderno Mangá Brasileiro [The Innovation of Modern Brazilian Manga]." Master's Diss., Universidade de São Caetano do Sul.

Gonçalo Júnior. 2010. *Maria Erótica e o Clamor do Sexo* [Maria Erótica and the Cry of Sex]. São Paulo: Peixe Grande, São Paulo.

Lopes, João H. 2010. *Elementos do Estilo Mangá* [Elements of the Manga Style]. Belém: s.n.

Luyten, Sonia B. 2000. *Mangá: O Poder dos Quadrinhos Japoneses* [Manga: The Power of Japanese Comics]. São Paulo: Hedra.

Monte, Sandra. 2010. *A Presença do Animê na TV Brasileira* [The Presence of Anime on Brazilian TV]. São Paulo: Laços.

Nagado, Alexandre. 2005. "O Mangá no Contexto da Cultura Pop Japonesa e Universal [Manga in the Context of Japanese Pop Culture and Universal]." In *Cultura Pop Japonesa: Mangá e Animê* [Japanese Pop Culture: Manga and Anime], edited by Sonia B. Luyten, 49–57. São Paulo: Hedra.

Pacievitch, Thais. 2008. "Imigração Japonesa no Brasil [Japanese Immigration to Brazil]." *InfoEscola*. http://www.infoescola.com/geografia/imigracao-japonesa-no-brasil.

Sato, Francisco N. 2005. "O Mangá e o Papel da Abrademi [Manga and the Role of Abrademi]." In *Cultura Pop Japonesa: Mangá e Animê* [Japanese Pop Culture: Manga and Anime], edited by Sonia B. Luyten, 59–63. São Paulo: Hedra.

Chapter 3
Scott Pilgrim vs. *MANGAMAN*: Two Approaches to the Negotiation of Cultural Difference

Aaron Pedinotti

Over recent decades, the incorporation of influences from Japanese manga into works of North American graphic fiction has involved a variety of approaches to issues of narrative structure, thematic content, and the rendering of visual motifs. In works that apply a manga-inspired aesthetic to commercially well-established materials, such as Marvel's Mangaverse of the previous decade,[1] the approach is often fairly superficial in nature, involving a straightforward grafting of elements of Japanese popular culture onto iconic American superheroes and their attendant storylines (Dunn 2001; Dunn and Dunstone 2002; Andrews 2006).[2] Another, similarly straightforward approach involves the insertion of North American characters into narratives whose core elements resemble those of established manga genres, such as stories involving the use of mecha vehicles and the defense of large urban areas from giant monsters.[3]

Beyond these direct incorporations lies a pair of relatively more complex approaches, both of which attempt to provide socially-inflected, thematic meta-comments on the processes of cross-cultural appropriation in which they are engaged. The first of these involves the depiction of North American settings in which the presence of manga elements is treated as an already-assimilated, background factor of their fictional world. This approach tends to convey the sense of a cultural space that is thoroughly saturated by manga motifs. In contrast, the second approach attempts to stage explicitly dialogical encounters

---

1   Editor's Note: See Chapter 9 for more information about Marvel's Mangaverse.
2   Also see Jill Thompson's *Death: At Death's Door*, an OEL manga-style comic that focuses on the character Death from Neil Gaiman's *Sandman* series (Thompson 2003).
3   See, for example, Frank Miller's two-part series for Dark Horse Comics, *Big Guy and Rusty the Boy Robot*, in which the American military uses a giant robot to defend Tokyo against a monster attack (Miller 1996). Also see the more recent graphic novel prequel to the film *Pacific Rim*, in which North American characters pilot giant mechas called "jaeggers" in order to defend East Asian cities from kaiju monsters (Beachman 2013).

between the universes of Japanese and American comics by deliberately highlighting the differences between them. The first approach, then, tends to focus on hybridity and blending at the expense of difference, while the second does exactly the reverse.

This chapter contrasts the narrative, thematic, visual, and paratextual elements of two works that exemplify the first and second approaches, respectively. These are Bryan Lee O'Malley's multi-volume *Scott Pilgrim* series (2004–10), published by Oni Press, and Scott Lyga's single-volume graphic novel *MANGAMAN* (2011), published by Houghton Mifflin Harcourt. In what follows, *Scott Pilgrim* is shown to depict an already manga-fied fictional North American cultural space in which a background ubiquity of Japanese pop-cultural elements has resulted in their assimilation into the aesthetic fabric of its fictional world. Alternately, *MANGAMAN* is shown to stage a highly aestheticized encounter between the universes of "American Comics" and "Japanese Manga," one that focuses explicitly on their differences.

While establishing this basic contrast, my chapter discusses the ways in which it relates to other, subsidiary differences between the texts. Most centrally, this includes their differing narrative treatment of interracial romantic relationships and the thematic and political significance of these depictions. It also includes their referencing of aesthetic and narrative influences, and the manner of their paratextual formatting as "manga," "comics," and/or "graphic novels." The discussion of paratextual elements situates the texts in their historical context, as exemplars of recent trends in American comic book publishing, and the insights derived from this focus on recent history provides further insights into the discussion of narrative and visual contents. In terms of its broader historical and geopolitical scope, my analysis is most significantly back-grounded by a nebulous and flexible form of twenty-first century North American global cultural hegemony, one which has older forms of empire in its developmental history without being entirely synonymous with them. Below, I argue that there are structuring inter-relationships at work between these various textual, paratextual, and historical factors. While doing so, I grant a degree of temporal and causal autonomy to different agendas, aesthetic intentions, and inter-textual processes, and decline to locate a single master determinant underlying them all. In the conclusion, I contrast the strengths and weaknesses of both approaches discussed here in light of their relevance to the formulation of a genuinely dialogical, politically progressive form of global manga, a task that involves a brief comparison of the fictional ontologies presented by each approach. As will become clear in what follows, these discussions allow room for a certain amount of sheer aesthetic pleasure-taking from the texts, not regardless of political considerations, but alongside them.

Scott Pilgrim versus ...

My discussion of *Scott Pilgrim* is best begun with a synoptic take on what might be called its overt, or author-intended, themes and contents, followed by a more closely-targeted discussion of certain of its recurrent motifs. Throughout its six volumes, this series traces the misadventures of a white, early twenty-something, Toronto-based slacker whose name occurs in the title of each volume. As an unmotivated, unemployed, dubiously-qualified bassist for a post-punk garage band, Scott is to some extent a throwback to the Gen X hipsters/slackers of the 1990s. But to a greater extent, he is also a creature of his own millennial generation. As such, he is chronically short on attention, addicted to videogames, and possessed of a mind so accustomed to indiscriminate linkage as to be literally open to intrusions from outside.

For the better portion of Volume 1, which is entitled *Scott Pilgrim's Precious Little Life*, the narrative establishes itself as a semi-serious, semi-comic tale about Scott and his group of quirky, twenty-something hipster/slacker friends. As such, it resembles countless other contemporary fictions that deal with the vicissitudes of middle-class young adulthood. From its early pages onwards, the series' overt thematic preoccupations include the specific flavors of narcissism, escapism, projection, emotional and sexual irresponsibility, loneliness, denial, and media-induced reality-confusion that often accompany the twenty-something phase of life. The central dramatic conflicts revolve around the main characters' efforts to cope with people who most exemplify these unpleasant tendencies and their struggles to become emotionally committed, responsible adults.

Although these themes and conflicts remain consistent throughout the series, the manner in which they are addressed changes rather drastically near the end of the inaugural volume, when the world of *Scott Pilgrim* is shown to be decidedly other to our own, and to strongly resemble a universe out of Japanese manga. This occurs when a public fistfight breaks out between Scott and a romantic rival, and the two are revealed to be capable of gravity-defying acts of hand-to-hand combat involving motion lines, force fields, exaggerated facial expressions, and the summoning of paranormal entities by the villain (O'Malley 2006, 168). From this incident onward, the series is frequently punctuated by manga-like fight scenes, including comedic combat with robots, samurai swordsmen, and giant foes.

With the arrival of these narrative elements, the series enters a narrower category of young adult fiction: those that use fantastical, science-fictional, and/or paranormal motifs to make metaphorically thematic statements about the dangers and challenges of adolescent and post-adolescent life. As such, *Scott Pilgrim* is the recent outgrowth of a multi-platform and cross-genre North American textual category that contains numerous works, including the early *X-Men* and *Spider-Man*, the *Teen Titans*, *The Faculty*, and *Buffy the Vampire Slayer*, among many others. Over the course of the past few decades, many of the texts in this category have grown increasingly ironic and playful in their use of genre motifs, often making self-reflexive comments about their own clichés and formulas.

While continuing this trend toward self-reflexive irony, *Scott Pilgrim* brings new materials into the mix. Through its incorporation of manga influences, it attempts to fuse elements derived from Japanese comics with the narrative and thematic tendencies of its American antecedents—an effort that is facilitated by the fact that the fused elements already have much in common with each other. For, like their American counterparts, many manga use their own roster of conventions to comment on aspects of adolescent and twenty-something existence, and of late, many have grown increasingly ironic and prone to self-commentary about the manner in which they do so.

Along with its spectacular fight scenes, the manner in which *Scott Pilgrim* carries out these aesthetic incorporations includes other visual and paratextual features. In every panel, the series' artwork is highly influenced by classic manga stylistics. This includes the presence of a black-and-white color scheme in the original trade paperback editions; the use of large, round eyes for each of the main protagonists; the use of motion lines and other visual signifiers of manga-like action and a generally cutesy aesthetics of character depiction.

At the level of the paratext, the original black-and-white editions were printed in a 5 × 7″ digest form, which in the world of North American trade publishing has become commercially and semiotically synonymous with the notion of "authentic manga" (Brienza 2009). And throughout the series, the narrative makes frequent nods to aspects of Japanese popular culture that, while not manga per se, are definitely manga-related. Scott's videogame preferences, for example, run toward Japanese products. When dreaming of himself as a game character, he resembles Link from *The Legend of Zelda* (O'Malley 2007, 51–2). And when his band has gathered to practice, he tells them that he has "learned the bass-line to Final Fantasy Two" (O'Malley 2012, 55).

When considered in light of the overt thematic concerns that were catalogued above, these manga-related elements seem to play something of a subordinate or supporting role, contributing to the story's messages regarding irresponsibility and escapism, and especially to its reflections on media-induced ambiguities about the nature of reality. Specifically, they point to a background cultural pervasiveness of superhero narratives, videogames, science fiction images, and Japanese comics that is so omnipresent as to have possibly altered or undermined the structure of reality itself. As such, this omnipresence is treated as a taken-for-granted feature of the text, a *fait accompli* enacted prior to its opening panel. Thus, when the first gravity-defying fight scene occurs, it manages to be somewhat surprising, without being much of a surprise.

Yet amid this accretion of inter-textual references, aesthetic hybridizations and thematic statements about the nature of contemporary media landscapes, other, more troubling tendencies are noticeably at play. These arise from the racial dynamics of *Scott Pilgrim*'s romantic subplots. When their underlying import is highlighted, these cast the series' incorporation of manga elements in a far more significant, interpretively central light. In order to see this, it is useful to reflect briefly on the general social profile of the characters that is revealed through a quick, superficial glance at the text. Such a glance reveals a number of smart-alecky, wisecracking, mostly white but sometimes not, mostly straight but sometimes gay, Canadian and American hipster kids.[4] As was the case in its textual predecessor, *Buffy the Vampire Slayer*, the use of nonwhite and homosexual side characters gives the character makeup of the series a liberal, inclusive look; but as scholars have also said of *Buffy*, this *pro forma*, politically correct form of inclusivity is subtended by ideological proclivities that to some extent contradict it, enforcing retrograde values and prejudices (Alderman and Seidel-Arpaci 2003). For reasons that will shortly be made clear, the same can be said of *Scott Pilgrim*'s use of manga elements. While these give the text an appearance of multicultural openness to a hip, trans-Pacific fusion of popular aesthetic forms, close examination of their narrative deployment reveals countervailing tendencies.

In order to get a sense of this, I now turn to a major structural feature of the series' overarching plot: Scott Pilgrim's conflict with "the seven evil exes." As used throughout the series, this phrase serves as a collective signifier for the former romantic partners of the young woman who is Scott's primary love interest for most of the narrative. This is the character Romana Flowers, a post-punk American hipster who has relocated to Toronto. Early in the series, she is revealed to have a sordid history of romantic involvement with less-than-pleasant personality types (O'Malley 2012, 162). When she flees the US for Canada, one of these former flames establishes a "league of evil exes" whose *raison d'etre* is to prevent her from having a satisfying relationship with anyone ever again. As Ramona's latest attempt at such a relationship, Scott becomes the object of the league's wrath. In order to be with her, he must defeat them all in single combat.

For present purposes, the primary interest of the league is its conspicuous inclusion of Asian members. One of these, a young Indian-American man named Matthew Patel, is the character who Scott fights in the previously-mentioned climactic scene from Volume 1. A few details of this particular scene are worthy of scrutiny. It begins when Patel crashes through the ceiling

---

4   The gay characters include Scott's friend and roommate Wallace Wells, and the guitarist for his band, Steven Stills. A nonwhite member of his peer-group includes his ex-girlfriend Knives Chao.

at a performance of Scott's band, attacking Scott while he is still onstage. During the ensuing fight, Scott pummels Patel, rapidly punching him 64 times, achieving a "new personal best" in the manner of a videogame player, and sending Patel flying upwards towards the ceiling from which he has descended (O'Malley 2011, 139). When Patel has recovered from this initial engagement, he breaks into a Bollywood-style musical number, during which he uses mystical powers to summon "demon hipster chicks" who levitate in the air behind him and throw mystical fireballs in Scott's direction (147–50). Scott's victory is achieved with the help of his friends and bandmates, who assemble behind him onstage and use bellicose dance moves to summon a force field that deflects the fireballs. Scott then delivers a death blow, causing Patel to burst into coins—the videogame-style of death that is eventually suffered by each of the seven evil exes (148–55).

Any honest assessment of this scene's (barely) subtextual racial implications would need to involve the following set of observations. First and foremost, it depicts a white young man angrily beating the bejesus out of a nonwhite young man, eventually leading to the latter's death. Second, in the course of this violent encounter, the nonwhite young man is portrayed in a highly stereotypical manner, and prevalent motifs of Indian popular culture are explicitly associated with his villainy. Third, this character's eventual defeat involves a racially-charged group confrontation in which the two camps break down into mostly white kids on one side and a human-demon bundling of Americanized Bollywood clichés on the other. Fourth, the manner of the white kids' victory involves the literal establishment of a boundary in the air, in which the force of penetration that is threatened by the hybrid aggressor is deflected, leading to his defeat. Rather significantly, this victorious group comprises the very assemblage of characters that, by virtue of its inclusion of some token nonwhite and homosexual members, is involved in the series' projection of a fashionably inclusive, cosmopolitan image. Through the narrative uses to which this group is put, we can discern a jarringly countervailing tendency, in which the supremacy of North American hipster whiteness is able to assert itself against a stereotypically-rendered nonwhite adversary.

This tendency is especially interesting when considered in light of another specific sequence that occurs as an interlude during the fight scene. In it, Ramona interrupts the action from the music venue's balcony, explaining to Scott and his friends the backstory of her previous involvement with Patel. This tale is accompanied by panels illustrating her story's contents:

> It was in the seventh grade. It was football season, and the little jocks were in high gear. For some reason they all wanted me … [Here a panel illustrates a group of white, football-playing jocks scoping out Ramona.] Matthew Patel was the only non-white, non-jock kid in school. Probably the only one for miles around,

or in the entire state, for all I know. So, *of course* ... [Emphasis mine. These words are accompanied by a sequence of panels in which Patel is depicted as a dark silhouette, stalking Ramona from behind a tree, leading up to a sequence in which Patel rather aggressively kisses Ramona with a disturbingly violent expression on his face.] We joined forces and took 'em all out. We were one hell of a team. Nothing could beat Mathew's mystical powers combined with my brute strength. [This is accompanied by a few panels in which Matthew and Ramona beat up the white jocks.] Nothing but pre-adolescent capriciousness. [Ramona walks away from Matthew in the hallway of a junior high school, flicking him the bird while he fumes in rage.] We only kissed the once, and we were quits after something like a week and a half. (O'Malley 2011, 143–5)

When cross-referenced with the rest of the fight scene and other aspects of the romantic subplots discussed below, this three-and-a-half page sequence is remarkably crowded with dubious racial suggestions. On Matthew Patel's side of things, there is the motif of the nonwhite, sexually-threatening stalker-male so obsessed with a young white woman that he cannot get over her for years (after an approximately ten-day fling in junior high). This is coupled, on Ramona's side, to a thoroughly unreflective, entitled (*"of course"*) conflation of dating "the only non-white, non-jock kid" with an act of alt-chic rebellion against the jock-dominated, normative social order of the American public education system. As conveyed by both its immediate visual depiction and the over-arching narrative fallout that flows from it, this conflation is shown to be loaded with danger for the white female character, leading to continued stalking and the violent assault of her boyfriend even into her twenties.

Additional romantic subplots shift the ethnic locus of former romantic partners from the Indian subcontinent to East Asian locales, and the manner in they do so connects quite interestingly to the influence of manga on the series. The shift is most glaringly evident in Scott's conflict with the penultimate pair of evil exes: a duo made up of Japanese twin brothers that Ramona once dated at the same time, named Ken and Kyle Katayanagi. From their introductory moments onward, the series is not kind in its depiction of these siblings. In the first panel in which they appear, they stand haughtily at a costume party, dressed up as themselves, with hostile expressions on their faces. Kyle wears all white clothing and stands with his arms folded in a superior posture, a caption to his left containing the words: "Kyle K. (Handsome Jerk)." His brother stands beside him, snobbishly sipping a glass of red wine. He wears a white headband and a sleeveless muscle shirt that rather loudly carries the sun and rays of the Japanese imperial flag on its front. His caption reads: "Ken K. (Perfect Asshat)." A picture on the wall behind them depicts a woman in a state of partial undress, and they are surrounded by a group of young white women who seem to be made giddy by their presence in the room (O'Malley 2009, 11).

Figure 3.1 The first appearance of the Katayanagi twins. From *Scott Pilgrim vs. the Universe* (2009)

Much like the Patel subplot, the subsequent depiction of the twins involves a pairing of pop-culturally inflected ethnic stereotypes to the impression of villainy. For the remainder of the costume party sequence, they attack Scott with a remote-controlled robot which resembles images from the work of legendary manga artist Osamu Tezuka (O'Malley 2009, 12–24). When this tactic fails, they resort to similarly manga-inspired karate kicks. During the sequence in which they do so, moreover, they have abducted one of Scott's female friends and dangled her in a cage in order to use her as bait (116–32). As in the case of Patel, this kidnapping involves stalking behaviors in which the twins are initially depicted as dark silhouettes tracking the young woman from behind, again resulting in the impression that nonwhite characters pose a semi-sexualized threat to young white women (99).

Even more so than in the case of Patel, Scott's battles with the twins involves the fore-fronting of ethnic antagonisms. During their initial encounter, the twins adopt a racially superior attitude to Scott, passive-aggressively gloating over the fact that "English is not our first language" and characterizing their use of proxy robotics as superior to the direct combat practiced by the Euro-Canadian "barbarians" of the series (O'Malley 2009, 12–13). For his part, Scott unleashes a fairly uncharacteristic torrent of sometimes racist verbal abuse on the twins, referring to them as "dicks," "identical turds," and "Japanese jokes," just before killing them both (126–7, 132). Overall, it is fair to say that the depiction of the twins is the most racially charged and troubling of any in the series.

Interestingly, however, the twins are not the only case in which Japanese culture and motifs derived from manga are strongly associated with the prospect of violent threat and sexualized danger. There is also the case of the series' arch-villain, Gideon Graves, a trendy nightclub owner and cultural capitalist who is the original organizer and mastermind of the league of evil exes. In the series' climatic showdown, Gideon fights with a katana blade, adopts the clenched, maniacal postures typical of manga villains, and eventually expands to a demonically super-human size and shape—all of which give an otaku flavor to his villainy (O'Malley 2010, 166–73).

On the other side of the romantic storyline, Scott also has an ex who, while not evil, is definitely stalker-like, prone to violence, and of East Asian ethnicity. This is Knives Chou, a Chinese-Canadian teenager Scott briefly dates and then unceremoniously dumps in favor of Ramona at the beginning of the series. After being dumped, Knives proceeds to follow Scott around, lurking outside his home, dating one of his friends, imitating Ramona's hairstyles, and periodically attacking Ramona in public using knives and martial arts. Although Chinese herself, Knives is proximately the source of further associations between *Japanese* motifs and threats of violence. This occurs when her father, angered at the effect that Scott has had on his daughter, attacks him with samurai swords, of which he is shown to be a collector (O'Malley 2007, 64–7, 150–53, 170–76).

Some of these examples can be read as straightforward nods to manga influences, but when cross-referenced with the series' depiction of other ex-partners and East Asian characters, deeper structural factors can be seen to be at play. In order to get a sense of what those factors might be, some brief review is in order. So far, I have shown that *Scott Pilgrim* occupies a double position in the history of North American pop-cultural narratives. On one level, the series is an outgrowth and continuation of a multi-modal textual lineage in which paranormal and sci-fi motifs are used as metaphors for young adult dilemmas. On another level, it is also an important example of a text that fuses visual and narrative elements of Japanese and American comics. Additionally, there is ample evidence that, like some of the predecessors in its American lineage, the series projects an image of multicultural openness while simultaneously exhibiting signs of racial antagonism in its subtexts. Specifically, a persistent, structural feature of the series' romantic subplots concerns the dumping of unstable, violently vengeful Asians by white characters who must subsequently defend their status as a couple against attacks from these nonwhite exes.

When attempting to explain each of these observations in a manner that takes their potential relevance to each other into account, it is difficult to ignore the probable salience of Bryan Lee O'Malley's mixed Korean and French-Canadian ethnic heritage. When all of the previously amassed evidence is considered in tandem, it seems fairly plausible to claim that a mixture of authorial tendencies derived from the unique social pressures implied by this heritage might be manifesting in the series. These might include a sympathetic gravitation toward multiculturalism countervailed by a lingering Korean and Korean diasporic hostility toward the Japanese; a resultantly complex and ambivalent set of anxieties about the artistic appropriation of Japanese styles; a similarly ambivalent awareness of the privilege and social power that attend inclusion in the internally hierarchical and contested category of whiteness; and a projection of complicated outsider feelings onto fictional members of other Asian ethnicities.

Rather than focusing upon these conjectural, individually-based possibilities of interpretation, however, I prefer to consider the series in light of a larger social and historical situation for which O'Malley might have been uniquely poised to serve as an expressive conduit. Simply put, this larger situation is the increasingly global reach and cultural influence of Japanese manga. *Scott Pilgrim* is a significant outgrowth of this increased influence; it was produced during the mass-market explosion of manga products in North American publishing markets throughout the first decade of this century. Casey Brienza (2009) has shown that this process involved the shift to an affordable digest template and the preservation the original right-to-left reading format of Japanese comics. When examined at the paratextual, visual, and narrative levels, *Scott Pilgrim* can be seen to refract the dynamics of this situation in a complex, double-edged manner. At the level of the paratext, it adopts the new size template of the digests without going right-to-left, thereby preserving the reading format of Western comics. The original artwork is black and white and strongly evokes manga styles, but its line work is a bit darker and more solid, and its depiction of motion a bit less fluid, than is the case in most mainstream Japanese comics. Lastly, as has been shown, its narratives comprise a mixture of North American and Japanese pop cultural influences. At each of these levels, then, the text both incorporates and exhibits signs of partial self-insulation against Japanese influences.

My contention is that these structural and functional overlaps comprise the multiple faces of an ambivalently hybrid response to the historical situation of the text. In making this claim, I also contend that this historical situation informs the series' narrative depiction of a world in which manga motifs have become naturalized features of everyday life. As such, it plays a related, structuring role in *Scott Pilgrim*'s displayed attitudes toward Asian characters. At the narrative level, the main feature of this response is as follows: throughout the series, a hip version of the white, heteronormative couple plays the role of a filtering institution in a ubiquitously manga-fied reality, signifying more than just its status as couple. The nature of this filtering function can be understood via the couple's narrative trajectory. Prior to the start of their relationship, Scott and Ramona engage romantically with East Asian characters, but they eventually come together to form an ethnically and culturally insulated unit that survives its encounter with Asian others with a white identity intact. It is significant, in this regard, that Ramona is an American and Scott a Canadian, and that both are Caucasians. Their coupling thereby secures a simultaneously cultural, national, and ethnically Euro-American association between the United States with Canada, rendering their romantic union a bulwark of joint North American white identity. In its role as filtering institution, the purpose of the Scott/Ramona dyad is to be flexible enough to flirt with nonwhite otherness in its youth while rejecting the disruptive allure of this otherness in adulthood. In this way, the unit that they form is able to respond to changes in the cultural conditions that surround it without being dissolved by them.

Considered in its historical context, this outcome is not difficult to interpret as an anxious, defensive subtextual response to the increased influence of manga upon North American popular culture, and particularly upon the cognitive and affective development of North American youth. This interpretation helps to explain the text's displayed attitudes toward Japanese characters and motifs, whose inclusion in the story results in repeated patterns of hostility and threat containment. Parallel maneuvers at the visual and paratextual levels allow otherness a partial admittance to the text while keeping its influence under control. Operating in this multi-pronged manner, *Scott Pilgrim* deploys a classically hegemonic strategy of incorporation on power's own terms, while still managing to seem superficially hip and culturally sensitive at the levels of its overt themes.

MANGAMAN

MANGAMAN, which was written by Barry Lyga and illustrated by Colleen Doran, is a much shorter work than the *Scott Pilgrim* series, comprising only a single, relatively slim volume. For this reason, its primary points of relevance to current concerns take less space to discuss. This black-and-white, 7 × 13" text tells the story of a young male character who comes from a world in which mecha battles with kaiju monsters and other goings-on typical of Japanese comics are routine features of daily life. Prior to the story's opening, this character is unexpectedly catapulted through a rift in space and time and ends up landing in a small American town called "Castleton," which at first appears to be located in the "real" world. The young man, whose name is Ryoko Kiyama, is housed at a military institution located in this town. Here he is watched over by a research scientist, named Doctor Capeletti, who is working on an enormous machine that, when finished, will be able to send Ryoko back to his home world and close the breach in space/time.

In the opening pages of the story, Ryoko is compelled to participate, against his own stated inclinations, in the youth culture of small town American teens. Having just been enrolled in the local high school, he is encouraged by Capeletti to attend the "Homegoing Party," a raucous event thrown by local youth at the beginning of each school year in a spirit of adolescent opposition to the prescribed "Homecoming" rituals (Lyga 2011, 1–3, 8). A sequence in the narrative run-up to this party introduces Ryoko's future love interest, Marissa Montaigne. As a high-school senior who has entered a phase of late-adolescent experimentation with her identity, Marissa has recently dumped her boringly popular jock boyfriend Chaz and started to wear unusual costumes to social events and to school. As she prepares for the "Homegoing Party," for example, she puts on a traditional Japanese gown and styles her hair in an accompanying fashion (3–6). At the party, she catches site of Ryoko as he is introduced to the local student population for the first time. Although this first contact is brief, the two take an immediate interest in each other (12–15). The rest of the narrative is structured around the process of Ryoko and Marissa getting to know each other while negotiating the social, intercultural, and ontological difficulties entailed by the fact that they literally come from two different worlds.

As the story progresses, these negotiations begin to involve a shifting sense of reality. In the beginning stages of the story, the narrative seems to maintain a sharp line of demarcation between the "reality" of Marissa's world and the fictional status of Ryoko's universe. This line is first established when it is revealed that "manga" actually exists as a form of mass-produced fiction in Marissa's reality, meaning that, for the residents of Castleton, Ryoko is literally a fictional character brought to life (Lyga 2011, 24). At one point, an antagonistic high school student pejoratively refers to him as "Mangaman," and after Marissa touches Ryoko's hand, she tells a friend that it "felt like reading" (30). Doctor Capaletti refers to the dimension rift that brings Ryoko to the town as an "extra-scientific event," indicating that there may not be a way of accounting for it within the scientific framework of his world's "reality" (24). And throughout most of the story, the majority of small town American characters maintain a physically consistent form, while Ryoko's appearance often shifts in the manner typical of manga characters. He explodes, for example, into exaggerated, cartoony expressions when he is feeling embarrassment, love, or sexual excitement (29, 32). Motion lines form in the air around him, take on solid form, and become precipitates that have to be cleaned up by the high school janitor. Rain clouds form over his head when he is sad, and his thoughts materialize in the air above him (27, 53, 29). As a result of these and other differences from Castleton's citizens, Ryoko is unable to grasp the codes and causal logics of his new surroundings. He exhibits surprise, for instance, when a fistfight with the jealous Chaz actually leads to physical harm (95). His unusual characteristics are noted as peculiarities by the residents of Castleton, most of whom label him as a freak. In the story's early stages, all of this reinforces the notion that they are of the "real world" and that Ryoko is a creature of fiction.

As the story progresses, however, this strict line of demarcation begins to dissolve and eventually collapses completely. This begins at the level of visual depiction. Increasingly throughout the narrative, the residents of Castleton come to be drawn in a stylized manner that is at once evocative of *Archie Comics* and Roy Lichtenstein's pop art. This style of depiction renders their appearances a combination of small town American clichés, combining aspects of conservative eras such as the 1950s and 1980s with contemporary fashions and references to current technology. During a scene in which Marissa's parents express their xenophobic worries about her involvement with Ryoko, for instance, they take on a blankly cartoonish appearance, as if they are reciting lines from a bygone era. Overall, however, the hairstyles, clothing, and interior décor seem not so much to be dated as to partake of a kind of pop timelessness. Marissa's ex-boyfriend Chaz is a combination of various jock stereotypes of different eras, and Marissa and her other acquaintances are also depicted in a slightly clichéd, historically collaged manner, summoning a comic book flavor of small town Americana.

On his side, Ryoko is also depicted in a manner that draws out and amplifies stylistic aspects of manga characters to a point that occasionally verges on caricature. This includes large eyes and a lithe, agile form, but is most particularly the case with regard to the sexual androgyny of his appearance, which is visually highlighted to the point of extremity. With his long, wavy black hair and pointy, high-set face, Ryoko sometimes seems more feminine than masculine, prompting stereotypically heteronormative and homophobic comments (e.g. "—a boy or a girl?"; "I don't know if I should kick its ass or screw it"; and "girl's hair—") from a crowd of mostly male American students during his public introduction at the Homegoing party (Lyga 2011, 14). At both the visual level and at the level of character responses, such instances subtly put the Americans on an ontological par with Ryoko, suggesting an encounter of clichéd identities and forms.

As they accrue throughout the volume, such stylizations insert a sense of "unreality"—or more accurately, of "pop *reality*"— into the world of Castleton. Near the end of the narrative, this culminates in the revelation that the town is situated in another type of comic book universe, possessed of its own naturalized motifs, rules, and structures. Quite significantly, it is Ryoko who demonstrates this, being in a position to notice it due to his origin in a different sort of universe. As he and Marissa go on a scenic nature walk near the middle of the story, he tells her that he can sometimes see future events before they happen. The reason, he explains, is that time moves differently in his world; the moments that make up time are sequenced in a right-to-left as opposed to left-to-right manner. Pointing to a car that is located outside of a panel frame, he asks Marissa if she can really see it, indicating that it is not "really there" but is rather somehow implied to her visual sensorium, and then calls her attention to the "white space" comprising the panel boundary where the car should be. He then reaches from a preceding panel into the one that follows it, tapping her on the shoulder and giving her a start (Lyga 2011, 60–61). Although initially alarmed by the implications of these discoveries, Marissa quickly grows to accept them. Realizing that her own world is comprised of panels with gaps between them, she learns how to enter the space between the panels and move around inside it, popping out of thin air into a girlfriend's bedroom and seeking out Ryoko when he is alone on a walk (69–72).

By the end of the volume, the de-naturalization of Marissa's reality is so complete that her own physical form undergoes a metamorphosis. This event is preceded and influenced by the fact that she has grown increasingly enamored with Ryoko and charmed by the aesthetics of his being. When nervousness causes huge sweat beads to break out on his head, for example, she tells him, "I don't know why, but that weird sweat thing you do is **adorable**" (Lyga 2011, 74). This aesthetically-inflected romance leads to a four-page erotic encounter between Marissa and Ryoko, drawn in a dreamy, collaged style that combines elements of Japanese and American graphic erotica (83–6).

Marissa's transformation occurs when, in the story's climatic sequence, she runs into the dimensional rift that leads to Ryoko's world, mistakenly believing that Ryoko has entered it himself. She is repelled from the rift before it closes, but when she reemerges, she has been transformed into an iconically cutesy manga girl, sporting huge round eyes, a mere pointy curve of a nose, a triangular smile, and her own tendency to shift forms in an affectively revealing manner. When Ryoko asks her how she feels, her eyes become glowingly exclamatory hearts, and she replies, "*PRETTY **AWESOME***" (Lyga 2011, 125). After sharing a swelling romantic kiss, the two set out to hunt kaiju and explore the world beyond Castleton.

Concluding Comparisons

There are clearly a number of significant differences between the narrative and visual contents of *Scott Pilgrim* and *MANGAMAN*. As demonstrated, the former exhibits thematically contradictory tendencies, displaying a surface sheen of multicultural inclusivity while seeming to deploy a subtextually racialized, hegemonic strategy at the level of its romantic subplots. In contrast, the central romantic plotline of *MANGAMAN* serves to undermine the naturalized privilege of a white, American world, while exposing the fragility and malleability of its norms, identities, and ontological assumptions and playfully critiquing the heteronormativity and xenophobia that attend these. In doing so, it concludes with the formation of an interracial, genre-crossing romantic relationship that contrasts starkly to *Scott Pilgrim*'s conclusive affirmation of a white couple's racially purified commitment to itself.

The paths to these contrasting resolutions unwind against larger narrative and visual backdrops that take different approaches to the influence of manga. *Scott Pilgrim* portrays a world in which already-incorporated, taken-for-granted manga elements have reached a cultural saturation point. *MANGAMAN*, on the other hand, treats manga and American comics as distinct universes with their own styles and manners of existence, drawing out and deliberately magnifying difference to a point of occasional near-caricature. The differences between these approaches manifests at the level of visual style. In *Scott Pilgrim*, the pencil work is hybrid through and through, combining American and Japanese elements in every panel, while *MANGAMAN* maintains a marked visual distinction between its "American" and "manga" characters and settings. And at the level of the paratext, *MANGAMAN* is formatted and sized as a traditional American graphic novel, rather than as a "manga" digest, as is *Scott Pilgrim*.

Another significant difference between the texts can be seen in the extent to which they cite their manga influences. In the case of *Scott Pilgrim*, there is very little direct referencing of manga artists, authors, or specific graphic works. Throughout the series, influence expresses itself as a general borrowing of styles and motifs. In contrast, *MANGAMAN* makes numerous explicit references to two important figures from the history of manga, Henry Yoshitaka Kiyama and Rumiko Takahashi. During a conversation between Ryoko and Doctor Capelletti, for example, the latter claims to have read works by both of these artists (Lyga 2011, 45). Later, in a nod to the central narrative gimmick of

Takahashi's popular *Ranma ½* series, Ryoko is revealed to have had a girlfriend on his home world who transformed from a girl into a boy (50–51). Ryoko's last name, moreover, is "Kiyama"—a reference to the eponymous artist signals a thematic overlap between *MANGAMAN* and the latter's most important work, *The Four Immigrants Manga* (1931). This early graphic novel tells the story of four young Japanese men, including Kiyama himself, who immigrated to San Francisco in the 1920s. Like *MANGAMAN*, it contains numerous social mishaps precipitated by the cultural displacement of a Japanese character operating in a less-than-hospitable American milieu. Thus, both tales are stories of Japanese immigration to America, one realist and the other fantastical.

Comparatively, then, *Scott Pilgrim* seems to presume a state of aesthetic assimilation that precludes the necessity of explicit reference to historical and artistic influences, whereas *MANGAMAN*'s direct concern with the issue of difference results in explicit citations of Japanese and Japanese-American manga lineages. Considered in light of the previous discussion, the former approach seems to dovetail with *Scott Pilgrim*'s hegemonic tendencies; by eliding the very histories that produced it, the series avoids the complex and fraught relationship of manga genres to issues of ethnic representation, cultural and national identity formation, immigrant experience, and the complexities entailed by processes of intercultural exchange and the globalization of popular culture.

For its part, *MANGAMAN* does not only engage its textual history, it also provides commentary on its contemporary moment and makes protopolitical suggestions concerning the future negotiation of manga's ethnic and national legacies by consumers and fans. For on one level, the story gives off strong implications about the ways in which the fictional worlds contained by graphic texts can be significantly related to cultures-of-origin without having to be absolutely tethered to them in any sense of ethnic, national, aesthetic, or individual identity. This is the significance of Marissa's metamorphosis. In becoming a manga girl, she does not become Japanese or relinquish the social facts of her whiteness and American-ness; yet this transformation nonetheless opens her up to new possibilities for aesthetic and personal engagement, and these possibilities retain an undeniable relationship to Japanese popular culture.

On another level, however, there is also a sense that the ethnic and national identities of graphic fictional characters are not entirely homologous with those of "real-world" humans. On this front, the text makes a particularly forceful and thematically pointed suggestion. This is that the fictional worlds in which manga, comics, and graphic novels are set possess an irreducible reality, immanent to themselves, that grants them a degree of ontological autonomy from the ostensibly "non-fictional" reality in which they are produced (see especially Lyga 2011, 70). Thus, the respectively "Japanese" and "American" identities of manga Ryoko and comic book Marissa are not exactly the same as the real-world versions of such identities. Rather, a sense emerges from the text that both character's identities are in some way real and fictional at the same time, and this implication is ultimately shown to be relevant to "reality" as such. For, by undermining the social and ontological primacy of two universes that believe themselves to be non-fictional, *MANGAMAN* very strongly implies that our own world is another real fictional universe comprised of contingent, arbitrary, flexible, and revisable social arrangements. Needless to say, these outcomes have bearing on the development of a politically and culturally sensitive approach to manga's increasingly global influence, and to the formation of new fan identities derived from works of manga.

Alongside such bearing, the story also makes metaphorical statements about the historic period in which it was produced. Like *Scott Pilgrim*, it can be seen to comment upon the increased influence of manga on North American culture, particularly with regard to the popularity of manga texts among young female readers. This is evident in Marissa's attraction to the cuteness of Ryoko's affective expressions, a process which references a significant aspect of manga's appeal to teen and young adult female consumers (Brienza 2011). It is also evident in the sudden and unexpected abruptness of her transformation into a manga version of herself. Considered in light of its broader socio-economic context, the speed of this transformation mirrors the speed with which the sales of manga have expanded in North American publishing markets, rapidly coming to influence the production of cartoons, movies, and videogames, and fomenting the rapid development of fan cultures in which strong personal identifications with manga characters are widespread.[5] With these socially-inflected metaphors, *MANGAMAN* depicts the flipside of the situation on which *Scott Pilgrim* also comments. Rather than presenting a reality in which manga is already culturally omnipresent, it focuses on the processes whereby this omnipresence is achieved and comments playfully on the cultural frictions produced by it.

In closing, then, I can add a few additional differences to those identified above. Throughout this section, I have shown that *Scott Pilgrim*'s approach to difference provides relatively superficial citations of its own Japanese influences. In an earlier section, I have also shown that it indulges an essentially postmodern ontology in which reality and fiction are seen to be indistinguishable from each other. In contrast, *MANGAMAN* pays explicit tribute to its influences, and in doing so, develops an ontology in which fictions retain ties to their cultures of origin while also maintaining a degree of semi-autonomy from them. While allowing room for experimentation with new identities and new forms of aesthetic incorporation, this difference entails sensitivity and respect for the specific histories and cultures from which these new forms and identities are derived. As a result, *MANGAMAN* seems to generate less dissonance between

---

5 To get a sense of the speed of this transformation, see Brienza (2009).

its overt and subtler thematic messages, as if the two had been more deliberately and coherently thought through in advance, and intentionally coupled to a progressive political agenda.

Taken together, these findings seem to warrant a conclusive endorsement of *MANGAMAN*'s relatively buffered and careful negotiation of difference. Yet any such endorsement needs to be considered in light of the historical situation in which both texts were produced, and to which each refers. For despite the apparent virtues of *MANGAMAN*'s approach, it is nonetheless the case that *Scott Pilgrim* seems to more accurately anticipate the cultural texture of the near future. Although small town parochialism provides a handy metaphor for numerous North American attitudes toward otherness, it has limits when applied to a situation in which manga has gone thoroughly mainstream in US and Canadian society. It would seem, then, that what is called for on both aesthetic and logistical grounds are texts that combine *MANGAMAN*'s political sensibilities with the portrayal of a cosmopolitan world similar to the one depicted in *Scott Pilgrim*. In this sort of text, the bellicose attitude of *versus* would yield to an appreciative syncretism of aesthetic traditions, and the habit of hegemonic dumping would give way to unrepentant kisses. As the influence of manga continues to expand its global reach, such a development could not fail to be *PRETTY **AWESOME.***

References

Alderman, Naoimi and Annette Seidel-Arpaci. 2003. "Imaginary Parasites of the Soul: Vampires and Representations of Blackness and Jewishness in the *Buffy/Angel*verse." *The Online International Journal of Buffy Studies* 3 (2). http://slayageonline.com/essays/slayage10/Alderman_&_Seidel-Arpaci.htm.

Andrews, Kaare. 2006. *Marvel Mangaverse, Volume 3: Spider Man, Legend of the Spider Clan*. New York: Marvel.

Beachmen, Travis. 2013. *Pacific Rim: Tales from Year Zero*. Burbank, CA: Legendary Comics.

Brienza, Casey. 2009. "Paratexts in Translation: Reinterpreting 'Manga' for the United States." *The International Journal of the Book* 6 (2): 13–20.

Brienza, Casey. 2011. "Manga Is for Girls: American Publishing Houses and the Localization of Japanese Comic Books." *Logos: Journal of the World Publishing Community* 22 (4): 41–53. doi:10.1163/095796512X625445.

Dunn, Ben. 2002. *Marvel Mangaverse, Volume 1*. New York: Marvel Comics.

Dunn, Ben, and Kevin Dunstone. 2003. *Marvel Mangaverse, Volume 2*. New York: Marvel Comics.

Kiyama, Henry Yoshitaka. 1999. *The Four Immigrants Manga: A Japanese Experience in San Francisco, 1904–1924*. Berkeley, CA: Stone Bridge Press.

Lyga, Scott. 2011. *MANGAMAN*. New York: Houghton Mifflin Harcourt.

Miller, Frank. 1995. *The Big Guy and Rusty the Boy Robot*. New York: Dark Horse Comics.

O'Malley, Brian Lee. 2007. *Scott Pilgrim, Volume 4: Scott Pilgrim Gets It Together*. Portland, OR: Oni Press.

O'Malley, Brian Lee. 2009. *Scott Pilgrim, Volume 5: Scott Pilgrim vs. The Universe*. Portland, OR: Oni Press.

O'Malley, Brian Lee. 2010. *Scott Pilgrim, Volume 6: Scott Pilgrim's Finest Hour*. Portland, OR: Oni Press.

O'Malley, Brian Lee. 2011. *Scott Pilgrim, Volume 1: Scott Pilgrim's Precious Little Life, Color Edition*. Portland, OR: Oni Press.

O'Malley, Brian Lee. 2012. *Scott Pilgrim, Volume 2: Scott Pilgrim vs. The World, Color Edition*. Portland, OR: Oni Press.

O'Malley, Brian Lee. 2013. *Scott Pilgrim, Volume 3: Scott Pilgrim & the Infinite Sadness, Color Edition*. Portland, OR: Oni Press.

Takahashi, Rumiko. 2003. *Ranma ½, Volume 1*. San Francisco: Viz Media.

Thompson, Jill. 2003. *Death: At Death's Door*. New York: DC Comics.

Chapter 4

Euromanga: Hybrid Styles and Stories in Transcultural Manga Production

Nicolle Lamerichs

From the nineteenth century onward, Europeans and Americans developed a strong cultural fascination for Asia, which is often referred to as "Orientalism." Classically, Orientalism refers to the power relationship between the West and its Eastern Other. This relationship, however, is uneven. Even today, Orientalism is presumed to be characterized by Western superiority and Eastern inferiority as a result of the internalized power regimes of colonialism (Said 1978). The relationship between the West and Japan, however, is more complex than Said's theory forebodes. The dialogue between Western countries such as the Netherlands and Japan is an intimate one where narratives, experiences, and memories constantly cross borders. One space where this flow is most clearly visible is in art and popular culture.

Historically, Japanese culture has been appropriated in Western impressionist art, Zen gardens, and architecture (Napier 2007). When World War II tarnished this culturally rich image, the image of Japan became more ambivalent and inspired both fear and curiosity. Today, the nation's global identity, which lingers between East and West, inspires Western corporate businesses, art, and media, as it represents a mixture of spiritual traditions, strong work ethic and family morals, as well as an advanced technocapitalist model (Ivy 1995; Wolferen 1995). This Orientalism—an ambiguous fascination for Japan's Otherness—is closely related to the reception and appropriation of Japanese popular culture in the West.

The cultural dynamics between Japan and the West cannot readily be signified as hegemonic forces but rather are complex flows that go back and forth between groups. An example of this widespread influence of Japan is manga, a visual language that originates in comics but has spread to animation ("anime"), games, and other consumer goods. Japan exports media products that are widely recognizable and hailed by consumers all over the world who align themselves with Japan's exotic, fantastical imagery (Smits and Cwiertka 2012). The compelling nature of Japanese culture has been dubbed "Cool Japan," a term that originates from Douglas McGray's article "Japan's Gross National Cool" for *Foreign Policy* (2002). Later adopted by Japanese politicians and policy makers, this concept refers to the country's pervasive soft power (Nye 2002).

The cultural influence of Japan has been amply theorized on a macro level; signified as "cultural globalism" (Burn 2006), "transculturalism" (Hills 2002; Jenkins 2006b, 156), or even a "global space" (McLelland 2001). On a micro level, the aforementioned studies explore the figure of the Anglo-American "otaku," the fan of Japanese popular culture. While the otaku is pathologized in Japan as a deviant and obsessive fan (Galbraith and Christodoulou 2012), in Western countries the term has been introduced to connote a more positive identity: the cult fan interested in Japanese content. The otaku is also a gatekeeper who makes Japanese content accessible. Since much Japanese content does not cross borders officially, Western fans are prone to, for instance, translating comics, games, or animation themselves (Denison 2011). The otaku is thus a liminal figure, someone who hovers between the official industries whose products s/he honors but, at the same time, always struggles to attain access to this culture at all.

The popular culture of manga thus already creates difficulties in terms of language, accessibility, and circulation. This cultural dynamic is uneven, particularly when considering that the concept of manga culture in the scholarly literature seems to suggest a hegemonic relationship in which Japan influences the West with its soft power. Still, it would be wrong to portray this dynamic solely as an influence from Japan's side, embraced by Western "Japanophiles." The Japanese are interested in Western countries and their narratives in their own right. Ito, Okabe, and Tsuji (2012, xiii) rightly point out that Osamu Tezuka, Japan's preeminent author, was inspired by Disney productions in his work, while today's most celebrated animator, Hayao Miyazaki, embraces European culture in his movies. Despite shared cultural imagery, however, Western and Eastern audiences are largely divided by local protocols, specific interests (e.g., in particular game genres), and language differences.

This chapter specifically examines the artistic influence of manga in the Netherlands and Germany to explore how Japanese popular culture migrates across media, cultures, and local traditions.[1] I use the concepts "transculturalism" and "transmediality" to account for these complex cultural dynamics between various local traditions. First, I will provide a more general outline. After that, I will trace the theoretical framework, discuss these two national contexts, and exemplify them with various case studies. Methodologically, this chapter provides a close reading of various Dutch and German Euromanga and the

---

1   It is important to note that the German and Dutch contexts are somewhat unique in that they both engaged in manga distribution, translation, and local production somewhat later than other European countries, such as France, Italy, and Spain (Jüngst 2004).

local contexts in which they emerge. My approach is a medium-specific one (Hayles 2004) that reads these comics in terms of their visual and narrative style, with close attention to elements such as paneling and their semiotic implications (McCloud 1993). I also examine the historical production contexts of these Euromanga. Such comics often emerge in fandom as small independent projects, but can also be initiated by, or professionalized into, mainstream publishing houses. In some cases, the language of manga is adopted by other comics artists to experiment with the style or convey criticism of their own culture or the East. This study is also partly based on my own involvement in the Dutch manga scene as an artist and editor of the circle OpenMinded.

Particularly, I shall focus on two cases that, each in their own way, mediate manga. First, I explore the manga publication *Oost West* (2009), in which multiple Dutch artists interpret Japanese culture and aesthetics. The project involved local doujinshi (amateur manga) artists as well as mainstream comics artists, all of whom created graphic novels that convey cultural themes and narratives of Japan. Second, I investigate the appropriation of "yaoi" and "yuri" doujinshi in Germany. By close-reading the anthology *Lemon Law* (2007–), I chart how German artists interpret the queer genres of manga culture and the ways their own national culture stands out.

Transmedia and Transcultural Fandom

In Western countries, manga projects often emerge as cult comics that draw fan audiences who are already familiar with Japanese popular culture. Especially in Europe, such comics projects are often small-scale and initiated by fans. However, in Japan, manga cannot be understood through its comics alone but as an elaborate "media mix," a combination and integration of different media platforms to sustain large franchises.

Increasingly, media content is spread across multiple media platforms, ranging from television and games to new media. Mass media in both East and West increasingly deploy transmedia designs that rely on promotional texts distributed across media platforms (Gillan 2010; Jenkins 2006a; Ross 2008). Transmedia design can also imply new narrative models; these, again, emerge both in Japan and in the West. Henry Jenkins (2006) has for instance coined the phrase "transmedia storytelling" as a model in which the industry distributes narrative content across different media platforms (e.g., television, games, animation). This model of franchising narratives and characters has been common in Japanese popular culture since the 1980s (Ito 2005). It relies on audience engagement to collect narrative content across media platforms and interpret the larger textual world. Jenkins' (2006b) example of this model is *The Matrix* franchise, where the game explores additional storylines that add to the meaning of the movie trilogy. He also mentions the Japanese game *Kingdom Hearts* (2002), a joint endeavor with Disney, as a best practice.

Other scholars, however, note that the Japanese model has become less geared towards grand, transmedia story worlds and more towards branding recognizable characters (Azuma 2009). Whereas Western transmedia storytelling may be described as all-encompassing and plot driven, the Japanese model is iconic and relies on tropes. However, both Asian and Western transmedia designs imply an active consumer who connects and interprets disaggregate parts of the narrative. In Western countries, the increased transmediality of the text is intimately tied to an increase in "participatory culture" around popular culture. Viewer activity is encouraged through web sites, competitions, and voting systems (Gillan 2010; Müller 2009). It is debatable whether such a model can be mapped onto Japanese popular culture, where participatory culture still appears to be a bottom-up affair, rather than a top-down formation motivated by the industry.

These fan cultures form communities that have been theorized as "fandom," an analytical term to describe the active audiences of popular culture. Fans are characterized by their creativity, online and offline sociality, and their affect for the media text. Since the 1970s, comics, television, and film fandoms have all emerged in rich, industrial countries such as North America and Japan. Increasingly, the fandoms related to Japanese content, e.g. "manga fandom," have been developing in the emerging economies of countries such as China, Thailand, and Brazil.[2] Though manga fandom is a global phenomenon, it is also closely linked to local identity. Many authors have described these flows of content as transcultural fandom (Hills 2002; Hitchcock Morimoto and Chin 2013) to suggest its crossovers between cultures rather than nation states. "Transcultural" implies a term "which at once is flexible enough to allow for a transnational orientation, yet leaves open the possibility of other orientations that may inform, or even drive, cross-border fandom" (Hitchcock Morimoto and Chin 2013, 93).

Indeed, the culture around anime constructs a "fantasyscape," a site of play and imagination (Napier 2007). Susan J. Napier (2007) summarizes the concept as "temporary alternative lifestyles that exist parallel to the mundane, which people enter and exit as they please" (Napier 2007, 11). Manga fandom itself can also readily be understood as a fantasyscape that connects kindred spirits, both in the fiction itself as well as in its social environments, such as the fan convention. Napier's terminology is derived from Arjun Appadurai's *Modernity at Large* (1996), most particularly his understanding of global media functioning as an ideological landscape or "mediascape." Appadurai (1996, 35) explains that these landscapes "tend to be image-centered, narrative-based accounts of strips

---

2 Editor's Note: See Chapter 2 for more information about global manga in Brazil and Chapter 10 for the Philippines.

of reality." Thus, the concept refers to the ideological underpinnings of media products, such as the news or television, or advertising itself, which influence our ideas of reality. The fantasyscape, however, puts this term to a more liberal use, suggesting that contemporary media, such as manga, are not about ideological persuasion but about connecting through narratives and the imagination. In the participatory culture of manga, reality and imagination come in various shades of gray—the visuals allow audiences to connect globally by means of fantasy.

Euromanga

The Euromanga that I investigate in this chapter are closely related to local anime fan cultures—but must not be equated with them. The anthologies that I focus on are professionally published comics, not independent or self-financed fan creations. I have provided an analysis of Western doujinshi elsewhere (see Lamerichs 2013). Nonetheless, I will briefly explain the doujinshi model, since these local works and their artists are clearly influenced by, or indeed have prior experience in, these contexts.

Doujinshi are often described as "amateur manga" (Kinsella 1998), amateur being a term that stems from the Latin *amare*, "to love." Nowadays, amateur implies engagement in non-professional activities, which partly resonates with doujinshi. These comics are non-professional in that they are often created as labors of love rather than strictly for financial gain. The term "doujinshi" is derived from the Japanese *doujin* (literally "same person," which refers to one or several persons that have a common interest or goal) and *shi* ("magazine" or "periodical"). Colloquially, then, "doujin" stands for the self-publication of fan works in mixed media (e.g., games, music, and comics) and represents the community aspect which brings the fans together. For my purposes, doujinshi refers to self-published, printed works, which includes comics, light novels, and art books.

Doujinshi can be homages to existing texts, inspired by anime, manga, game, and even Western texts (e.g., *Harry Potter*, *CSI*). Some, conversely, belong to the "original" genre, meaning that they feature characters and stories that the artist conceived of him- or herself. Historically, doujinshi developed as an important fan practice in Japan in the 1970s, and this practice is intimately linked to the popularity of certain fan conventions, most notably Comiket. In Japan, the line between fandom and industry is blurry since doujinshi are also produced by professional artists. Moreover, many influential manga artists in Japan started out in the doujinshi scene and participated in it even after their professional debuts (e.g., CLAMP; Minami Ozaki of *Zetsuai 1989*).

Similarly, the production contexts of Euromanga blur the lines between fandom and the creative industries. A clear example of these experimental production models is the Italian series *Sky Doll* (2000–), a space adventure that integrates aspects of Japanese visual features and storytelling. *Sky Doll*'s production takes inspiration from Japanese production models in terms of transmediality. For instance, in their *Space Ship Collection* (2007), artists Alessandro Barbucci and Barbara Canepa engaged professional artists in drawing derivative *Sky Doll* art. What is unique about the project, though, is the way in which they regulated the production of these artworks and provided scripts for the artists to work with. These creations are not presented as fan made but as part of the official *Sky Doll* franchise.

In subsequent sections, I focus specifically on the manga-inspired comics that emerged in the Netherlands and Germany. However, it is important to note that I perceive these to be part of a wider trend of transcultural comics that combine different local styles and traditions. These comics point towards a global interest in Japanese popular culture that cannot simply be understood as a soft power. The aesthetics and narratives of Japan also empower local artists, who adopt the language of manga to innovate their own local comics industries. On top of that, manga tropes help these comics artists address those audiences that are often overlooked in the European comics scene, such as adolescent female readers.

Dutch Windmills and Bento Boxes

Historically, Dutch manga experienced its first wave in the late nineties in fanzines such as *Onomaga*, the magazine of the fan club Oranda no Manga, *FaniManga* (1997), and *AniWay* (1998). These magazines often included fan comics inspired by manga, ranging from "yonkoma," four-panel gag comics, to lengthier sequential art. Such comics also appeared in commercial magazines, initiated by companies rather than fans. An example of this is *AnimeniA*, published by the company Gamesworld (now known as Futurezone) that specialized in the distribution of videogames. Simultaneously, Léon van Hooijdonk reported to me on November 3, 2012 that solo artists such as Karin Barend and André Massee distributed self-published works for free or for modest prices at the earliest Dutch fan conventions. The earliest Dutch fan manga show tendencies towards original comics rather than fan art, an important characteristic of Dutch doujinshi which persists even today. But with the exception of *AniWay*, many of these fanzines disappeared after a few issues.

In 2001, when Goldfish Factory was founded, Dutch doujinshi experienced its second wave. These artists had elected to organize themselves according to the Japanese model of artist groups or "circles," which usually consist of various artists but can also be one individual. Doujinshi became used more often as a term by Dutch artists, not only for those works that were non-profit, but also for professional art that was manga-inspired. The foundation of four major circles, OpenMinded (2004), Cheesecake Studios (2004), Howling Riot

(2004), and Neutral (2004), coincided with *AniWay*'s Fanthology contest, a competition that published the best Dutch fan manga. While OpenMinded and Neutral specialized in shoujo genres, including yaoi and yuri, Cheesecake Studios and Howling Riot were characterized by their interest in shounen.

This second wave in Dutch manga, characterized by the emergence of circles, also had several other features. For starters, the Dutch artists largely published their works in English in order to reach a broader audience. Some circles attended conventions abroad in Belgium or Germany, sometimes under the common collective banner Mangafique. This group was central for promoting Dutch manga, not only by attending a wide range of fan conventions, but also by bringing Dutch manga to other comics conventions and expos. Such Dutch comics markets were commonly structured around popular genres, specifically European comics and Western graphic novels, while manga had a marginal place at these events. The organization Mangafique, however, aimed to create visibility for manga at these events, as well as promote cultural diversity. They also hoped to draw younger audiences to these events.

Dutch artists have largely focused on original characters and stories, though some fan art and parodies have also been published. Goldfish Factory for instance has published a series of *Sailor Moon* (1992) parodies since 2001, while Neutral specialized in drawing doujinshi of CLAMP series such as *xxxHOLiC* (2003–11) since it was founded in 2004. It is striking that the Dutch scene has focused largely on creating original art, though, and also seems to value this deeply. This can be explained partly by the fact that Dutch artists also sold their work outside of strictly anime and manga fandom scenes at other comics venues.

In the Dutch context, fandom and professional comics scenes often come together. The anthology *Oost West* [East West] (2008) is an example of these interventions between manga culture and fandom, one that I would now like to elaborate a bit further. *Oost West* is a collaboration of professional Dutch artists as well as Dutch doujinshi artists and art students. I see this work as an exemplar of the Dutch manga scene since it also included graphic novel artists that explored Japanese content and styles. This diversity, I would argue, is characteristic of the Dutch manga scene.

Oost West is a 178-page standalone volume that reflects on the cultural crossovers between the Netherlands and Japan. The title clearly suggests a dialogue between the West and the Eastern Other. *Oost West* features many artists that debuted in Dutch manga fandom, such as André Massee and Marissa Delbressine. The anthology, from the comics publishing house Beedee, is in Dutch. Thus, it appeals to the Dutch comics scene rather than a broad, international fan community. This can be contrasted to Dutch doujinshi, which are commonly published in English to make sure that international audiences can read them.

Figure 4.1 *Oost West* (2009). Cover illustration by Marissa Delbressine

The comics in *Oost West* are printed in grayscale and often contain screen tones and dynamic, cinematographic paneling. However, within the character designs and backgrounds, some artists clearly adopt mainstream manga aesthetics with highly stylized, detailed characters, while others draw in a more realistic style. In this blend of Eastern and Dutch culture, a clear transcultural dialogue emerges that I will discuss by going into several important narrative and aesthetic themes in the anthology.

The cover by Marissa Delbressine already contextualizes the anthology as a meeting ground of cultures. Colored in dark purple shadows, a female figure seductively looks at the viewer (Figure 4.1). Her hand touches a shoji screen and though her pose would suggest shyness, her gaze is brutal. Her sword, visualized most clearly in her shadow, characterizes her as a ninja, crouched in a hidden compartment and ready to assassinate her target. Upon closer observation, the image is rife with Dutch symbols, such as the windmill tattooed onto her upper arm. This motif is repeated in the background of Dutch tiles, decorated with the same symbol. This Dutch image echoes the fascination that European painters have long had with Japanese women. As such, the illustration is emblematic not only of Dutch manga fandom, but of the specific transcultural tradition in which it is rooted.

Oost West has several distinct features that reveal the Dutch interpretation and appropriation of manga styles and storytelling. For starters, several stories are set in contemporary Japan and visualize its characteristics from a European point of view. "Morgen" [Tomorrow], by Alice and Mike, is set in a crowded Japanese subway where humans as well as small, cute monsters are seated. This exaggeration stresses the cultural imagination of Japan by the Dutch as a crowded, modern country, connected by vast networks of trains and subways. Other comics, such as "Icarus," by Marissa Delbressine, visualize a large urban terrain with towering, highrise buildings and billboards. Kino-kun's "Pockey Grabe and Mountain Dew" is set largely in a Japanese convenience store, Yoyogi Park, and Shibuya. In these comics, Japan and its pop culture is associated with urbanity, consumerism, and with its specific means of transportation, such as subways or *shinkansen* bullet trains.

Moreover, the Dutch artists mediate common themes of Japanese popular culture. Specific genres and tropes which are associated with Japan form lines throughout the anthology. Several post-apocalyptic and science fiction stories are included throughout the comic. Olivier Heiligers' "Messiah" displays a visual style that is clearly inspired by the designs of Akira Toriyama and Leiji Matsumoto. André Massee's "Groeistuipen" [Growing Pains] also alludes to shounen manga storytelling conventions by focusing on the quest of three boys that assemble a magical artifact. Several of the comics sport hybrid characters and monsters, which create transmedial relations with series such as *Pokémon* and *Digimon*, among the first anime to be broadcast in the Netherlands. Dutch artists are clearly inspired by the fantastical elements of manga, especially manga's alternative settings, characters, and creatures.

Furthermore, the comics are highly self-reflexive and intertextual, thereby explicitly addressing the Dutch people that read the anthology. Many of the comics contain references to well-known characters of Japanese media mix franchises in the background, such as Pikachu. Others purposely dress their characters in the Japanese street style of the Gothic Lolita, such as the colorful protagonists in "Morgen" by Alice and Mike. Other stories are set in fan cultures themselves, such as the aforementioned "Pockey Grabe and Mountain Dew," which narrates the story of two fans who meet out-of-character in a convenience store and then compete with each other in a cosplay contest. The collection creates visibility and awareness of the practices of manga fans while also presuming a knowledgeable reader.

Throughout the comics, an aesthetic of cuteness emerges in the soft monsters and wide-eyed manga tropes. As Ngai (2005) argues, when observing Takashi Murakami's artwork, cuteness has transgressive potential because it can also package uncomfortable truths more readily. Cuteness, then, not only suggests vulnerability and helplessness, but also aggression and power (Ngai 2005, 283). *Oost West* reveals a similar discourse, especially in "Toys in the Attic," by Schwantz and Wortel, which follows a manic child in a toy store. Taunted by wide-eyed, fluffy plushies, he kills all the customers with a katana. The comic can be compared to the *South Park* episode "Chimpokémon" (1999), a parody of *Pokémon* in which the children are enticed to buy all the toys produced by an evil corporation from Japan. What these two stories have in common is a critique of global capitalism and obsessive consumerism. Though the examples are Japanese, these concerns of standardization can also stem from the West, as suggested by the popular concept "McDonaldization" (Ritzer 1993).

Thus, cuteness becomes a site for transgression in these Dutch productions. *Oost West* is not only a tribute, but also a critique of particular Japanese values, such as its intense consumerism and pressures on youth. So, while cuteness can be critical, it is also a visual device that labels these heterogeneous Dutch comics as manga. It grants artistic license to comics producers. Thus, aesthetic devices become a key mediator of cultural values—a semiotic tool that bridges East and West.

The Fantasyscape of German Yaoi

Historically, the context of German manga[3] is fundamentally different from its neighboring country, the Netherlands. In Germany, manga has been widely popularized and translated, and anime has been amply broadcasted on national television. German publishing houses have translated and published manga extensively since the 1990s, though several titles were released before this decade.

In terms of translation, *Barefoot Gen* was first published in Germany in the late 1980s. Though manga were sporadically translated in the years to follow, the publication of *Dragon Ball* (1996) by Carlsen Comics quickly led to more

---

3   Editor's Note: See Chapter 8 for more about gothic German manga.

publications. The late 1990s in particular were characterized by the publication of many different manga by companies such as Egmont Ehapa and Carlsen Comics. This coincided with the broadcasting of major anime series such as *Sailor Moon* as well as a crisis in the German comics market (Malone 2000, 23). But the translation and publication of Japanese comics in Germany became especially profitable the new millennium. In 2005, the revenue of the German manga industry was €70 million, which was a 6.9 percent increase compared to 2004 (Knumann 2006). The growth of the book publishing industry as a whole, meanwhile, was only 1 percent. In other words, manga quickly became a dominant comics medium in Germany. This is opposed to the limited visibility of manga in the Netherlands, where it is considered a niche medium at best.

Similar to Dutch manga, German manga was pioneered in fan magazines such as *AnimaniA* (since 1994) and *MangasZene* (2001–06). Germany, however, developed a thriving publishing culture in which local manga artists have been scouted by means of contests and their work published by companies such as Carlsen Comics. As Paul Malone (2010) writes, "The local publishers rapidly capitalized on its appeal to female readers and began fostering local manga artists in Germany. These are mainly young women producing *shoujo* manga, and increasingly integrating popular boys' love elements into their work."

This possibility of becoming a professional manga artist heavily shaped the discourse and distribution of German manga. Fans quickly professionalized their output in the late 1990s, grouping together into official publishing houses such as Schwarzer Turm and Fireangels that were not solely a labor of love. These publishing houses strived to pay their artists and were more than independent, non-commercial groups. This professionalism also meant that printed comics were not seen as amateur objects originating from the context of a specific space of learning and self-improvement, such as in the Netherlands or Japan. In Germany, printed works are often equated with professionally published works and thus had to have a certain quality.

Those who were excluded from publishing therefore focused more on online portfolios, at platforms such as deviantART, or created web manga. Specifically the German fan forum Animexx.de has been a key platform in the distribution of self-created manga for many years, where budding artists could display their art and receive feedback.[4] It also became common among German artists to share their art among friends in con booklets, e.g. sketch books brought to conventions in which other fans draw commissions for free.

For a long time, independently published comics did not flourish in Germany, where professional expectations had to be met and an amount of financial compensation for artists was expected. In the past few years, however, there has been a shift in German fandom. In a personal communication on February 19,

---

4 Editor's Note: See Chapter 8 for more information about Animexx.de.

2013, Fireangels editor Anne Delseit speaks of a "renaissance of doujinshi" as different independent artists are now slowly organizing into casual artist groups and circles, comparable to the Japanese production model. The large publishing companies now carefully set their professional status apart from independent groups and circles, but they also struggle with this distinction. Both parties, publishing houses and circles, are present at fan conventions and need clientele.

The production of German manga, as Malone (2010) writes, was very much connected to policies surrounding sexual and violent media content. A climate of moral panic has surrounded manga since 2008, when new policies and regulations prohibited the depiction of underage, fictional characters in sexualized situations, under the assumption that these depictions were in fact expressions of child pornography. This political discourse was integrated into the German manga and also led to innovative comics that particularly addressed child abuse and the sexual depiction of underage characters.

While there are many German manga (or "Germanga") to choose from, I decided to base my analysis on several comics in the anthology *Lemon Law* by Fireangels. This ongoing anthology series has five volumes at the time of this writing, with the sixth due in 2014. Fireangels specializes in queer manga, most particularly yaoi (McLelland 2005; Thorn 2004). These genres include gay romance and are primarily created by and for women. Its lesbian counterpart, yuri, is less visible in popular culture in Japan and other countries. Nonetheless, Fireangels has published some yuri comics as well. Similar to Japan, the German yaoi artists and authors appear to be all women. Yet in spite of this focus on yaoi and yuri, queer romance is often not the main genre characteristic. In fact, the anthology sports historical fiction, science fiction, slice-of-life, and fantasy stories in which gay romance is but one theme. The success of *Lemon Law*, I would argue, reflects the overall German interest in yaoi.

Lemon Law is printed in grayscale but includes several colored pages. It has a prototypical tankoubon B6 format, which is an unusual format in most Western countries. (The Dutch manga *Oost West*, for instance, is printed in B5 format, which is more standard in Europe.) In terms of aesthetics, *Lemon Law* appears to be more faithful to the visual conventions of manga than *Oost West*. Some styles appear to be more inspired by stories that flourished 1970s and 1980s (see Figure 4.2), while others display the conventions of contemporary boys' love (see Figure 4.3). Overall, *Lemon Law* is a blend of styles but one that remains true to the characteristics of manga while incorporating a few elements of traditional European comics or graphic novels.

When analyzing the series, several themes stand out, compared to *Oost West*. For starters, the anthologies hardly feature any stories that are set in Japan. Instead, they offer fantasy settings, modern and historical versions of Europe, or unspecified places. Many of the stories are firmly rooted in a German or European tradition. "Emerald Rising," by Marlicious, features a young boy

Figure 4.2 Minzpyjama, "Octavian," *Lemon Law*, Volume 5 (2012, 124)

Figure 4.3   Anne Delseit and Sai Nan, "China Blue," *Lemon Law*, Volume 4 (2011, 37)

with French parents who has moved to a new country, supposedly Germany. The comic integrates many French sentences, expressions, and stereotypical references to French culture, such as jokes about baguettes. The Other in this comic is not Japan, but the neighboring country France, suggesting that local manga form a complex vessel of inter- and transnational images and tropes. Historical fascination, however, grounds several of the other stories. "Octavian," by Minzpyjama, is set at the court of Vienna, characterized by its powdered wigs and detailed sceneries. The young Octavian, dubbed the "Rosenkavalier von Wien [Rose Cavalier of Vienna]" meets a famous count, but their affair is met with the jealousy of another man. In this case, local history is mediated through the exotic style of manga and eroticized. Through the iconic style of shoujo manga from the 1970s and 1980s, the artist explores German and Austrian history. Despite its emphasis on romance and sexuality, yaoi functions as a powerful tool for rewriting in these cases, similar to other types of feminist writing which have historically relied on appropriation and parody.

In other cases, the German artists blend manga storytelling with other repertoires. Several of the comics deconstruct genre repertoires that are common in Western crime fiction, procedural drama, or superhero comics. "China Blue," by Anne Delseit and Sai Nan, is a hard-boiled detective story set in a town controlled by an Asian underworld. The artists blend Japanese visuals with a type of storytelling reminiscent of American film noir. In similar fashion, "Coined," by the Dutch artist Marissa Delbressine, parodies classic superhero comics and also shows that Japanese styles can easily be combined with other genres and media. In other words, the artists and authors of the *Lemon Law* anthologies do not merely reproduce manga tropes but instead combine them with their own local cultures and traditions, as well as with other non-Japanese sources.

These and other stories suggest that *Lemon Law* not only mediates manga visually, but displays similar interests in queer characters, cult storytelling, and characterization. The characters and stories are iconic and cater to a specific niche audience, interested in the chemistry between male characters. The settings serve as a background in which these relationships unfold, and particular tropes, such as the hero and the villain, are deconstructed and eventually queered. Fireangels is only one publishing company of out of several in Germany that create local yaoi and yuri. The widespread nature of German yaoi suggests that manga is not only embraced as a visual culture, but that its specific genres may also sustain further creative development and exploration. Yaoi, then, may be one fantasyscape that brings together narrative tropes and audiences from different cultural backgrounds.

Conclusion

This chapter has shown that manga is a complex phenomenon in continental Europe with a unique history of appropriation and remediation. The doujinshi groups and manga publishers from Germany and the Netherlands evince a deep fascination for Eastern culture that is constantly reinvigorated. The dynamics of these local manga can only be understood through a transcultural framework that takes into account the local context as well as the appropriation of foreign cultural capital. Euromanga have developed unique local traditions and styles that inform their cultural context and readership.

Manga, however, is more than a particular medium or style for these artists. It is also a culture in which particular hierarchies and gatekeepers in comics production are contested. The participatory culture of manga allows European artists to experiment with creative styles and foreign models of comics creation and distribution, such as doujinshi circles. This democratic model is clearly foregrounded in the practices of both Dutch and German manga artists and cannot be separated from the emergence of manga fandom. Yet while these local manga may often originate in such subcultures, they do not stand in isolation from the cultures and practices of the professional comics industry at large. Dutch manga artists are often active in independent doujinshi scenes that thrive around particular fan magazines and circles, but individual artists also work together with other comics artists on larger projects. In Germany, however, manga are often professionally published, and the artists are more consciously faithful to the look and feel of mainstream manga.

One can conclude that manga is not merely mimicked or parodied in these local subcultural contexts, but incorporated within a particular mainstream comics culture. Within these scenes, manga tropes and production models function as a source of innovation and experimentation. German and Dutch artists are clearly drawn to specific genres and tropes from Japanese popular culture, such as the homoerotic yaoi. Through this genre, Western artists can comment on the heteronormativity of Western popular culture and create alternative stories about gender and sexuality. In *Lemon Law*, however, romances and erotica also appear to take the backseat in favor of building a unique story world or text.

What comics artists take from the culture of manga, then, are its vast fantasyscapes that appeal to the imagination and transgress the conventions of their local fictional media. The artists and writers also tend to group themselves in similar fashion to the circles in Japan, suggesting that collaborative production and participation are central to this medium across national boundaries. Manga is not merely a medium then, but also a learning space that inspires creativity. Overall, these budding manga artists bring the cult sensibility of manga to

Western markets. The discourse on manga has to be diversified to take these local expressions into account.

Acknowledgment

I would like to thank Nele Noppe for her comments on this article.

References

Appadurai, Arjun. 1996. *Modernity at Large: Cultural Dimensions of Globalization*. Public Worlds. Minneapolis, MN: University of Minnesota Press.

Azuma, Hiroki. 2009. *Otaku: Japan's Database Animals*. Minneapolis, MN: University of Minnesota Press.

Denison, Rayna. 2011. "Anime Fandom and the Liminal Spaces between Fan Creativity and Piracy." *International Journal of Cultural Studies* 14 (5): 449–66. doi:10.1177/1367877910394565.

Galbraith, Patrick W. 2012. *Otaku Spaces*. Seattle: Chin Music Press.

Gillan, Jennifer. 2010. *Television and New Media: Must-Click TV*. London: Routledge.

Hayles, N. Katherine. 2004. "Print Is Flat, Code Is Deep: The Importance of Media-Specific Analysis." *Poetics Today* 25 (1): 67–90.

Hills, Matt. 2002. "Transcultural 'Otaku': Japanese Representations of Fandom and Representations of Japan in Anime/Manga Fan Cultures." Paper presented at *Media in Transition 2: Globalization and Convergence*, MIT, May 10–12. http://cmsw.mit.edu/mit2/Abstracts/MattHillspaper.pdf.

Hitchcock Morimoto, Lori, and Bertha Chin. 2013. "Towards a Theory of Transcultural Fandom." *Participations: Journal of Audience and Reception Studies* 10 (1): 92–108.

Ito, Mizuko. 2005. "Technologies of the Childhood Imagination: Yugioh, Media Mixes, and Everyday Cultural Production." In *Structures of Participation in Digital Culture*, edited by Joe Karaganis and Natalie Jeremijenko, 86–111. Durham, NC: Duke University Press.

Ito, Mizuko, Daisuke Okabe, and Izumi Tsuji, eds. 2012. *Fandom Unbound: Otaku Culture in a Connected World*. New Haven: Yale University Press.

Ivy, Marilyn. 1995. *Discourses of the Vanishing: Modernity, Phantasm, Japan*. Chicago: University of Chicago Press.

Jenkins, Henry. 2006. *Convergence Culture: Where Old and New Media Collide*. New York: NYU Press.

Jüngst, Heike. 2004. "Japanese Comics in Germany." *Perspectives: Studies in Translatology* 12 (2): 83–105.

Kinsella, Sharon. 1998. "Japanese Subculture in the 1990s: Otaku and the Amateur Manga Movement." *Journal of Japanese Studies* 24 (4): 289–316

Knümann, Bastian. 2006. "Deutsche Mangabranche Boomt Weiterhin." *Handelsblatt*, April 5. http://www.handelsblatt.com/panorama/kultur-litera tur/manga-und-anime-deutsche-mangabranche-boomt-weiterhin/2637798. html.

Lamerichs, Nicolle. 2013. "The Cultural Dynamic of Doujinshi and Cosplay: Local Anime Fandom in Japan, USA and Europe." *Participations: Journal of Audience and Reception Studies* 10 (1): 154–76.

Malone, Paul M. 2010. "From BRAVO to Animexx.de to Export: Capitalizing on German Boys' Love Fandom, Culturally, Socially and Economically." In *Boys' Love Manga: Essays on the Sexual Ambiguity and Cross-Cultural Fandom of the Genre*, by Antonia Levi, Mark McHarry, and Dru Pagliassotti, 23–43. Jefferson, NC: McFarland & Co.

Malone, Paul M. 2013. "Transplanted Boys' Love Conventions and Anti-'Shota' Polemics in a German Manga: Fahr Sindram's 'Losing Neverland.'" *Transformative Works and Cultures* 12. http://journal.transformativeworks.org/index.php/twc/article/view/434/395.

McCloud, Scott. 1993. *Understanding Comics: The Invisible Art*. New York: HarperCollins.

McGray, Douglas. 2002. "Japan's Gross National Cool." *Foreign Policy* June/July: 44–54.

McLelland, Mark. 2005. "The World of Yaoi: The Internet, Censorship and the Global 'Boys' Love' Fandom." *The Australian Feminist Law Journal* 23: 61–77.

Müller, Ego. 2009. "Spaces of Participation: Interactive Television and the Reshaping of the Relationship between Production and Consumption." In *Digital Material: Tracing New Media in Everyday Life and Technology*, edited by Marianne van den Boomen, 49–64. Amsterdam: Amsterdam University Press.

Napier, Susan J. 2007. *From Impressionism to Anime: Japan as Fantasy and Fan Cult in the Mind of the West*. New York: Palgrave.

Ngai, Sianne. 2005. "The Cuteness of the Avant-Garde." *Critical Inquiry* 31 (4): 811–47.

Nye, Joseph S. 2004. *Soft Power: The Means to Success in World Politics*. New York: Public Affairs.

Ritzer, George. 1993. *The McDonaldization of Society: An Investigation into the Changing Character of Contemporary Social Life*. Newbury Park, CA: Pine Forge Press.

Ross, Sharon Marie. 2008. *Beyond the Box: Television and the Internet*. Malden, MA: Blackwell.

Said, Edward W. 1978. *Orientalism*. New York: Vintage.

Smits, Ivo, and Katarzyna Cwiertka. 2012. *Hello Kitty En Gothic Lolita's: Schattigheidscultuur Uit Japan* [Hello Kitty and Gothic Lolitas: Cuteness Culture from Japan]. Amsterdam: Amsterdam University Press.

Thorn, Matthew. 2004. "Girls and Women Getting out of Hand: The Pleasure and Politics of Japan's Amateur Comic Community." In *Fanning the Flames: Fans and Consumer Culture in Contemporary Japan*, edited by William M. Kelly, 169–87. Albany: SUNY Press.

Wolferen, K.G. van. 1995. *Japan: De Onzichtbare Drijfveren Van Een Wereldmacht* [Japan: The Invisible Motives of a World Power]. Amsterdam: Muntinga.

Chapter 5
"Manga is Not Pizza": The Performance of Ethno-racial Authenticity and the Politics of American Anime and Manga Fandom in Svetlana Chmakova's *Dramacon*

Casey Brienza

At the very height of the US manga market in the first decade of the twenty-first century, just before the global financial crisis hit publishers hard at the end of 2008 (Brienza 2009a), the research firm ICv2 surveyed bookstores and comics shops across North America and produced a list of the "Top 50 Manga Properties" for 2007. Included were four so-called Original English Language, or "OEL," manga. In its analysis of the list, the following was noted:

> While OEL titles have in general provoked negative reactions from hardcore fans who consider "OEL manga" to be an oxymoron, it is worth noting that some of them have been selling quite well, and that in spite of formidable competition from an unprecedented number of "true" manga releases from Japan, four OEL titles managed to make the list ... (*ICv2 Guide to Manga* 2008)

One of these four titles, ranked at #41, was Svetlana Chmakova's *Dramacon*, a three-volume series published by Tokyopop from 2005 to 2007 and reprinted in an omnibus "Ultimate Edition" in 2008. And besides being a bestseller in spite of "negative reactions from hardcore fans," it also happens to be a fascinating window into the very same politics of American anime and manga fandom which, in some corners, would prefer it had never existed in the first place. But what, exactly, is the source of the controversy to which ICv2 is alluding to here, and why is it so very important to some readers for there be a such thing as "true" manga in the first place?

This chapter is an attempt to answer those questions and understand their wider sociological ramifications. After outlining a brief history of OEL manga in the United States, I draw upon Goffman's dramaturgical analysis and Alexander's cultural pragmatics to explore the ways in which American anime and manga fandom debates the meaning of the word, "manga." Beginning with a pivotal scene in the second volume of Chmakova's *Dramacon* and using it as a point of departure, I proceed with an in-depth analysis of a 52-page anime forum debate about OEL manga to understand how and why manga is being defined. There are five distinct categories of meaning attached to manga, ranging from quality to style. By reconnecting these meanings to *Dramacon*'s depiction of con culture, I show that American anime and manga fandom is dependent upon the convincing performance of ethno-racial authenticity, which, as an interpretive category, prematurely forecloses the creative and cultural possibilities of a complexly connected global society.

Theoretical Framework

Dramaturgical analysis and theories of cultural performance are, appropriately enough, absolutely essential to understanding the politics of fandom in *Dramacon*. The word drama originates from the Ancient Greek word for "action" and is used specifically to refer to storytelling in a performative mode, such as in theatrical or televised productions. As a genre, drama attempts to portray serious emotions and themes in a realistic manner, but used colloquially it can conversely refer to exaggerated, even ridiculous, emotional conflict. And indeed, there are certainly shades of both of these in Chmakova's choice of title for her manga.

However, Chmakova is not by any means the only writer to appropriate the language of the stage. Because the performance of a drama typically presupposes the involvement of multiple actors working together in the collaborative production of meaning-making, sociologists have also taken theoretical inspiration from dramatic practice and conventions. Erving Goffman (1959; 1974) was the first to deploy the language of the theater in sociological analysis, arguing that people actively manage their self-presentation and assume certain "roles" in particular settings based upon the impressions upon others they want to make. While hugely influential in the field, it perhaps places too much emphasis upon the strategic, planned nature of all human interaction, implying that people either actively conceal their real selves or, alternatively, have no real identity outside of the deliberate, staged performances of their various roles. Furthermore, Goffman's analysis was confined to micro-social interaction and is therefore not good at accounting for structural inequalities or the collective exercise of social power.

More recently, Jeffrey Alexander (2011) has worked toward addressing these limitations by expanding upon Goffman's dramaturgical analysis in his theoretical work on performance and cultural pragmatics. In a fragmented and complex modern society, he argues, the elements of a social performance must be "re-fused" to become convincing and effective. This requires "psychological identification and cultural extension" (Alexander 2011, 53). The better the re-fusion is, the more the performance resembles ritual, i.e. "episodes of repeated and simplified cultural communication in which the direct partners to a social interaction, and those observing it, share a mutual belief in the descriptive and prescriptive validity of the communication's symbolic contents and accept the authenticity of one another's intentions" (Alexander 2011, 25). Of particular importance to me in this context is Alexander (2011, 13)'s elucidation of authenticity as "an interpretive category rather than an ontological state" which "results from processes of social construction." As shall be demonstrated, central to the culture of American anime and manga fandom is the social construction of Japan as an authentically discrete, ethno-racial category.

A Brief History of OEL Manga

Before proceeding with my analysis, it is worth a short digression to discuss the publishing history of so-called OEL manga such as *Dramacon*. Now, granted, there have been "manga-influenced" American comics for as long—and perhaps even longer—than there have been Japanese manga published in the United States. *Elfquest* artist Wendy Pini and *A Distant Soil* creator Colleen Doran are but two veteran comics creators who have cited manga among their influences. Antarctic Press, specializing in manga-influenced content, was founded in 1984. (By way of comparison, the first Japanese manga to be even partially published in English translation was Kenji Nakazawa's *Barefoot Gen*, serialized from 1980 to 1982.) Central Park Media (CPM), primarily an anime localization company, also published manga, and its first in the 1990s was actually an original, US-produced adaptation of the Japanese anime *Dirty Pair*. Fred Gallagher's webcomic *Megatokyo*, which debuted in 2000, is also manga-influenced and has been collected in print by several different publishers, including Studio Ironcat, CMX, Dark Horse, and even, in Japanese translation, Kodansha.

The specific term "OEL manga" is widely believed to have been coined by anime and manga critic Carlo Santos on his personal blog, which he defines as "a type of comics (sequential art) that incorporates distinctive elements of manga (comics originating from Japan) but originally scripted in the English language" (Santos 2005). However, it became closely associated with the now defunct Los Angeles-based independent publishing house Tokyopop, one of the most prominent experimenters with manga-influenced comics. When the company was still called Mixx Entertainment, it published *Sushi Girl*, first released in ten installments in the shoujo manga mangazine *Smile* and reprinted in a graphic novel edition in 1998. Though drawn by the artistic duo Tavicat, the copyright to *Sushi Girl* was owned solely by company founder Stu Levy (Simons n.d.).

Facing a climate of increased competition in the early 2000s for the best licenses from Japan—especially from Viz Media, co-owned by two of Japan's three biggest publishers, Shogakukan and Shueisha, and Del Rey Manga, which had a co-branding publishing arrangement with the third, Kodansha—Tokyopop began to cast about for other sustainable publishing options. One of these was to start cultivating homegrown talent, and the publisher launched its twice-annual, later annual, "Rising Stars of Manga" competition in 2002. Winners and finalists would be encouraged to produce their own three volume series. Tokyopop also set ambitious quotas for numbers of new OEL titles to be released annually. Due to the theoretical potential for spin-offs and other franchising, copyright and subsidiary rights were contractually shared between the creator and the publisher. Some commentators pointed cynically to Stu Levy's Hollywood ambitions,[1] but there is no question that being published by Tokyopop did launch some artists' careers. In any case, by the time the publisher folded in 2011, over 50 OEL series had been published. Besides *Dramacon*, other notable Tokyopop OEL manga included *Bizenghast* by M. Alice LeGrow, *Van Von Hunter* by Mike Schwark and Ron Kaulfersch, *The Dreaming* by Queenie Chan, *East Coast Rising* by Becky Cloonan, and *MBQ* by Felipe Smith.

As the market for manga expanded rapidly in the middle of the first decade of the twenty-first century, several new presses focused on publishing OEL manga. The most prominent of these was Seven Seas Entertainment, founded by Jason DeAngelis, who decided he would rather start his own publishing company than sign his intellectual property over to Stu Levy. DeAngelis' own *No Man's Land* was one of its earliest releases, as was *Aoi House* by Adam Arnold, another Seven Seas staffer. Other small, indie press players in the OEL manga field included Yaoi Press (boys' love) and SelfMadeHero (adaptations of plays by Shakespeare). Several trade presses, such as St Martin's Press, Penguin, and Thomas Nelson, which do not otherwise publish Japanese titles or much in the way of comics content, period, also got into the game during manga's North American boom years, experimenting with their own in-house "manga." The graphic novel and manga imprint of Hachette USA, Yen Press, had, from its inception in 2007, intentions to publish both Japanese manga and Korean manhwa in translation,

---

1   This comment, taken from the "OEL manga jumping the shark" Anime News Network forum topic analyzed later in the chapter, is typical: "Meanwhile, one of the whole points of OEL manga is that they're TokyoPop originals and TokyoPop maintains creative rights over them for optioning into movies and other mediums. Do you see the little game they're playing there? This OEL manga bit is more looking like a scam for cheap IP and content for other media and not like a proper publishing company" (The Xenos, August 14, 2008).

as well as OEL titles. The most prominent of these thus far, the first volume of *Twilight: The Graphic Novel*, for example, boasted a 350,000 first print run, the biggest for any manga or graphic novel to date in the North American market (Memmott 2010). Though not officially labeled manga anywhere, its Korean artist Young Kim relies heavily upon the visual conventions of Japanese manga.

Although the term itself has fallen out of usage in the industry and there has been no consensus since then about what it should be called instead, publishing OEL manga has become *de rigueur* post-2007. In fact, by 2011, the year of Tokyopop's closure, *all* manga publishers still active, with the exception of Vertical and the new Kodansha Comics, had added original English language manga to their lists. It could therefore be argued that normalization has eliminated the need to make categorical distinctions. Or perhaps the term continues to be so potentially incendiary that publishers would rather occupy the nebulous space of definitional ambiguity than take any position on an issue that is bound to displease *somebody*. As long as the books sell, who cares? Yet oddly enough, one artist actually penned a bestselling OEL manga series which tackled the definitional debate head on. Her name was Svetlana Chmakova.

About the Author

Svetlana Chmakova was born on October 7, 1979 in the former Soviet Union. In 1996, at the age of 16, she emigrated from Russia to Canada with her family, where she completed high school and a degree in Classical Animation at Sheridan College in Ontario. She cites translated editions of *Elfquest* by Richard and Wendy Pini as an early creative influence, as well as American comics such as *A Distant Soil* and *Sandman* and English-translated manga such as *Ranma ½*, *Oh My Goddess!*, and *Vampire Princess Miyu* (Coville 2006).

Prior to her professional debut in manga, Chmakova regularly exhibited and sold her work at anime conventions and other indie comics events such as the Toronto Comic Arts Festival (TCAF). She also published webcomics, such as *Chasing Rainbows* for Girlamatic.com and *Nightsilver* for Wirepop.com. This early, online work prompted Tokyopop editor Mark Paniccia to invite her to pitch an OEL manga project to his employer that would eventually become the three-part series *Dramacon*. When Paniccia moved on to an editorship at Marvel Comics, another Tokyopop editor, Lillian Diaz-Przybyl,[2] took charge of the project (Chmakova 2008). Volume One was published in 2005, Volume Two in

---

2 Diaz-Przybyl would subsequently become a force in the US manga industry in her own right and after leaving Tokyopop in 2011 she partnered with Magda Erik-Soussi, Rebecca Scoble, and Jill Astley to launch Chromatic Press. Editor's Note: See Chapter 1 for more information about Chromatic Press, written by Erik-Soussi herself.

2006, and Volume Three in 2007. An omnibus "Ultimate Edition" collecting all three volumes of the series was published in 2008. The series was named one of the Best Comics of 2005 by *Publishers Weekly* and, as noted in the beginning of this chapter, one of the Top 50 Manga Properties in 2007 by the research firm ICv2. It was also nominated for a Special Recognition Eisner Award in 2007, the US comics industry's top honor.

The commercial and critical success of *Dramacon* reportedly helped keep Tokyopop afloat financially during the mid-2000s, and it opened up new professional horizons for Chmakova as a global manga artist. She acquired representation from Judith Hansen of Hansen Literary Agency, a literary agent specializing in the emerging graphic novel category, broke ties with Tokyopop, and signed a deal with the then newly launched Yen Press for her follow-up original series, *Nightschool*, which began serialization in the magazine *Yen+* in 2007. Since then, she has also worked on Yen Press's manga adaptation of James Patterson's young adult series *Witch & Wizard*.

Plot Summary

According to Chmakova (2008, 607), *Dramacon* "was inspired by a particular incident at a con I used to frequent." While sitting behind her table at the Artists' Alley, she reports having "spotted a really cool cosplayer—the same guy two years in a row. We never spoke or even met, but he caught my eye and I wondered what his story might be, were he a manga character and the con his story." And indeed, this scenario is this slice-of-life romance manga's initial conceit: The shy teenager and aspiring manga script writer Christie Leroux attends her very first anime convention with her artist boyfriend Derek Hollman. Derek is outgoing and loves flirting with the other female con attendees, leading to increasing tensions between the young couple. Christie thus finds herself attracted to the mysterious, mirrored-shades-wearing cosplayer Matt Green, whom she first spots from her table in Artists' Alley. She and Matt become acquainted, and eventually he interprets some of the weirder aspects of anime con culture, introduces her to his companions, and offers her some unsolicited relationship advice. The denouement of the first volume is an escalating argument between Christie and Derek which ends in attempted rape and Matt punching Derek. Christie spends the last day of the con in Matt's room. Though it was a difficult few days, there were plenty of good times too, and Christie resolves to return to Yatta Anime Con next year.

The subsequent two volumes of the series recount Christie's con attendance in successive years. Christie has dumped Derek professionally as well and now collaborates with Bethany, a gifted but hardworking artist whose mother does not approve of manga as a career choice. The duo's obvious creative potential attracts the benevolent attention and encouragement of Lida Zeff, Mangapop's star Western artist. Meanwhile, the romance between Christie and Matt lurches along in fits and starts until the inevitable picture-perfect happy end at the conclusion of the third book.

All in all, *Dramacon* deploys the themes, styles, and tropes typical of mainstream shoujo manga in Japan, and the plot in its basic outlines, while reasonably skilled and well-paced, is not especially remarkable. In fact, fictional stories featuring manga creators as protagonists are quite common in Japan,[3] since, as storytellers elsewhere, Japanese artists are good at writing what they know. What *are* remarkable, however, are Chmakova's astute observations and representations of North American anime and manga fan and con culture and the sorts of social interactions which might be expected to occur in it. Of particular note is one short scene, placed almost directly in the middle of the middle volume of the series. This scene is, in a very literal sense, right at the heart of *Dramacon*.

It begins with Lida who, having stopped by the Artists' Alley looking for Christie, strikes up a chat with Bethany. While Lida is at Christie's and Bethany's table, a young girl wearing a sailor-style school uniform costume and a boy of similar apparent age wearing a "Yo-Gi-U" t-shirt stop to look at the wares on offer. The girl wants to make a purchase, but the boy, hearing her use the word "manga" is skeptical, saying, "That's not manga" and then calling the second of his female companions a "retard" when she argues with him (Chmakova 2008, 251).

When Lida, whom the second girl recognizes excitedly as "Lida-san," the "manga artist," tries to intervene in the escalating argument, the boy, his arms crossed over his chest, grouses, "Aw, fer crying out loud … Her stuff isn't manga either" (Chmakova 2008, 251). Lida's reply is nonchalant: "Hon, we can call it fried cheese if we want to—last I checked this was a free country" (Chmakova 2008, 252). The boy is stunned into silence for a panel. Then the debate continues. Because this scene is so important, I have transcribed the dialogue in full:

Girl #2: You're such a loser, Jim. This is totally manga! Look, see? Chibis!

Girl #1: Um, guys … Come on …

Boy (Jim): It's not! Manga! [sic]

Girl #2: Why not?!

---

3 One especially well-known recent example is the *Weekly Shonen Jump* series, *Bakuman*. Other examples published in English include *Comic Party*, *Genshiken*, *Otomen*, and *Fall in Love Like a Comic*.

Boy (Jim): Because she's not Japanese!! Manga is a Japanese artform! [sic]

Lida: So if a non-Japanese person draws it, it's not manga?

Boy (Jim): Exactly! Get it now??

Lida: Applying this logic to something else we all know and love ... A pizza is not a pizza unless it's baked by an Italian in Italy. Yes?

Boy (Jim): ... ...

Boy (Jim): Manga is not pizza.

Lida: Yes, well, nothing in this world is perfect.

Boy (Jim): Are you all ****ing stupid??!!!

Lida: Whoa, language!

Boy (Jim): Shut up!! Manga is Japanese!!!

Lida: Kid, calm do—

Boy (Jim): You're not Japanese!! So you can't draw manga!

Boy (Jim, pointing at Bethany): She's not Japanese either!! She's not even white!! (Chmakova 2008, 252–4)

At this point, the boy's mother intervenes, apologizes to Lida and Bethany, and takes him away. Watching them go, Lida remarks, "Kinda like being back home and reading some anime forums. Minus the part where a parent shows up, heh" (Chmakova 2008, 259).

This exchange, undoubtedly based upon Chmakova's own personal experiences as a Russian-Canadian manga artist, is devastating, and it captures succinctly the performative competition for symbolic dominance over the definition of the word manga in American anime and manga fandom. Lida, representing the American manga publishing industry and very much in line with their general position on this subject (see Brienza 2014), argues that anything at all can be called manga if it is convenient and/or desirable to do so. Others, such as Girl #2, represented here as a moderate voice, think that manga is a particular visual style and narrative language—hence the reference to "chibis." However, these are not the views which are made most prominent in the *Dramacon* scene. Rather, according to the position so shrilly and stridently advanced by fans such as Jim, manga must be produced by a Japanese person. Some would go further still, arguing, as Lida suggests by her reference to "an Italian in Italy" that to be manga it must also have been produced in Japan. Indeed, as noted in the introduction to this collection and in Santos' definition earlier in this chapter, manga is often defined in the English vernacular as comics from Japan, or, in the strictest sense, comics which were originally produced and published in Japan. The race of the manga artist under such conditions would, presumably, be immaterial.

Nevertheless, the prominence of the racialized argument being made here cannot be overemphasized. Due to Japan's perceived ethnic and racial homogeneity,[4] the default assumption would be that most manga originally produced and published in Japan would indeed be created by a Japanese artist. Non-Japanese artists publishing all-original work in Japan are exceptional, and to date the only American to do so with a major publishing house is Felipe Smith (Brienza 2013a). Yet this exchange would also suggest that a comic drawn by a Japanese person and published outside of Japan in the first instance, whether in the United States, France, or South Korea, would also be "manga." Clearly, ethno-racial identification is being expressly privileged over geographic location of origin in the definition of authentic manga, and this is being argued loudly and in no uncertain terms by some fans. Why? What purpose does this serve? If they feel so strongly about it, there must be a reason. Unfortunately, the *Dramacon* scene itself provides no clear answers.

Kinda Like Reading "Some Anime Forums"

In the final bit of the scene, Lida observes that this altercation is similar to discussions that have been had on online anime forums. These discussions, one may glean from her comment, can become heated, complete with juvenile behavior such as name calling. As it turns out, similar debates have indeed occurred on online forums catering to real-world anime and manga fans. A good, indicative example comes from Anime News Network, the largest and most-trafficked English-language anime news, reviews, and information site on the internet. The site has an active discussion board, and on March 28, 2007, a forum participant started a new discussion thread titled, "OEL manga jumping the shark." The thread was popular and continued for 51 further pages of

---

[4] Sociologists such as John Lie (2001) have argued persuasively that Japan's supposed racial and ethnic homogeneity is a post-WWII ideological construction, and that modern Japanese society is, in fact, a multiethnic one.

postings until the moderator, having received complaints regarding accusations of racism, locked it on August 28, 2008.

Even cursory inspection of this discussion reveals that it does indeed proceed along similar discursive lines as the ones outlined in *Dramacon* by Chmakova. Although the topic title would suggest that the discussion focuses on whether or not OEL manga is just a fad that is now beginning to die out, in fact the vast bulk of the postings are devoted to defining the word "manga" and whether or not titles produced outside of Japan can—or should—be called manga too. Indeed, the "manga is not pizza" comment is referenced explicitly in the fourth post. From this forum topic, it is possible to identify five distinct lines of argument about how to define manga. Three of these are recognizable from *Dramacon*, while the other two may be thought of as replies to the assertions introduced there. I will discuss each in turn.[5]

Manga as Marketing Function

"So now manga's a format again?" (The Xenos, August 18, 2008)

"I try to not get into these OEL pissing matches, because all this debating really has no affect [sic] on sales at all. If a book can appeal to the right readers, then it can do quite well for itself no matter where it comes from. OEL is shelved with manga for the same reason that Korean manhwa, Chinese manhua, and Japanese light novels are--it is meant to appeal to the same target audience. The word "manga" has become a word that bookstores use to know where to shelve books. That's really all there is to it." (adam_omega, August 18, 2008)

The first definition of manga suggested on the forum thread I will discuss here aligns most closely to that used by the publishing industry. As described in Brienza (2009b), the trim size and price point pioneered by Tokyopop in 2002 for its "100% Authentic Manga" line was quickly appropriated by other publishers to advertise their books as "manga." Bookstores began to shelve these similarly-sized books together, and by 2005 or so discrete "Manga" sections had become fixtures in the major chains. The "adam_omega" quoted above is Adam Arnold, Senior Production Editor of Seven Seas, one of the indie US publishers specializing in OEL manga, and his contribution to "these OEL pissing matches" is representative of the current industry view on terminology. As Lida pointed out, it is a free country, publishers are free to call their books what they wish, and it so happens that the word manga has acquired a useful marketing function. By labeling their books as "manga," publishers help to

---

5   In interest of fidelity, all extracted quotes from the forum postings throughout this chapter preserve as much as possible the poster's own spelling and text formatting.

ensure that bookstores know where to shelve them. This, in turn, maximizes sales because the customers browsing the manga section are the intended target audience. Usage of word "manga," in other words, has nothing do with content or the contexts of production; it is, rather, all about the context of reception. Of course, this definition locates the source of epistemological authority in the realm of commerce, and for cultural goods such as manga there are enduring tensions between artistic and capitalist imperatives.

Manga as Style

"[OEL]'re English language comics that are *particularly influenced* by Japanese storytelling traditions." (Ayokillyou, March 31, 2008)

"I thought [manga] was a style of art which is a form of storytelling? What is this?" (The Xenos, August 18, 2008)

"If you've read enough manga, your eyes will instantly pick out what is Japanese and what the imitators are." (Shadowrun20XX, August 18, 2008)

"What specific parameters meet this magical, generic and stereotypical style you keep mentioning? Big eyes? Small mouths? Speed lines? Sweat drops?" (Hellkorn, August 19, 2008)

"Analyzing manga on a visual perspective without geographical limitation is more OPEN. This openness will bring about a greater range of creative potential. Here's a question for you: **Is the creation of manga limited to a specific ethnic group?**" (KyuuA4, August 20, 2008)

It therefore ought to go without saying that this first definition of manga as a marketing category is not universally accepted. As in *Dramacon*, some manga fans are unwilling to accept the premise that US-based publishers ought to be allowed to call American-made comics manga merely because it is efficacious or in their financial best interests to do so. Instead, they argue, there is something characteristic about the style of art and/or storytelling that is distinctly manga-like, and only comics produced in this style can and should be referred to as manga. So, for example, if it has "chibis," as proposed by Girl #2 in *Dramacon*, then it is manga. Moreover, defining manga as some sort of narrative or visual style pioneered in Japan but not necessarily confined to that country has the advantage, as noted by KyuuA4, of not limiting manga creation to a specific ethnic group. But, as Hellkorn suggests with a series of rhetorical questions, given the sheer diversity of manga published in the post-WWII period in Japan, it is virtually impossible to comprehensively define what constitutes the "manga style." Some Japanese comics might feature characters with "stereotypical" "big eyes" and "small mouths," but many others do not. Debates about what "manga style" truly is are never resolved, and a more objective, empirical way of defining manga—which does not have any underlying authoritarian, capitalist motive—is therefore sought.

Manga as Japanese

> "OEL cannot be called manga because manga is a Japanese word and OEL is in English." (mistress_rebi, March 29, 2007)

> "I actually agree that manga is Japan-only. It has a clear definition." (Jackmace Ryo, August 19, 2008)

> "[M]anga are Japanese comics. Japanese comics are comics that were created for a Japanese audience by comic artists who work in the Japanese comic industry." (Tamaria, August 20, 2008)

> "TokyoPop used to print Sailor Moon as single issue comic books. So, yeah, there are Sailor Moon comics [sic] books and Sailor Moon graphic novels. And yet both of those are still manga." (The Xenos, August 19, 2008)

To escape subjective judgments about style, some fans, like Jim, take the view that manga is Japanese. It has nothing to do with format, style, or whatever Americans working in the publishing industry like Adam Arnold might think. If the comic was originally published in Japan, it is manga. This would seem to be a straightforward definition, yet in practice, due to Japan's perceived ethno-racial and linguistic homogeneity and the relative parochialism of the manga publishing field there, it also carries implicit baggage. Jim's comment, "You're not Japanese!! So you can't draw manga!," is salient. Comics originally published in Japan would be presumed to have been created by a person of Japanese ethnicity and written in the Japanese language. But if someone Japanese publishes a comic outside of Japan, is it manga? If someone non-Japanese publishes a comic inside Japan, is it manga? If, say, non-Japanese artist Felipe Smith publishes an original title with Tokyopop and a second, in virtually the same visual style, with Kodansha, does the latter count as manga while the former does not? To define manga simply as having been first published in Japan provides straightforward answers to all of these questions, but those answers do not seem entirely satisfactory in practice. Certainly it does not work in the interests of those working in publishing or those people outside of Japan who would aspire to create something they might someday hope to call manga.

Manga as Quality

"Most OEL published is crap that's not worth my time or money." (digitalkikka, April 1, 2007)

"Bad manga is just that. Bad manga. As for comic, they're worse **visually** than any manga. **Which cartoon/animated cat would you prefer to look at: Garfield, or Chii (from Chi's Sweet Home)?** It's sad how we can say Quality isn't a factor—but—it does [sic]. Thsoe [sic] who deny this are lying to themselves." (KyuuA4, July 24, 2008)

"Nobody objects to the concept, it's the bad comics and dry emulations we object too [sic]. And since OEL manga is pretty much dominated by amateur level comics, the terminology is not doing anyone any good." (Tamaria, August 15, 2008)

Amid debates about whether or not manga is 1) a marketing category, 2) a style, or 3) a comic from Japan, a fourth tacit definition of manga begins to surface. Although Chmakova does not directly address this one in *Dramacon*, it haunts the text with its absence. Certainly, it is hard to imagine that she would be unaware of it, and that it would not be a source of considerable anxiety for her in her professional career. Manga, in the view of some fans, is a high quality product, while comics, such as those produced in the United States, are inherently and categorically inferior. This is most obvious in the quote above from KyuuA4, who argues that "comics" are just "worse visually" than "manga," and people who deny that this debate about the meaning of manga is not really about "quality" are "lying to themselves." In this view, OEL manga—because they are not from Japan—are of poor quality. And indeed, many commenters on the Anime News Network thread reflexively refer to OEL manga as "crap," "dry emulations," and "amateur level comics."

Why Do You Care So Much?!

"So you're saying that the average otaku[6] is pretty much racist? Honestly, I don't think I can argue against that generalization. I hope most fans are better than that, but I do notice a scary pro-Japan anti-American trend in way too much of the fandom." (The Xenos, July 30, 2008)

---

6   The Japanese word "otaku" and has its own fascinating and contentious cultural history. For more information, see Hiroki Azuma (2009). In the context of this chapter, its usage may be understood as synonymous with "anime and manga fan."

"There is only one reason why this discussion continues: There are people who do not want to be associated with American comics, so they insist on using the worth [sic] manga to describe the things they draw/the drawings they like." (Tamaria, August 13, 2008)

"I know most people's lives suck so they tend to connect themselves to various things in order to feel special somehow (a band, a sports team, a clothing line, whatever). And that they feel a need to protect whatever they've "connected" themselves to in order to make it seem (and thus themselves) superior. But seriously, if you want to connect yourself to something and then start fights over it, make it the usual religion or politics or some crap, not art ..." (Ultenth, August 22, 2008)

Inevitably, once the "manga as quality" argument, and variations thereof that seem to disproportionately denigrate OEL manga, surfaces, *ad hominem* accusations of racism quickly follow. However, because there are no proverbial parents to intervene, the conversation does not stop there. If the first definition explored in this chapter was about what the word manga does for producers, the fifth and final definition of manga is less of a formalized dictionary definition *per se* and more focused upon the distinctive work the term does for fans. So what, precisely, is that work? It is, following Bourdieu (1984), doing the work of creating and maintaining social distinction: They are, as Ultenth says, linking their social and personal identities to manga in order to feel "special" or "superior." However, this does not explain why some fans object so vociferously to any definition of manga that does not preserve its exclusive Japaneseness, manga as something that can only be made in Japan by Japanese people. Tamaria, who is not from the United States, suggests with an outsider's perspective that American fans need manga to be Japanese because they do not want to be identified with American comics or even, The Xenos suggests, with the United States, period.

Con Culture and the Politics of Fandom

"Also, you're getting confused again. Comic influenced manga would be fore [sic] stuff like JoJo or even Trigun. You likely meant to say manga influenced comics." (The Xenos, August 5, 2008)

Is there any merit to this last armchair—or perhaps I should say "swivel desk chair"—interpretation of the motivation of American anime and manga fans in debating the definition of manga? Yes, in my view, there is. After all, to truly understand a culture and how it works, it is "imperative to uncover not only what is insistently present, but the characteristic absences and rigidities—what cannot be thought, or what is systematically 'outside'" (Born 2004, 15). And in these 52 pages of debate about whether or not OEL manga can actually be called manga in the first place if they are formatted, marketed, and/or styled like Japanese manga but not actually from Japan, there is one very characteristic absence, one striking discursive omission: Japanese manga themselves are not stylistically or culturally "pure" and free of non-Japanese influence. The so-called God of Manga Osamu Tezuka himself, for example, was famously inspired by Betty Boop and Disney cartoons (Schodt 2007), and countless Japanese manga creators have both acknowledged and unacknowledged artistic influences originating from outside their home country. While this fact is very rarely recognized during the course of the discussion, as in this lonely passing mention by The Xenos on August 5, 2008, it is not used as evidence to support or dismiss any argument in favor of one definition over another. This conspicuous omission is, on the surface of things, odd. If all manga artists, no matter where they are, are wont to draw upon an international set of creative influences, why is this not a talking point against those who would say that manga can only be Japanese? Why, moreover, are those who believe manga is a style not pointing out that, in the same way American artists occasionally used stereotyped Japanese visual and narrative techniques, Japanese artists occasionally deploy American ones? And what, finally, in such a regime of stylistic transnational flow, can ever be truly "Japanese"? These sorts of questions are never posed on the forum thread, nor are they answered. Clearly, they are systematically "outside" for a very good reason.

To understand what that reason is, it is worth stepping back away from the pages of anime forums and returning to the pages of *Dramacon* and its representation, more broadly, of con culture and the politics of fandom. Although the love story around which the books are constructed is recognizably clichéd ("drama" purely in the colloquial sense), the setting and the sorts of social interactions within it manifestly are not. The heated argument Jim has with Lida, so similar to very real debates on "some anime forums," is indicative, and one further aspect of the OEL manga, depicted in loving detail, stands out—the convention setting itself.

"Yattacon," a portmanteau of "yatta," which is Japanese for "hooray," and "con," short for convention, does not actually exist. In its general contours, however, as a once-annual anime and manga fan convention held at a single large convention center venue over the course of several days, it most closely resembles Anime Expo at the LA Convention Center or Otakon at the Baltimore Convention Center, the two largest US-based anime cons. (Chmakova's "local" con in Toronto is Anime North, and while its social scene is undoubtedly similar, it has been multi-sited since 2004, and is therefore a less obvious analogue.) Attendance at these cons number in the tens of thousands, and participants will typically overnight in nearby hotels, which may become their own impromptu party scenes. Apart from the Artists' Alley, where Christie spends much of her time, there is a Dealers' Room; an informative and entertaining program of panels and workshops during the day, run both by other fans and by industry professionals; and, in the evening, contests and social opportunities such as dances. At Yattacon, the dance is called a Masquerade.

The use of the word Masquerade for a dance is also telling because dressing up is an important part of con culture. The practice is called costume play, or "cosplay," and attendees come to cons dressed up as characters from anime and manga. Sometimes, but not always, they will assume some of the personality traits of their chosen characters, playacting and posing for photos with other "in-world" characters from the same series. Many of the characters in *Dramacon* are depicted primarily, or even entirely, in costume, including Matt, his sister Sandra (who specializes in costume design), and even Christie herself in later volumes.

It would, in short, be a stretch *not* to apply a dramaturgical analysis and see the con as a stage upon which the attendees perform particular roles especially suited for the occasion. And through these fans' performative acts, then, is the culture of their fandom created and maintained. But what is particularly striking about the con setting in *Dramacon* is how much of a world apart Yattacon is. It is a space away from home, away from work, away from school. People who otherwise reside on opposite ends of the country come together in a co-present assemblage that otherwise exists nowhere else. In fact, there is no plot away from the con; the story develops entirely within the narrow, geographic and temporal space of the con itself. The actors may well even be thought of as entirely different people away from the con.

These clear boundaries between the con and everyday life, I would contend, are absolutely essential to understanding the politics of American anime and manga fandom because it is uniquely within this demarcated space that social possibilities, such as, say, Christie and Matt's star-crossed, storybook perfect romantic relationship, can happen. Put differently, such dreams come true are not outside the realm of fantasy *because* the fantasy has been so carefully constructed and made real, *and a crucial component to this construction is the production of symbolic boundaries*. Spatial boundaries alone, while potent from a practical perspective, are not sufficient to keep it wholly separate, as the appearance and unwelcome interventions of parents at various stages throughout *Dramacon* would attest.

This is where the relevance of the debates about the definition of manga resurface. The con may be a unique space of social possibility, but it is a finite one, and being only a few days of the year means that the fandom's social cohesion needs to be maintained and reinforced through other means. One of these means is through online interaction on dedicated social networking sites such as the Anime News Network forums. Via these virtual means, a collectively arrived-at understanding of the proverbial objects of the fans' affection (Brienza 2013b), such as manga, serve to reinforce boundaries between fan and non-fan through their articulation across national, and especially ethno-racial, lines. These boundaries are thus kept secure at all times and places, not just within the three-day window of the con assemblage. Not "wanting to be associated with American comics" is an extension of wanting to keep fandom separate from normal—a.k.a. American—life. For some fans, therefore, manga must be "authentically" Japanese; to be otherwise is to threaten the sanctity of the boundaries between everyday life and fandom. This is why they become so passionate and emotional about their convictions. Their very ontological security in fandom is at stake.

Clearly, this constructed authenticity does not exist for purposes of racial discrimination. Nevertheless, there are pernicious side effects. By artificially essentializing the category of Japaneseness, complexities of group identity, affiliation, and influence are elided. Anyone whose identity, whether personally selected or ascribed, troubles that clear line between ordinary America and fandom may be resented—even mobbed. When Jim, in a rage, redirects his frustration at being challenged about manga's essential Japaneseness towards Bethany's status as a nonwhite person, the unintended consequences of the anxiety of anime and manga fans about ethno-racial authenticity could not be more obvious—and ugly. America is still a profoundly unequal and racialized society, and even within fandom not all people have equal access and opportunity. Only *white* American fans are permitted to obliterate their everyday selves and realign their identities to Japanese cultural goods in order to feel superior and imaginatively expand their horizons of possibilities. Because it reminds fans that their collectively enacted spaces of especial possibility are imperfect, Bethany's, and quite possibly Chmakova's own, hyphenated identities are an unwelcome reminder that fandom is not a utopia. Indeed, I would argue, truly constructing such a space through performance of ethno-racial authenticity is quite simply impossible. The real world has always already intruded.

American anime and manga fandom is, ultimately, a fantasy of somewhere else, where I can be other than myself; where I will be with people who are like me; and where I will find fulfillment on a horizontally-organized plane of social, cultural, and emotional possibilities. Yet these possibilities are constrained by the interpretive category of authenticity upon which they are performed. Jim was right, in the end: Manga is not pizza. Although OEL manga can become bestsellers, they cannot be just like pizza as long as the constitutive politics of North American anime and manga fandom require, in the construction and maintenance of symbolic boundaries, that contemporary cultural goods to be purely one thing, produced in one place, by one people. Chmakova's commercial and critical success in her career proves that there is genuine opportunity in the field for global manga, but for now the *real* possibilities of a globalized, cosmopolitanized, hybridized, and ever more complexly connected world remain just beyond the limits of fan fantasy.

References

Alexander, Jeffrey C. 2011. *Performance and Power*. Cambridge: Polity.

Azuma, Hiroki. 2009. *Otaku: Japan's Database Animals*. Minneapolis, MN: University of Minnesota Press.

Bourdieu, Pierre. 1984. *Distinction: A Social Critique of the Judgement of Taste*. Cambridge, MA: Harvard University Press.

Brienza, Casey. 2009a. "Books, Not Comics: Publishing Fields, Globalization, and Japanese Manga in the United States." *Publishing Research Quarterly* 25 (2): 101–17. doi:10.1007/s12109-009-9114-2.

Brienza, Casey. 2009b. "Paratexts in Translation: Reinterpreting 'Manga' for the United States." *The International Journal of the Book* 6 (2): 13–20.

Brienza, Casey. 2013a. "Beyond B&W? The Global Manga of Felipe Smith." *Black Comics: Politics of Race and Representation*, edited by Sheena C. Howard and Ronald L. Jackson II, 79–94. London: Bloomsbury.

Brienza, Casey. 2013b. "Objects of Otaku Affection: Animism, Anime Fandom, and the Gods of … Consumerism?" In *Handbook of Contemporary Animism*, edited by Graham Harvey, 479–90. London: Routledge.

Brienza, Casey. 2014. "Did Manga Conquer America? Implications for the Cultural Policy of 'Cool Japan.'" *International Journal of Cultural Policy* 20 (4): 383–98. doi:10.1080/10286632.2013.856893.

Chmakova, Svetlana. 2008. *Dramacon Ultimate Edition*. Los Angeles: Tokyopop.

Coville, Jamie. 2006. "Svetlana Chmakova Interview." *Coville's Clubhouse*, April. http://www.collectortimes.com/2006_04/Clubhouse2.html.

Goffman, Erving. 1959. *The Presentation of Self in Everyday Life*. New York: Doubleday.

Goffman, Erving. 1974. *Frame Analysis: An Essay on the Organization of Experience*. New York: Harper & Row.

ICv2 Guide to Manga. 2008. "Naruto on Top in 2007: ICv2 Top 50 Manga Properties."

Lie, John. 2001. *Multiethnic Japan*. Cambridge, MA: Harvard University Press.

Santos, Carlo. 2005. "No Blood For OEL." *Irresponsible Pictures*, September 17. http://comipress.com/backstage/incomplete/patachu/Irresponsible-Picture/irresponsible.patachu.com/2005/09/no-blood-for-oel.html.

Schodt, Frederik L. 2007. *The Astro Boy Essays: Osamu Tezuka, Mighty Atom, and the Manga/Anime Revolution.* Berkeley, CA: Stone Bridge Press.
Simons, Rikki. n.d. "FAQ." *Studio Tavicat.* http://www.tavicat.com/faq.html.

Chapter 6
On Everyday Life: Frédéric Boilet and the Nouvelle Manga Movement

Tiago Canário

Over the past several decades, slice-of-life stories have been increasing in the contemporary field of comic books. Interesting changes started in the West with the underground movement of the 1960s and 1970s, when cartoonists' lives themselves became a subject (Beaty 2009), a stark contrast from, and challenge to, the domain of superhero action-adventure stories. That new perspective gave space to narratives far removed from the heroic experience. They were based on the subject of common, everyday life.

That period was essential to the consolidation and maturation of the comics medium, which made possible the notion of comics as product not just for children but also for grown men and women (Groensteen 1996; Miller 2007). Such a narrative approach, based on writing about everyday life, tried to prove that comics are not just for kids (Schneider 2010). They began to explore the ordinary moments.

Throughout this same period, more prominent than the attention given to authors' biographies, Western countries experienced a large increase in the import and consumption of Japanese media, particularly in the 1990s (Moliné 2004; Gravett 2004). From this contact with the East, another influence emerged. Due to the massive expansion of the market for manga during the end of the last century, a vast number of experiments in anime and manga localization, both authorized licensed translations/adaptations and unauthorized scanlations and fansubs, appeared.

The West saw then two new paradigms in comics emerging: slice-of-life stories and manga from Japan. This chapter explores an initiative at the intersection of these two paradigms, Nouvelle Manga. The Nouvelle Manga Movement appeared to attempt to deal with new cultural challenges. It offered a curious aesthetic program interested in everyday life and ordinary characters, while also drawing upon Japanese manga and French cinema as its main sources of inspiration.

The chapter proposes an investigation of this movement through analysis of the Nouvelle Manga manifestos, discussions around *Nouvelle Vague* (i.e. New

Wave) cinema,[1] and finally conceptions about the nature of artistic modernity itself. Although there have been many previous studies of the *Nouvelle Vague* Movement (e.g. Ahmed 2010; Ranz 2010; Trifonova 2012; Vollmar 2007), my aim here is to examine the questions, problems, and solutions introduced by it, as well as to understand some exchanges that blurred cultural boundaries and created dialogues between East and West.

The Beginnings of Nouvelle Manga

The French comic artist Frédéric Boilet released his book, titled *Yukiko no Hourensou* [Yukiko's Spinach] in Japanese and *L'Épinard de Yukiko* in French, in 2001 while living in Japan. It was published in France, where it was primarily seen as a manga, and in Japan, where it was seen as a *bande dessinée*. It drew much attention from readers and critics. In both countries, it was published under a new genre label: Nouvelle Manga. Within a few years, it has been translated into Spanish, German, English, Portuguese, Chinese, Italian, Korean, and Polish, and these editions also explored the meaning of the new label.

The Nouvelle Manga genre had first appeared two years before the release of *Yukiko's Spinach*. At that time, the terminology was slightly different, but the basic idea was the same. In 1999, the editor and art critic Kiyoshi Kusumi proposed the label *Manga Nouvelle Vague* [New Wave Manga] in the *Comickers* magazine. Kusumi created the term, based on Boilet's graphic novels published in Japan. His narratives were somewhere between the intersection of Japanese manga and French comics and films. The pre-existing genre categories for comics and manga did not seem to capture this sort of work, and for this reason Kusumi attempted this new coinage.

Starting from the editor's perception and drawing from reflections on and debates with other French and Japanese artists and their works, Boilet proceeded to write the "Nouvelle Manga Manifesto" in August 2001. He used a brief version of Kusumi's term to name a curious trend that was emerging at the time. As described by Boilet, "[T]he term 'Manga Nouvelle Vague'—promptly shortened to 'Nouvelle Manga'—was used at first to describe my own graphic novels, perceived by the Japanese as graphically close to *BD* but read like manga, and recalling the spirit of French cinema" (Boilet 2007, 1). So, *Manga Nouvelle Vague* became just "Nouvelle Manga" [New Manga].

Yet despite the success of *Yukiko's Spinach*, this book cannot be recognized as the first ever Nouvelle Manga work. Boilet's previous comic books had seemed

---

1   Editor's Note: It would be conventional to translate *Nouvelle Vague* as "New Wave" for the purposes of English-language scholarship. However, the term has been left in the original French throughout this chapter intentionally in order to underscore the linguistic resonance with Nouvelle Manga.

to develop similar aesthetic patterns, as Kusumi had argued, and other authors' previous works also explored analogous narrative choices. The movement, thus, was seen as bringing together different but comparable authorial aesthetics. They were distinct and separate works but nonetheless had similarities.

In his first manifesto, Boilet (2001) points out the existence of Nouvelle Manga as an aesthetic proposal situated between manga and *bandes dessinées*, citing similarities between contemporary comics artists, like the Japanese Jirô Taniguchi (*L'Homme qui marche*, 1995; *Le Promeneur*, 2006), Kan Takahama (*Kinderbook*, 2004; *L'Eau amère*, 2009), and Kiriko Nananan (*Blue*, 1997; *Strawberry Shortcakes*, 2002), and the French Fabrice Neaud (*Journal*, 1992–2002), Frédéric Poincelet (*Essai de sentimentalisme*, 2001; *Mon bel amour*, 2006), and Aurélia Aurita (*Fraise et chocolat*, 2006), among others. This was, in short proposing a transnational movement which married two of the largest national markets for comics in the world. It should be noted at this stage that this was to change in his second manifesto (Boilet 2007), as will be seen later on. But for the time being, the historical precedent, as well as authorial and textual underpinnings, of the movement were strengthened.

Conscious of the cultural impact of its proposal, a big event was put together to raise audience awareness of the movement. During the time the first text was written, aggressive marketing strategies were planned to introduce the movement at exhibitions, installations, interventions, and lectures. An international event called *L'Événement Nouvelle Manga* [The Nouvelle Manga Event] was also held between September 29 and October 14, 2001 in Tokyo.

The campaign's main attraction was an exhibition of works by French and Japanese artists linked to the movement, which was open to the public for all 15 days. This exhibition, called simply *Nouvelle Manga*, was organized by the Tokyo National University of Fine Arts and Music, with support from the Japan Foundation, Institut Franco-Japonais de Tokyo, French Embassy in Japan, and Japan Arts Council. Located in the Masaki Kinekan room, the event exhibited original pages of comics by David B., Matthieu Blanchin, Frédéric Boilet, Yôji Fukuyama, Emmanuel Guibert, Fabrice Neaud, Loïc Néhou, Frédéric Poincelet, Jirô Taniguchi, and Naito Yamada. Boilet explains to Bastide (2001) that the exhibition chose a traditional Japanese décor, with tatami mats, low tables, natural lighting, and a request for visitors to be barefoot in the room. The original pages were shown on the tables, so the visitors could accommodate themselves on the tatami and read them slowly, in a horizontal display, instead of the common vertical one. The room had originally been made for exhibitions of *emakimonos*, Japanese picture scrolls, with the intention of extending the time for contemplation and encouraging a slow and detailed reading.

In the first week (August 29 to September 7), a live exhibition-performance called *La Maison de la Nouvelle Manga* [The Nouvelle Manga House] was held as well. In an atelier decorated by the interior designer Satoko Kojima, the public was able to watch David B., Frédéric Boilet, Fabrice Neaud, Loïc Néhou, and

Walter & Yuka working on some pages. Accompanied by translators, the artists took turns in the atelier to demonstrate their techniques and talk to the public. The *Maison* also presented original pages by Joann Sfar, Nicolas de Crécy, Christophe Blain, and Émile Bravo, known as part of the new generation of Franco-Belgian comics artists.

The two final exhibitions associated with *L'Événement Nouvelle Manga* were the *Installation Fabrice Neaud* [Fabrice Neaud Installation] and the *Exposition Au coin des rues* [At the Corner of the Exhibition]. The first was an installation which ran from September 29 to October 14 recreating Neaud's workplace in a small apartment, by using original pages, materials, and objects that inspired him in his relationship with everyday life, all portrayed on the autobiographical *Journal*. The *Exposition Au coin des rues*, meanwhile, showed pages by French and Japanese authors in public and private spaces, museums, galleries, temples, and commercial storefronts in the Nezu, Sendagi, Yanada, and Ueno neighborhoods.

The Institut Franco-Japonais de Tokyo also organized a conference on October 4 with David B., Frédéric Boilet, Fabrice Neaud, and Naito Yamada. Open to the public, the debate aimed to introduce French artists to Japan and create a dialogue between Japanese works and their own. Finally, comic books by artists involved in *L'Événement Nouvelle Manga* were put up for sale in the three exhibition rooms. There were books by French and Japanese artists, focusing on the new works, a partnership between l'Association, the French publisher Ego comme X, Tokyo Geijutsu Daigaku Museum Shop, and the *Comix 2000* and *Lapin* magazines.

Every visitor received a 32-page catalogue with the manifesto and introductory profiles of the participating artists, followed by some of their comic book pages. In an interview, Boilet told Bastide with great pleasure that:

> As such, it has already produced its first fruits, since, due to it, a small neighborhood association could do what no other professional, agent, publisher, organization or Japanese or French institution, even during the Année de la France au Japon, in 1998, had previously dared to try: a fifteen days festival about BD and manga in the heart of Tokyo, monopolizing four quarters, showing four exhibitions, one of them at the Tokyo National University of Fine Arts and Music ... (Bastide 2001, 1)[2]

---

2 Original text: "En tant que tel, il a d'ores et déjà porté ses premiers fruits, puisque c'est grâce à lui qu'une petite association de quartier a pu faire ce qu'aucun professionnel, agent ou éditeur, organisme, institution française ou japonaise, pas même l'Année de la France au Japon en 1998, n'avaient osé tenter jusqu'alors : quinze jours de festival autour de la BD et de la *manga* au cœur de Tôkyô, monopolisant quatre quartiers, présentant quatre expositions dont une aux Beaux-Arts et invitant trois auteurs / éditeurs français de tout premier plan!" (Unless otherwise indicated, translations are those of the author.)

L'Événement Nouvelle Manga gained attention from the *Asahi Shimbun* and *Yomiuri Shimbun* newspapers, two of the five most important Japanese newspapers; *Aera* magazine; fashion and literary magazines such as *Da Vinci, Pen, Figaro Japon, Ginza,* and *Mr. High Fashion*; and the NHK television channel. It was also covered by *Comickers*, which interviewed Fabrice Neaud and David B., *The Japan Times*, and many other French- and English-language specialist and niche publications.

Nouvelle Manga, therefore, was becoming a category for marketing purposes in its own right, connecting authors, the public, and publishers. This marketing started in earnest with the publication of *Yukiko's Spinach*. The book was released in a simultaneous publication in France (Ego comme X, September 2001) and Japan (Ohta Shuppan, August 2001). In Spain, the publisher Ponent Mon[3] was actually created because of the movement. According to the description on their website (Ponent Mon n.d.):

> Ponent Mon is a company established in 2003, which was started with a focus on the publishing of works framed under a new way to understand comics, the "Nouvelle Manga," headed by Frédéric Boilet. It brought together the best of European comics based on aesthetics, and more mature issues which came from manga. Since that time, and intending to satisfy the most exquisite tastes of discerning readers, the publisher has expanded its boundaries by publishing authors such as Étienne Davodeau, Emmanuel Gibert, Nicolas de Crécy, David B., Joann Sfar, Lewis Trondheim, or Émile Bravo in its European comics style, besides editing more experimental and avant-garde artists of contemporary manga production, as such Inio Asano or Hideo Yamamoto, and not forgetting to recover the classic horror manga, [by authors] such as Kazuo Umezu or Seiichi Hayashi.[4]

---

3 Editor's Note: The UK-based Fanfare has published many of Ponent Mon's books, including most of the Nouvelle Manga titles mentioned in this chapter, in English translation.

4 Original text: "Ponent Mon es una empresa fundada en 2003 que en sus comienzos se centró en la publicación de obras encuadradas en una nueva forma de entender el cómic, el 'Nouvelle Manga' encabezado por Frédéric Boilet, que unía lo mejor del cómic europeo con la estética y temática más adulta del manga. A partir de ese momento y con la intención de satisfacer los gustos más exquisitos de los lectores más exigentes, la editorial amplió sus fronteras publicando autores del calibre de Étienne Davodeau, Emmanuel Gibert, Nicolas de Crécy, David B., Joann Sfar, Lewis Trondheim o Émile Bravo en su línea de cómic europeo, además de editar a los autores más experimentales y vanguardistas del manga actual como Inio Asano o Hideo Yamamoto, sin olvidar la recuperación de grandes clásicos olvidados del manga de terror como Kazuo Umezz o Seiichi Hayashi."

Everyday Life in Boilet's Nouvelle Manga Manifestos

To understand the Nouvelle Manga aesthetic proposal and the reasons for the movement's emergence, it is essential to understand the manifestos. In the first one, released in 2001, the conclusion seems summarize the movement's intent:

> The Nouvelle Manga aims to be an expression of this complicity, the Franco-Japanese prolongation of French BD d'auteur and « la » manga (the Japanese BD d'auteur): an author's initiative (as opposed to a publisher's or import library's initiative that would inevitably lead to translations—or imports—of best-sellers) whose goal would be, by creating a bridge between the two genres, to present the readers with the best of the two countries' BDs and manga, and not just what sells most. This in the universal realm of daily life : be it autobiographical, documentary or fictional.[5] (Boilet 2001, 3)

This small excerpt offers clues for understanding Nouvelle Manga. In the beginning, it underlines the context in which the movement occurs, characterized by works that exist as contrasts to the movement's aesthetic proposal. The dissatisfaction with contemporary mainstream publishing is a central point, and it defines the comics artists in the French industry as those who "… are first and foremost illustrators, often more preoccupied with graphics than with scenario" (Boilet 2001, 1). And indeed, Franco-Belgian works do give much attention to illustrations. Adventure narratives, characterized by heroic protagonists and the extraordinary, dominated the market until the early 1990s.

However, this situation has changed with the rise of new small publishers. These presses made possible the emergence of new comic books, more concerned about everyday life, whether fictional or autobiographical. These new players were artist cooperatives focused on narrative and visual experimentation, and they stayed away from major mainstream publishers (Beaty 2009; Trifonova 2012). They published authorial works interested in exploring the limits of visual storytelling. Trifonova (2012) attributes this influence to the French *Nouvelle Vague*, during which the visual arts became a strong influence on culture, despite the previous domination of the literary arts.

The text of the manifesto is very critical of its contemporary Franco-Belgian works, especially those produced by major publishers: "… an album with skilful or fashionable drawings will always find buyers in France, even if the story is lousy or stupid" (Boilet 2001, 1). On the other hand, new works known as *"nouvelle bd"* could offer a more objective dialogue with everyday life and the readers' own contexts, which make them interesting to different groups. If the artists were

---

5   Editor's Note: This is a verbatim quote, not a translation. The original punctuation in the passage has been preserved in all its particulars.

inspired by their own lives, people could find similarities between those and their own day-to-day experiences, family relationships, dates, etc. (Miller 2007).

Boilet argues further that "universality is generally found in a kitchen or at the bottom of a garden, only rarely on Mars or Alpha Centauri" (2001, 1). So even if fictional narratives have some links with reality that readers could identify themselves with, slice-of-life narratives try to create a meaningful connection between text and reader by appealing to a familiar background. But this emphatically does not mean to imply simplicity; there is plenty of complexity and contradiction. Indeed, everyday life is formed by the improvised way in which men and women deal with their daily activities (Certeau 1998; Sheringham 2006), especially the most common of them. Sheringham (2006) underlines the day-by-day as a complex domain of human possibilities. When narrated, it creates "... stories that challenge any accurate plot description, often deprived of special events and inhabited by characters doing nothing more than living out their own routines" (Schneider 2010).

Following authors like Umberto Eco (1994) and Wolfgang Iser (1996; 1999), it may be argued that the readers' response to the Nouvelle Manga text creates an aesthetic effect, thereby completing the work itself. A narrative organizes a reality, but with a lot of gaps, which are offered to readers who include themselves and their own references in the reading process. Those pauses in the text give space to readers' imagination, creating an interactive process. They enter in the narrative to formulate its connections. Both authors are interested in the process of mediated communication, starting with the reception of the text. Although this is a study about Nouvelle Manga, not novels, such theories help to better understand the "advantage" discussed in the manifesto: "While comic strips and comic books are commercially designed to keep boredom away at all costs, the freedom brought by independent comics opens the doors to new forms of reader engagement other than instant immersion" (Schneider 2012, 106). More than simply appealing through a very familiar subject, everyday life narratives tend to create a fragmented and unclear collage of facts.

These concepts help to understand the potential of the manifesto's ideas about success in the cultural field. It asserts the economic viability of the movement based on the universality of its subjects. Nevertheless, more than the possible new audience's interest, this pamphleteering proposal points to another consequence: Foreign readers might see these works as closer to the French cinema and Japanese manga, both of which are able to cross national boundaries better than many comics put out by the major Franco-Belgian publishers.

Franco-Belgian comics production previous to the 1990s (or those outside of the *nouvelle bd*) favored a more specific range of subjects, including science fiction, action-adventure, and historical fiction, while on the other hand Japanese manga often chose everyday life subjects (Gravett 2004; Groensteen 1991; Moliné 2004). Boilet believes that this is why they became so famous and highly-regarded among different groups of people, by offering not just a vast range of subjects, but a significant amount of day-by-day situations, even if just a small part of such diversity is seen in the West.[6] In the French context, the manifesto points out some of those manga focused on everyday life, like Jirô Taniguchi's graphic novels. A new "term" is even proposed to characterize these manga. The text uses the French articles "le" (masculine) and "la" (feminine) to make clear the difference. "Le manga" is used to identify mainstream commercial manga titles, while "la manga" refers to artistic manga, narratives free from market demands.

The manifesto defines manga as a style that highlights story and narration, with a wide range of subjects, fluidity, and techniques to suggest feelings and sensations to the readers. "In Japan, a mangaka is someone who wants, above all, to tell stories, as opposed to those authors of *bandes dessinées* 'BDs' in France who generally become comic book artists through an interest in drawing" (Boilet 2001, 1). Along similar lines, Scott McCloud (1994) describes the Japanese techniques of narration as the "art of intervals." He believes that they have cyclic and labyrinthine narrative structures, with the use of wanderings and gaps, which calls for reader's inferences—far from the standard ideal of objectivity in Western visual culture. Gaps are, therefore, essential. In this particular representation of time, "manga lend themselves to a subtle game of reticence" (Groensteen 1991, 43).[7] Therry Groensteen, similarly, sees Japanese comics as an art of editing because of their ability to contract and expand dramatic passages of the narrative (by panel articulations and page layouts especially). Such an art of intervals, then, gives more space to the interactive process and the reader's imagination, as in Eco's and Iser's reader response theory.

Japanese and French comics have recognized traditions, but in some works the differences are not so clear. The Nouvelle Manga manifesto argues that since the 1990s, a variety of efforts show that cross-national influence is possible, especially after some exchange programs for artists. For example, the Japanese publisher Kodansha invited authors from Spain, France, and United States to be part of the manga line of its *Morning* and *Afternoon* magazines, which stimulated new graphic experiences. There was even a Manga Fellowship Program helping foreign comics artists living in Japan (Moliné 2004). Between them, names like George Gladir and Guy Jeans (penname of Robert Whiting) became known for their transcultural narratives. Gladir, in collaboration with the Japanese artist Tetsuya Oyama, published anecdotes about Chinese and

---

6 However, it is worth noting that, in fact, most of the Japanese manga published in Western countries since the 1990s are of a more mainstream sort, due in part to the immediately preceding rise in popularity of Japanese anime, which was exported starting in the 1960s (Gravett 2004; Luyten 2011; Moliné 2004).

7 Original text: "... les manga se prêtent au jeu subtil de la réticence."

Japanese behavior. Jeans, in collaboration with Minoru Hiramatsu, explored the adventures of an African-American baseball player living in Japan (Gravett 2004). The American artist Paul Pope described his experience as: "World Comics, that's how the Japanese thought about it. They told me that their goal was to create a comic style that would be universal, the style of the 21st century understood by all readers" (Gravett 2004, 157). Japanese creators also went to different countries. Taiyo Matsumoto, for example, studied in France. Due to the new perspectives of this international group of comics artists, similarities between Franco-Belgian and Japanese works emerged.

Those works, in turn, set a precedent for giving more space to authorial experimentation through the exploration of different subjects and narrative strategies (and not so attached to their own national traditions). A kind of *Nouvelle Vague* spirit and in-dialogue with the Japanese manga production (whose consumption was growing fast at that point) emerged, and a group of narratives created a disruption in readers' expectations—while containing enough similarities to glimpse a common purpose, even if they were not originally organized as a single group or genre category. And finally, in trying to perform their opposition to mainstream comics production, they explored a new niche market, which could be even stronger if organized as a movement. That was, I would argue, one of the most significant consequences of the movement. It enabled, for example, the creation of the publisher Ponent Mon, which started as a showcase for those artists (some of them not so well known previously).

Other events were subsequently organized in different countries, such as Brazil.[8] In 2007, during the Fifth Feira Internacional de Quadrinhos [International Exhibition of Comics], there was a tribute to Japanese comics. At that event, the Portuguese-language version of the second manifesto was released, with some Nouvelle Manga artists present. Also in the same year, a similar exhibition was held in Barcelona. Boilet was keen to highlight the transcultural attributes of the movement: "The term Nouvelle Manga might refer to the consciousness and initiatives from European, Japanese, or American authors who could follow it: I am starting this idea, this proposition, but its achievement obviously doesn't depend only on me" (quoted in Bastide 2001).[9]

This aspect of the movement was made explicit in the text of the second manifesto, "Nouvelle Manga in 2007" (first written in 2006 and updated in 2007), where Boilet asserts that the differences between the national comics of the United States, Japan, and France/Belgium are replaced in Nouvelle Manga

---

8   Editor's Note: See Chapter 2 for more information about manga in Brazil.

9   Original text: "Le terme Nouvelle Manga pourrait en désigner la conscience, et les initiatives d'auteurs européens, japonais ou américains qui pourraient l'accompagner : c'est une idée que je lance, une proposition, mais dont la concrétisation ne dépend évidemment pas que de moi."

by strong editorial and authorial perspectives. But if the difference between those traditions was a central point in the first manifesto, the second one gave more space to the marketing issue. Publisher-driven works are seen as based on nostalgic references and repetitive conventions, both in stories and in drawings. Author-driven books, in contrast, would be more audacious, blurring boundaries between major national publishers (Boilet 2007). The second manifesto argues that this distinction is clearer than the first one.

Nouvelle Manga, therefore, proposes to express the universality of these author-driven comic books. The movement is an initiative to break up geographical and cultural limits, through the creation and publication of autobiographical, documentary, or fictional trivial narratives. It is a question about "propositions," with efforts of displacement, communication, and mutual understanding (Bastide 2001). It aims to create links and bring together artists, publishers, and readers, as in the collective intention that characterized L'Événement Nouvelle Manga. Such connections require a vast amount of work, which is why Boilet asserts that the movement is more like a proposition whose execution depends on different agents.

In terms of aesthetic discussion, the movement encourages the creation of a graphic novel between manga and *bande dessinées*, with the French cinematic spirit, to promote works interested in ordinary life. As Boilet says,

> It is, in fact, more about authorial BD and manga than alternative BD and manga. Of course, the market laws place the authorial works among the independent publishers, but the pages from artists in rupture with the commercial system and attached to everyday life could have their place in a publication or exhibition, such as Nouvelle Manga au Japon. (Quoted in Bastide 2001, 4)[10]

The movement, moreover, recognizes in itself a wish for change that involves legitimate publishing opportunities and release events to make new conferences and exhibitions possible. It works as a sort of artistic distinction which helps lesser known artists:

> Furthermore, the label Nouvelle Manga can also currently be applied to several publishers worldwide : Casterman, Ego Comme X and Les Impressions Nouvelles in France, Akashi Shoten, Asukashinsha and Ohta Shuppan in Japan, Ponent Mon in Spain, Fanfare in the UK and US, Coconino Press in Italy, Dala

---

10   Original text: "… il s'agit moins en fait de BD et manga alternatives que, tout simplement, de BD et manga d'auteur. Bien sûr, la loi du marché veut que ces dernières se trouvent plutôt chez les éditeurs indépendants, mais des pages d'artistes rompus aux circuits commerciaux mais attachés au quotidien pourraient avoir leur place dans une édition, ou une exposition, Nouvelle Manga au Japon."

Publishing in Taiwan, Casa 21 and Conrad Editora in Brazil. They have dedicated themselves to publishing programs which are independent of geography and genre, aiming to present their readers with the best international graphic novels, original or translated works by such established masters as Emmanuel Guibert and Jirô Taniguchi, as well as those by newcomers and innovators such as Aurélia Aurita from France and Little Fish from Japan. (Boilet 2007, 1)

The second manifesto was an interesting turning point in the perception of the movement. In the first manifesto, even if it did not specify any traits exclusive to either manga or *bande dessinées*, the discussion does not give real attention to works beyond these main comics traditions; it, rather, constructs a proposal based on these traditions. The discussion in the second manifesto, however, is different. That later text returns to the movement a few years later, indicating a response to its initial reception and the public's interests, and highlights the promotion of authorial comic books on everyday life by artists from different national markets beyond Japan or France, like Brazilian, Italian, and Taiwanese ones. The opposition between publishers' commercial imperatives and Nouvelle Manga's global expansion become clearer. The Nouvelle Manga artists' "desire for change," with the release of graphic novels and the introduction of the movement to the general public, is made explicit. No longer just a group of artists who happen to have similar interests, it seemed to be an effort to recognize a contemporary desire for change *through* the coming together of artists with similar interests.

Nouvelle Vague and Nouvelle Manga

Trying to explicate the movement, Boilet (2001, 2) explains: "The term Nouvelle Manga was thus born in Japan to define my picture stories that are neither completely BD nor completely manga, and that remind of the tone of French cinema." His works drew critics' attention because of their resemblance to the French cinema movement; the narratives recognized as part of the Nouvelle Manga Movement take as their main theme a subject which was always celebrated by the French cinema—ordinary, day-to-day life. There are even references to Jean-Pierre Léaud, one of the most remarkable *dramatis personae* of the *Nouvelle Vague*, in both Frédéric Boilet's *Love Hotel* and *Yukiko's Spinach*.

For the French film industry, this focus on alternative subjects was needed to distance itself from the ubiquitous and mainstream Hollywood cinema, but this change took some time to reach comics (Trifonova 2012). The cinematographic movement had influence on more than just the Nouvelle Manga's conceptions, though. To understand why this is so, some background is necessary.

Michel Marie's *A Nouvelle Vague e Godard* [Godard's New Wave] (2011) characterizes the late 1950s, in France, as a place saturated by a perception of cinema as entertainment. *Nouvelle Vague* was a paradigmatic rupture in cinema's social status. Previously, there was little concern for or interest in experimentation, and big international films with movie stars, high budgets, and renowned directors were the order of the day. It was a busy but creatively stagnated field of cultural production—well-financed but artistically impoverished studios dominated (Marie 2011).

The cinematographic movement was launched by a new generation to establish a new voice. This period went on until 1963 with the sharp decline in audience numbers. Yet despite being short-lived, it was really meaningful. More than 160 new directors were able to showcase their ideas. The *Nouvelle Vague* aesthetic proposal covered everything from scripts to film endings and focused first and foremost on the creator's artistic and authorial freedom. This group of new authors crossed the boundaries between amateurism and professionalism, documentaries and fiction, with autobiographical inspiration and treatments on society's new morality.

According to Marie (2011), the technical subversions of the movement were: 1) the director was also the screenwriter; 2) he/she worked on improvised dialogues and acting; 3) natural settings were preferred over artificial studio settings; 4) the staff was small, with few workers engaged; 5) the sound was recorded on the sets, a direct sound; 6) there was no heavy lighting; and 7) characters were played by non-professional actors or professionals directed in a careless way. Truffaut considered the *Nouvelle Vague*'s film narration more personal, with storytelling being the directors' main interest (Gillain 1990). This subjectivity works especially on the dialogue and the characters' relationships, but the movement also demanded new screenwriters to develop the *scénario-dispositif* [scenario-device]. This kind of ideal script opened up space for random actions, unexpected events, and a sudden flow of ideas to happen during shooting (Marie 2011).

The movement's dogma was known as the *politique des auteurs* [policy of authors], whose foundations were proposed by François Truffaut's 1954 essay, "*Une Certaine Tendance du Cinéma Fraínçais* [A Certain Tendency of the French Cinema]." In a way, it became the movement's own manifesto against the old French cinema. The esteem of Truffaut's idea was increased by support from other critics like Godard and Éric Rohmer, and it became formalized as a policy of authors. This policy proposed that: 1) the director is the only author in the film; 2) some directors are authors, but others will never be, because of a distinction based on judgments of value; and 3) a failed film made by an author will be always better than another made by a mere director.

If the previous films were impersonal, subjected to the pressure of producers, foreign actors, distributors, and large numbers of staff, the new ones were simpler, with low costs and ordinary themes. The movement argued that when script and direction were controlled by the same person, the film would be able to reflect that individual's unique personality. No matter what the circumstances were, the result would reflect the author (Gillain 1990).

So, by focusing on treatments of what authors personally know and believe, the *Nouvelle Vague* movement was a place for experimentation and efforts to capture the contemporary moment. That, in essence, was the same creative spark to be perceived by Nouvelle Manga's readers. Nouvelle Manga was to represent authorial freedom, working on the boundaries of amateurism and professionalism, and taking inspiration from one's own autobiography and interpersonal relationships. Furthermore, Nouvelle Manga, like the French cinema movement, stays away from conventional narratives and linear structures, instead exploring a mix of perception, imagination, and thinking, with moments of self-reflection and intertextuality. These manga explore a wide range of genres but are more interested in ambience and mood than in dramatization.

The Nouvelle Manga manifestos also mirrored the emblematic opposition between authorial works and mainstream commercial works (although they avoid the explicit skepticism of the French directors). In both cases, though, the concept of authorship is central. In the comic book movement, it no longer works as a force against processes of globalization, as was the case for *Nouvelle Vague* cinema, but as a narrative writing project immersed in—and even hastening—these very processes (Trifanova 2012). The author is now the one interested in traversing cultural boundaries to create a universal vision of everyday life.

The narrative construction of Nouvelle Manga works to create aesthetic effects somehow similar to the effects from the *scénario-dispositif* of *Nouvelle Vague*, which was interested in the recording of unexpected events. If the *Nouvelle Vague* films dealt with improvisations, then the *Nouvelle Manga* comic books seem to do the same—or attempt to simulate it. The works create an impression of randomness that recalls the haphazardness and the improvisation of French films (far away from the common and formulaic closed scripts). Those fragmented actions, apparently random flow, detailed small instants, and suppression of others all work together as narrative devices to emulate this haphazardness. So, these glimpses of everyday life read like stumbles in the narrative. Suddenly, the reader finds an intimate moment, a deviation, or something seemingly uninteresting. There is a kind of deconstructive construction of characters. They are developed through this haphazardness, rather than through their personal goals or major decisions.

In sum, the focus of the Nouvelle Manga movement, taking its inspiration from the *Nouvelle Vague* movement in cinema, is on ordinary, everyday life, a space for trivialities and oscillations, even wasting time. This space is usually inhabited by ordinary men and women, anonymous characters based on a wandering, haphazard rhetoric, with their own diegetic existence related to gaps and inhabited places (Highmore 2002). Like a *flâneur*, they create a discontinuous, non-linear, and accidental discourse by their wandering. The characters express themselves in the diegetic world, while giving a form to the space.

The Avant-Garde Spirit

Thus, the *Nouvelle Manga* can be thought of as having reclaimed a *Nouvelle Vague* spirit that was no longer popular in France but was nonetheless still very much a part of French-language readers' cultural repertoire. The structures of the manifestos are, however, less about scaffolding a new aesthetic program than about criticism of existing ones. They are written with a clear, strongly-worded, even combative, discourse and are openly skeptical of the contemporary production of the works that are outside of the movement. Furthermore, their structure (like manifestos) and the offering of an aesthetic program (which they assume is more fair and sophisticated, compared to mainstream comics) recalls not just the *Nouvelle Vague*, but the concept of artistic modernity itself, and especially the avant-garde movements.

Gilberto Mendonça Telles (1983) explains such movements as part of the intellectual concerns that marked the first decades of the twentieth century. In that period, different groups and artists, in the European context especially, tried to interpret changes in their society. Their interpretations ranged from negativity about the past to the active pursuit of ushering in a new order for the future. Those movements were different from each other, but all of them worked in an attempt to understand social change and propose new aesthetics to accompany that change. The *–isms*, such as the refusal of all the current aesthetic values, e.g. Dadaism, or construction over destruction, e.g. Cubism, were interested in the renewal of artistic sensibility to create a more coherent discourse about society (Read 1969).

Graça Aranha (1983) defines the sensibility of modern art in the West as a project centered on subjectivism, in contrast to the two previous centuries based on Romanticism. The individual and his or her emotions and interpretations came to the foreground. The artist was also assigned a central role. Due of the influence of Romanticism, artists began to be seen as geniuses free to express themselves. Particularly in the case of avant-garde, they responsible for leading cultural change (Foucault 1992).

Although not subject to the paradigmatic shifts of the early twentieth century, Nouvelle Manga nonetheless had its own controversies to confront. In the context of these notions of artistic freedom, heterogeneity of cultural production becomes inevitable. Each artist can only follow his or her own impulses, feelings, and intuition (Telles 1983). Something similar seems to happen in Nouvelle Manga, and this can make it quite difficult to nail down precisely what the medium *is* and, crucially, is *not*. Yet by identifying the aesthetic failure of other comics, Nouvelle Manga somehow manages to appear as an organizing trend. It denies the current popular aesthetic values and proposes experiments, to effect an artistic rupture and reinterpret society. Similar to the virtuosity of the avant-garde movements, Nouvelle Manga sees itself as the place for authentic works responsible for the renewal of sensibility, in a pamphleteering—and almost dogmatic—frame. Put differently, the movement seems to justify its own emergence through the very existence of its creative output.

Conclusion: A Decade Later

The Nouvelle Manga Movement draws upon multiple European intellectual traditions. Although it happens decades later, it seems to retake part of the avant-garde spirit by attempting to change the horizon of expectations. It also links the *Nouvelle Vague* Movement in cinema to manga and *bande dessinées*. Finally, it also attempts to produce aesthetic distance, in Jauss's (1994) terms.

Sales figures for French, Japanese, and American manga consumption help to understand the readers' horizons of expectation. In Japan in 2012, 25.4 percent of the publishing market earnings came from manga. An equivalent to USD $2.88 billion was earned. The shounen manga series *One Piece* was the single bestselling title, with 23.46 million copies sold. It was followed by *Kuroko's Basketball* (8.07 million copies) and *Naruto* (6.49 million copies). In North America, an estimated USD $700–730 million were earned on graphic novel sales in the same year. DC and Marvel, the two main publishers, represented 74.34 percent of the market. The three bestselling titles were *The Walking Dead*, *Uncanny X-Men*, and *Avengers vs. X-Men*. The French comics market, meanwhile, earned €418.6 million, 10 percent of that total from just by three Japanese manga series, *Naruto*, *One Piece*, and *Fairy Tail*. These sales figures help to elucidate not just the economic impact of the comic book market in different national territories, but also the dominance of mainstream action, superhero, and science fiction series. In light of these figures, the importance of the Nouvelle Manga Movement as a marketing strategy for its authors is underscored.

Since the Nouvelle Manga Movement began just over a decade ago, there has not been another event like *L'Événement Nouvelle Manga*. Nevertheless, its ideas had interesting ramifications in the publishing space. Anthologies like *Japon: Le Japon Vu par 17 Auteurs* [Japan: Japan Viewed by 17 Authors] (2005), *Corée: La Corée Vue par 12 Auteurs* [Korea: Korea Viewed by 12 Authors] (2006), *Chine: Régards Croisés* [China: Viewpoints] (2009), and *Quelques Jours en France* [A Few Days in France] (2009) have been released in successive years, and in all of them, international groups of comics artists were invited to experience everyday life in different cities and then turn that into short stories for the anthologies. These collections of authorial points of view remember the iconic *Paris vu par...* (1965), a touchstone of the *Nouvelle Vague*. They explore various styles and themes, in subjective narratives. Although published without the explicit Nouvelle Manga label, they seem to develop the purpose of the movement: to create globalized works of manga about the everyday life. There even was the collective album

Manga Nouvelle Vague (2005), which introduces itself in the foreword as: "The avant-garde of Japanese comic books. Precursors of autofictions made into cartoons. Authorial manga ... In brief, the best of modernity."[11] In short, all of these titles are part of the corpus of works named "*la manga*" by the manifestos.

While the movement is no longer in the spotlight, it has not died out. The exchanges between artists from Japan, Korea, China, and France are very significant. It is hard to know the precise impact of the movement, but the collective interest in it is as clear as the light it shed on some artists, making itself a platform for them. Publishers have been releasing author-focused works on slice-of-life stories exploring narrative innovation, which means the development of authorial freedom and the fusion between professionalism and amateurism and fiction and documentary remain.

Even if it is not fully possible to determine the extent of the Nouvelle Manga Movement's efforts, more important than trying to verify the extent of its influence, however, is how it is essential to recognize it as an initiative to promote artists who did not previously have the spotlight. And just as significant is the participation in the exchange of different aesthetic narratives between the West and the East. The aesthetic innovations of Nouvelle Manga were not purely the genre's own invention. However, the movement became an important platform for such ideas, using its own force to promote them in events, exhibitions, and in the publication of new titles.

At times, the movement seems to be something intangible, difficult to grasp. Notwithstanding, it has helped to create transnational artistic exchange and develop an alternative aesthetic discourse. Despite of the criticality of Boilet's manifestos, it was an attempt to reorganize and reenergize global manga production. It highlighted different and distant authors, promoting and creating spaces for dialogue between them. It was the recognition of an international effort, uninterested in the differences of national comics traditions but rather the common points of each extraordinary yet ordinary person's life.

References

Ahmed, Maaheen. 2010. "Reading (and Looking at) *Mariko Parade*—A Methodological Suggestion for Understanding Contemporary Graphic Narratives." *Global Manga Studies* 2: 119–33.

Bastide, Julian. 2001. "Le Bilan de la Nouvelle Manga [The Review of Nouvelle Manga]." *Animeland*. http://www.boilet.net/fr/nouvellemanga_bilan_1.html.

---

11   Original text: "... l'avant-garde de la bande dessinée japonaise. Des précurseurs de l'autoficcion dessinée. Du manga d'auteur ... Bref, le must de la modernité."

Beaty, Bart. 2009. "Autobiography as Authenticity." *A Comics Studies Reader*, edited by Jeet Heer and Kent Worcester, 226–35. Jackson: *University Press of Mississippi*.

Berniere, Vincent, and Josefh Ghons. 2005. "La Nouvelle Vague Manga [The New Wave Manga]." In: *Manga Nouvelle Vague*. Bruxelas: Casterman.

Boilet, Frédéric. 2001. "Nouvelle Manga Manifesto." http://www.boilet.net/am/nouvellemanga_manifeste_1.html.

Boilet, Frédéric. 2006. "Nouvelle Manga in 2007." http://www.boilet.net/am/nouvellemanga_2006.html.

Certeau, Michel de. 1998. *A Invenção do Cotidiano* [The Invention of Everyday]. Petrópolis: Vozes.

Eco, Umberto. 1994. *Seis Passeios pelo Bosque da Ficção* [Six Walks in the Fictional Woods]. São Paulo: Companhia das Letras.

Foucault, Michel. 1992. *O Que é um Autor?* [What Is an Author?]. Rio de Janeiro: Passagens.

Gillain, Anne. 1990. *Cinema Segundo François Truffaut* [Second Cinema François Truffaut]. Rio de Janeiro: Nova Fronteira.

Gravett, Paul. 2004. *Manga: 60 Years of Japanese Comics*. New York: Collins Design.

Groensteen, Thierry. 1991. *L'univers des Manga: Une Introduction à la Bande Dessinée Japonaise* [The Universe of Manga: An Introduction to the Japanese Graphic Novel]. Bruxelas: Casterman.

Groensteen, Thierry. 1996. "Les Petites Cases du Moi: l'Autobiographie en Eande Dessinée [The Small Boxes of Me: Autobiography in Comics]." *9e Art* 1: 58–83.

Highmore, Ben. 2002. *Everyday Life and Cultural Theory*. London: Routledge.

Iser, Wolfgang. 1996. *O Ato da Leitura: Uma Teoria do Efeito Estético* [The Act of Reading: A Theory of Aesthetic Effect]. Volume 1. São Paulo: Ed. 34.

Iser, Wolfgang. 1999. *O Ato da Leitura: Uma Teoria do Efeito Estético* [The Act of Reading: A Theory of Aesthetic Effect]. Volume 2. São Paulo: Ed. 34.

Jauss, Hans Robert. 1994. *A História da Literatura como Provocação à Teoria Literária* [The History of Literature as a Provocation to Literary Theory]. São Paulo: Ática.

Luyten, Sonia B. 2000. *Mangá: O Poder dos Quadrinhos Japoneses* [Manga: The Power of Japanese Comics]. São Paulo: Hedra.

Luyten, Sonia B. 2005. *Cultura Pop Japonesa* [Japanese Pop Culture]. São Paulo: Hedra.

Marie, Michel. 2001. *La Nouvelle Vague e Godard* [Godard's New Wave]. Campinas: Editora Papirus.

McCloud, Scott. 1994. *Understanding Comics: The Invisible Art*. Reprint edition. New York: HarperCollins.

Miller, Ann. 2007. *Reading Bande Dessinée: Critical Approaches to French-language Comic Strip*. Bristol: Intellect.

Moliné, Alfons. 2004. *O Grande Livro dos Mangás* [The Big Book of Manga]. São Paulo: Editora JBC.

Okakura, Kazuko. 2008. *O Livro do Chá* [The Book of Tea]. São Paulo: Estação Liberdade.

Ponent Mon. "Quiénes Somos? [Who Are We?]." http://www.ponentmon.com/comics-castellano/quienes-somos.html.

Ranz, Olalla Hernández. 2007. "Nouvelle Manga, Mon Amour: Reflexiones sobre la Narración Gráfica de Historias Cotidianas [Nouvelle Manga, Mon Amour: Reflections on the Graphic Narration of Stories of Daily Life]." *Bellaterra Journal of Teaching & Learning Language & Literature* 2 (1): 35–50.

Read, Herbert. 1969. *A Filosofia da Arte Moderna* [The Philosophy of Modern Art]. Lisboa: Editora Ulisseia.

Schneider, Greice. 2010. "Comics and Everyday Life: from Ennui to Contemplation." *European Comic Art* 3 (1): 37–64.

Schneider, Greice. 2012a. "Lost Gazes, Detached Minds: Strategies of Disengagement in the Work of Adrian Tomine." *Scandinavian Journal of Comic Art* 1 (2): 58–81.

Schneider, Greice. 2012b. "What Happens When Nothing Happens: Boredom and Everyday Life in Contemporary Comics." PhD diss., Katholieke Universiteit Leuven.

Sheringham, Michael. 2006. *Everyday Life*. Oxford: Oxford University Press.

Trifonova, Temenuga. 2012. "Nouvelle Manga and Cinema." *Studies in Comics* 3 (1): 47–62.

Truffaut, François. 1954. "A Certain Tendency of the French Cinema." In *Movies and Methods*, edited by Bill Nichols, 224–35. Berkeley: University of California Press.

Vollmar, Rob. 2007. "Frederic Boilet and the Nouvelle Manga Revolution." *The Free Library*. http://www.thefreelibrary.com/Frederic+Boilet+and+the+Nouvelle+Manga+revolution.-a0160279687.

Chapter 7
An American Manga Artist's Journey Down a Road Less Drawn

David Blanchard

As we move further into a future age of globalization of cultures, my experiences have shown me that an idea may start in one place—but will most assuredly migrate to another place that may be around the corner or the other far flung side of the planet. Once the idea arrives where it is going, someone will seek to give their unique take on the concept, striving to make the idea their own. With ideas, things always seem different on the surface, maybe even completely alien and incomprehensible. Most stay away, but there are those who will scratch at it and dig deeper and find themselves amazed in wonder and crave more; we are all engaged in a revolving door of culture whether we know it or not. An idea sparked in your mind most likely came from one sparked in someone else's and so forth and so on. On the forefront of this is manga, a style of comic book illustration that started on the island nation of Japan. Manga has spread the world over and influenced countless creations outside its place of origin. Only recently, though, have the contributions of manga artists from outside Japan started to gain recognition. As an American manga artist, I know this all too well. Here I will relate my personal experiences as an artist, writer, and publisher of manga, and show why there is indeed manga from beyond Japan.

As an American artist I can only really speak with any assertiveness on the concept of American manga, although many other countries have taken the style under their respective cultural wings. I will start with a little background about myself and the time I first joined the global manga movement. I started practicing and learning all I could about the art of manga the year before I entered high school at the age of 14. This was in the mid to late 1990s, during a time that manga and anime were becoming more widely known in the United States. The proverbial genie of artistic influence had been let out of the bottle and would never be put back in again. During the year 2000, while still in high school, some like-minded friends and I formed a small studio of artists and writers and started releasing works. These early works reflected what we thought manga was and wanted manga to be all about. At this time, the number of artists being influenced by and wanting to create manga seemed to be on the rise, and a plethora of works, ranging from amateur web art to comics published by large companies, started to emerge. It seemed like a new artistic movement was set to take the stage. In the beginning, the climate was positive and accepting; people were just looking to have fun, and if they liked a certain manga styled work they didn't care where in the world it came from.

However, as things started to grow larger, paradigms began to slowly shift. As artists and companies started to make—or realize they could make—money and turn manga into a business that they could devote a large portion of their lives to, debates started as to whether or not artists from outside Japan could create manga at all. Some suggested that because Japan is considered so culturally different from other parts of the world, an artist not born and raised in Japan would simply not be able to wrap their heads around this foreign style of storytelling. While we refuted that claim, questions began to arise about what we ought to call manga done outside of Japan. At first, the idea was that it's all manga, so just call it manga. But artists and fans still wanted to make some sort of distinction. I was for this as an artist; I too wanted some distinction—if only to be able to say, "Look what we can do; we're just as good as anybody else!" The first idea was to take the name of the country you are from and just put manga after it. In my case, this would make the artwork I did American manga. Of course, the terminology would vary for each artist, depending on what part of the world they inhabited. The word manga used on its own would be reserved for denoting works of Japanese origin. However, many people found this to be politically incorrect, and a whole host of terms started to emerge, and the one most people settled on in the United States was OEL, or Original English Language, manga. The problem with this and other terms was that it started to give the feeling that manga from outside Japan was inferior or fake, made to cash in on the newfound popularity of the medium. This is when manga purists started to pop up, echoing precisely that sentiment—that manga can only come from Japan. That debate went back and forth, with people picking their sides, but for artists like myself it was for the most part just an annoyance. Who cared what this art was called or whether it was real or fake?

I do not know if the collapse of the global economy or the fallout of the anime industry in the United States aided in this or if it just happened to coincide, but within my personal circles things just seemed to hit the doldrums after 2008. It wasn't that works of manga stopped; it was just that no one seemed to be crusading and pushing for manga by artists outside Japan as much as they had used to, and the movement stagnated. Artists I knew either got out of the business entirely or no longer talked that openly about ideas that they had or projects that they were working on. This persisted up until quite recently. Now, however, thing are on the upswing again, and with the rebranding of what we do as "global manga," it looks like the world is finally taking notice of the artists that for the most part have been left in the shadows of this artistic style.

Hitokiri: A Lesson in How to Get (Self-)Published

Now, with that out of the way, I will discuss in more detail what is involved in the actual creation of this artwork. While I have worked and collaborated with other creators in the past, I am usually a solo act, doing everything from concept to publication myself. *Hitokiri* is the first manga I did which was intended to be a multivolume graphic novel series. Before this project I had primarily worked on literary mecha science fiction stories. With *Hitokiri* I expanded into the action-horror genre. *Hitokiri* is a werewolf story. The idea came about in 2002; at the time, I had been coming across a wealth of stories in all different forms of media whose main premise was about vampires hunting other vampires. I thought to myself, "I don't think that I have seen this concept done with werewolves hunting other werewolves." It struck me that werewolf depictions always seemed to be of drooling, snarling beasts playing second fiddle to the romantic vampires. So I set out to make a story that elevated the werewolf. The basic concept for the main character, whose name was that of the title of the series, was a werewolf hunter that was scratched but never fully turned into a wolf and instead became a human werewolf hybrid. In the story, werewolves only go to hell if they taint their souls by eating human flesh and blood. So to avoid this and get his revenge, he hunts and eats other undead creatures instead.

    Artistically, my first concept for the look of the character was for him to stay in a personified wolf form and not to transform back and forth with the phases of the moon. His garb was that of black plate armor, gauntlets, cape, and a four point hat adorned by a pentagram and feather plume. Hitokiri's primary armament was a sword with the appearance of a misshapen cross, since the character felt betrayed by God. Personality-wise the character was a quiet individual of few words. The setting of the story was that of a medieval fantasy world. In the redraft, the hat, cape, and sword were kept, but instead he now wore a trench coat with a black suit; only the chest plate from the armor remained from the original design. The gauntlets were changed from black to blue in any color art, and pentagrams were placed on each side of them. Hitokiri now also held a small silver cross in his mouth as one might a tooth pick. His arsenal was complemented with a machine pistol and a Gatling pistol, a fictional weapon I designed for the manga that is like a handheld version of a Gatling gun. Hitokiri's personality became the polar opposite of his initial conception; he became very sarcastic, vaguely evil, and borderline psychotic. The setting was updated to be more or less contemporary, with a slight Gothic feel to some elements.[1] These changes were made because I felt the original

---

    1   Editor's Note: It is intriguing to note that, despite Cavcic's argument in Chapter 8 that the Gothic mode has particular appeal to women, Blanchard is also here evincing an attraction to Gothic elements in manga.

Figure 7.1 *Hitokiri Volume 1*, by David Blanchard

clothing design and character personality was too plain. The new concepts then clashed with the setting, and besides, I also thought I would have more elements to draw on from a contemporary setting. The mix of old and new pieces to the character's outfit and weapons helped to create the impression that he was actually hundreds of years old. He was keeping things he liked and updating only when he felt like it. This is the feel I wanted for the main character.

With the main character and supporting cast concept art done I started in on actually illustrating the manga itself. This being the first book I had ever created in manga style, it shows my naiveté and lack of certain nuances of the art form. For example, anyone who is a manga fan for a decent length of time knows that grayscale in most manga is done using tone sheets; the artist takes premade sheets with tones of grayscale or grayscale patterns and presses them onto the paper where they want that tone or pattern to be. At this time, my access to manga was limited, and I was taking greater influence from Japanese animation, so I had never heard of tone sheets. Up until this point in my life, my artistic experience had been more in the field of fine arts, so I thought all the grayscale was being done by pencil shading. So there I sat, painstakingly recreating shades and patterns by hand with a pencil. It took up a grueling amount of time.

With the first draft of chapter one complete, I took it with me to a weekly meet up of friends and fellow creators to get their thoughts on it. They liked it but suggested that one problem was that they thought the sound effects were cheesy. This was not directed solely at my work but at the medium in general. This point was brought up by several artists, and a conversation ensued about how to deal with the fact that most people find sound effects in comic books to be cheesy. So I went back and did a second draft. This time, I eliminated the sound effects by taking them out completely. The feedback the second time around at the weekly gathering was that while the cheesiness was gone, something seemed to be lacking without the sound effects. My creative solution, when I finished a third draft, was to replace the sound effects, but this time to use only Japanese sound effects. The consensus, finally, was that this worked. Plus, given that the book was designed for the English-speaking world and most of people reading the book probably couldn't read Japanese, they got a sound effect on the pages which, through their own deductive reasoning, could come to their own conclusions about what was happening on the page, what the sound was supposed to be. This avoided the cheesiness by just having what was to most people an indecipherable glyph on the page. It also helped with the overall aesthetic feel of the piece. Since *Hitokiri* was supposed to be a manga, the Japanese sound effects, coupled with monochrome artwork and the decision to orient the paneling from right-to-left, made it what people were expecting it to be.

The entire first volume took almost a year to complete, starting in December 2002 and finishing in November 2003. Once I had a finished book, however, the question was what to do with it? I had access to some distribution and retail outlets, but they were all small scale, and I wanted to try and progress to a higher level. So at the suggestion of a friend, I submitted a copy to Image Comics. At the time, Image Comics was seen as a company that was into newer concepts and might be more open to a book done in manga style; this was a time when manga's popularity had gone skywards and seemed to have hit American comic book publishers out of the blue, outselling their books in droves. Most American comic book publishers were trying to swing the pendulum back, so to speak. They just rejected manga and wanted nothing to do with it because they saw it as a threat to the traditional American comic book art. I received no response, which is how things usually go; the volume of submissions a company receives is more than they can respond to individually. Only those artists and projects that they have an interest in pursuing are the ones that get an answer. I, like many others then and now, waited months and months for a response that never came. That's how I got my answer: "No, sorry. We have no interest at this time."

While waiting to hear from Image Comics, I started in on a second volume of the series and some other ideas I had been tossing around in my head. Knowing that it was unlikely going to get a positive response from Image, I started running what was completed of *Hitokiri* as a webcomics series in the spring of 2004. For the next two years, this is how *Hitokiri* got out into the world. It was difficult, with little return. In 2006, after being re-inspired by some new artist friends, I went back and redrew and cleaned up the original artwork in the first volume. This time around, I was able to get the book into print, but like before response was limited. Although *Hitokiri* started off decently, its sales soon slowed to a crawl. In 2008, I submitted *Hitokiri* to the 4th International Manga Awards for best manga from outside Japan. While *Hitokiri* did not win and I never found out what place the book actually came in the competition, just submitting it helped give the story a nice profile boost. Then, with the rise of e-readers and e-book downloads, *Hitokiri* finally started to find its audience. For a time, *Hitokiri* even became the number one selling horror manga on the Kobo Books e-book retail site from December 2012 until April 2013, after which it dropped to second place and has remained there since. My favorite thing about *Hitokiri* is that I have received several letters from aspiring artists telling me how much they love the artwork and asking for advice. I always try to respond with the most helpful information I can. This is the part I love about the work the most: that a piece that took so long to complete, that took so long to get out into the world, and so long to find its audience, has brought fun and inspiration to manga fans, future manga artists, and just artists in general. That is a great legacy for any artist and/or work of art.

Swinger Ace/Sam Swinger: A Lesson in Unfinished Projects

For the next project I was involved in, a friend and sometimes co-collaborator Taylor Field approached me sometime in late 2002 to early 2003 to help him flesh out the story for a character he had come up with called *Swinger Ace*. The character was a zoot suit-wearing superhero that was in part based on an idealized version of Taylor's alternate swinger personality he liked to use when out for the evening. The basic concept for the story and character was that of a comedy about an uncool, nerdy office worker who would be transformed into a suave ladies' man superhero. Most of the creation of this character and his world actually took place in my kitchen between the hours of 10:30 pm and 1 am. At the time, I was working late and wouldn't get off until 10 pm. So Taylor would meet me after work, and we would head back to my place, which was just up the road. Then, over a pot of late night tea, we would get to work. One of us would set the concept for the scene, and because we could both be very sarcastic and played well off of each other, we would start where one of us would say some sort of one liner, and the other would respond with another one liner. We would just go back and forth like that, and eventually, with a little fine tuning, we would have an entire scene. In this way, we came up with the stories for the character.

During one particular late night session, Taylor said that he wanted to do a scene where the main character was meeting an informant, but he wanted him to meet the informant in a church and while waiting falls asleep and has a dream about Jesus confronting Judas. He wanted the scene to be like one out of *The Sopranos*. Taylor started the scene off with Jesus saying, "I don't know which one of you betrayed me but come clean and I'll forgive you." I made the suggestion that Judas should be wearing a wire. The scene then continued with Jesus asking Judas if he was the one and Judas denying it, only to have Jesus ripping Judas' shirt open, thereby revealing the wire. Taylor then started into Jesus' line of, "How could you? I treated you like a brother," and then Judas' response of, "Jesus, I'm sorry; please forgive me. Oh, God." To which I instantly add without really even thinking, "Don't bring my father into this." Taylor immediately snapped back, "He can't save you now." The scene then moved to the main character waking up and telling a priest about his dream and the priest having to explain that that wasn't the way that happened. This is perhaps the best example of how we worked on coming up with ideas and scenes for this story.

Now, while we had some ideas for events in the story, we still did not have an opening or, important in this case because Swinger Ace was to be a superhero, an origin story. As we talked more and added to the project, the name of the character changed from Swinger Ace to Sam Swinger and the title became *It's the Adventures of Sam Swinger*. We decided on starting off with the character in an office and him being the token guy everyone else makes fun of and has no luck with the girls. After another humiliating day at the office, Sam leaves to drown his sorrows in booze. The idea of what follows explains how he got his powers. The concept was to be that he would be given a set of wishes to get his powers and equipment. We wanted the wish granter to be summoned from an empty liquor bottle of some kind, but we didn't want to use a genie. Finally it was decided that we wanted a wish granter that was from a previous era and could be seen as a person who embodied the feel of the sense of coolness we were going for, and we decided to have the spirit of Dean Martin be the wish granter. The spirit of Dean Martin gives Sam superpowers, thereby turning him into Sam Swinger with a supped up car, a sidekick, and a magic pocket watch. With these, Sam Swinger hits the streets.

Unfortunately, this ended up just being one of those projects that never saw fruition for one reason or another. A rough draft of about half of the first volume was completed, and that is all that came to be. Other projects and distractions kept Taylor and me busy, and it just kept being put on the back burner with the intent that we would get back to it. But in the end, we never did. I hate when this happens. For me, the only way a character or a story dies is if the work is never completed. Here was a wacky, off-the-wall story that I think people would have really liked and enjoyed, but now all that was ever completed sits in a file on my computer's desktop and stares back at me from time to time whenever there are thoughts or talk about at least trying to complete the first volume of *Sam Swinger*. This is a perfect example of what may befall a project, and it does happen occasionally. Most of the time there's no way to see it coming. I bring this up because there are probably untold scores of manga stories that for one reason or another have never been completed. As a writer, it is your job to do your best to guide these tales to their completion. Of course, even writing this chapter makes me think once again about trying to complete *Sam Swinger*. Who knows? Maybe this time Sam Swinger will finally get to hit the streets in earnest.

Sharknado: A Lesson in Licensing and Intellectual Property Rights

As a manga artist, I have found it increasingly difficult to get published, so I decided to venture into self-publishing. I started selling and distributing books digitally and within a short amount of time was actually making a steady income. I formed my own company, Perfect Commando Productions, around this model of publishing, even picking up other creators' works to publish. This leads me to a project that I am helming solely as a publisher at the moment. As I started to plan this chapter, this project was still in the early stages. Most smaller comic book publishers in the United States make the bulk of their income by obtaining the rights to adapt other pre-existing entertainment media properties into comic books. This new project would be Perfect Commando Productions' first attempt to gain the rights to a property that was not created from scratch in-house.

The property in question is a film by the name *Sharknado*. The film premiered on the Syfy Channel in the summer of 2013. The plot of the film is about a waterspout that lifts sharks out of the ocean and deposits them in Los Angeles. The main characters gather up friends and family and try to escape from the city as the sharks rain down upon them.

This film unexpectedly and quickly gained a cult and social media following. After watching it, the gears in my head started turning, and I thought it would be perfect for a manga adaption. I wanted to write stories about other characters within that universe. However, at this time, I had a lot of work already going on, and given the rapid popularity of the film, I figured someone had to already beaten me to it. A few months later, my work schedule cleared up, and I revisited *Sharknado*, trying to find out if there had been any comics or graphic novel adaptations, or if it had been announced that a studio was working on any with a pending release in the near future. I found no information about anyone having obtained the rights to it or having been commissioned to adapt the film. So I got in contact with the studio that made the film, The Asylum. They were very interested in my proposal to turn the film into a graphic novel and wanted to move on it.

However, the film had been commissioned by the Syfy Channel, and the Syfy Channel and its parent company NBC Universal actually held the rights to the film. The Asylum forwarded my request, and I was introduced to Jeffrey Li, the Vice President of the Syfy Channel. Mr. Li and I then spent the next four days emailing one another, but our schedules were at odds, especially since this was the week of Thanksgiving. We were unable to set up a phone meeting, and Mr. Li was getting ready to go out on vacation starting the day before Thanksgiving. He handed me off to the company Earthbound, which handles licensing of the Syfy Channel's properties. I was able to arrange a phone meeting, which was just a brief introductory phone call; Milin Shah was the individual in charge. He explained how they had huge success with *Sharknado*, and people were getting permission to do t-shirts, lunchboxes, key chains, and all other sorts of materials to tie in with the film. But no one had come to them wanting to do a graphic novel. I had apparently caught them out of left field. Whereas everyone else was just looking to slap the brand name and image on an item, I was looking to create something that would help build their franchise. Mr. Shah and Mr. Li wanted to move on this idea quickly because they were going to be doing a huge marketing campaign for the release of the sequel coming out in the summer of 2014 and they wanted to capitalize on its fans' anticipation as much as possible.

Mr. Shah then sent me a DMT, Deal Memo Template, and said to fill it out and to send it back with a company profile for my business. A company profile is a document showing what your company does, what companies it has worked with, where and how you sell your products, and where you advertise. When I opened the DMT and went through it there was a lot of information that they were asking for but that I didn't have. The document asked about who I was going to have manufacture the books and a Free on Board royalty rate, a transport fee. None of this I felt applied to my company as it is a digital publishing company. So I spoke with Mr. Shah again, explaining my position and the situation and asking him for clarification. He explained that the DMT was a general catch-all document because an official final draft contract from NBC Universal can take up to six to eight weeks to draw up and complete. The DMT was a legally binding document showing an agreement had been reached so that parties could start development of products and properties immediately, without further six-to-eight-week delay. Moreover, he explained that the only areas on the document that they were actually concerned with was the sections dealing with how long I wanted a license for, what the royalties on the sale of each book would be, how much I would guarantee in sales, and how much I was willing to advance on the guarantee. I filled out the DMT and sent it along with the other necessary paperwork back to Earthbound, who would then forward it to the Syfy Channel. Once and if the Syfy Channel accepts my offer and signs off on it, I will then begin the process of creating graphic novels based on the film.

That is where I was left at for weeks because of the Christmas and New Year's holidays, waiting to hear back, waiting to hear if the answer is yes, or no, and if no then will further negotiations take place? Or is the deal dead like the many hapless victims in the film? Finally, I emailed them to see what was happening, and I was told that they were still discussing the offer and would get back to me at the end of the week. When the answer came back, it was no. Earthbound told me that Syfy would not except any offer if the advance was not at least a certain amount. This amount was far more than I could put up. I figured the deal was dead. But then a family member said that they thought that this was a great opportunity and would loan me some money and that I should try to get Syfy back to the negotiating table. So I countered Syfy with an offer of a few thousand less than what they wanted. They still were not satisfied, but Mr. Shah told me he was working on them. A couple weeks passed, and I would have to email them to see what was happening. They would ask me to send a list of titles that I've published. A few more weeks passed, and I would email them again. They would ask me for something else related to properties I have worked on. Then everything would go silent for a few weeks until I would try emailing them again.

As time went on, I was starting to get the distinct feeling that they were hoping that I would just go away and that I was not a large enough company for them to work with. So finally, I decided to try and bring the deal to a close whether or not it was a success and move on. I upped my offer by a few thousand dollars. The cycle of waiting a couple of weeks resumed once again, but at the same time the family member that offered to loan me money, when I brought up the latest news regarding the deal, had seemingly forgotten about having ever made me this offer. That left me negotiating a deal with funds I did not have and no ideas about where to come up with it. Syfy then asked me to give them three personal success stories about my company; I did that, telling them about *Hitokiri*, *Éirinn Go Brách*, and *Geisha*, titles I worked on either as a publisher or a publisher/artist. Syfy then came back with a counteroffer: I would put up the total amount for what I had proposed as a guarantee in sales, and they would forgo any future royalties.

This was the best offer I thought that I was going to be able get from them, but I still had to figure out how to come up with the funding. I decided to try and secure investors for the project. I was able to find three initially, one of them a seasoned investor who was a huge fan of the movie. However, as things were coming to a close, he and another investor decided to opt out at the last minute. Instead, I had to take out a small business loan. The loan, plus the funding from my remaining investor and my own out of pocket contribution, was enough to cover the new agreed upon advance. I told Syfy that I was good to go and accepted the deal. They sent over a new revised Deal Memo Template for me to sign.

As things stand right now, I tentatively have the license and am waiting for the final contract to arrive. I have already started concept art for the book that Syfy will need to approve, and if all goes well, *Sharknado* with be the first licensed property obtained by Perfect Commando Productions, the first Syfy original movie adapted to manga that I know of, and one of only a handful of American properties adapted into an OEL manga. The anticipated release date is currently scheduled for the summer of 2014.[2]

Conclusion: Learning on the Road Less Drawn?

Manga in Japan has a history spanning approximately 60 years, but in the rest of the world it is young, new, and, in some cases, being born again. Whether or not manga created outside Japan is seen as an imitation, a fusion, or purely "manga" is a philosophical argument with champions and detractors on both

---

2 Editor's Note: *Sharknado 2: The Second One* premiered on July 30, 2014 to the highest ratings ever achieved by a SyFy Channel original movie (Pennington 2014). On the basis of this continued success, a third *Sharknado* movie is expected to debut in the summer of 2015 (Rife 2014). By the close of 2014, however, David Blanchard's proposed *Sharknado* manga had not been published.

sides. Each artist, writer, and publisher will have their own interpretation. The manga boom of the early 2000s saw the rise of manga by American artists, but it also saw this talent squandered by companies out to make some quick cash. These companies took advantage of a lot of young artists and stymied their careers. The manga boom has ended, but at the same time there seems to be a renewed interest in the artists who choose to take pencil to paper and sketch out their manga dreams. I see this in talk online from people looking and asking for manga done in English or just for manga from anywhere other than Japan just because they want to see what it is like and are fascinated by it. I like to think that this is the start of these works gaining greater acceptance. However, the majority of this interest seems to originate from places other than the United States. My books sell the greatest number of copies in Canada, followed by various European countries. My home country of the United States, despite its larger total population, fluctuates between second and third place and at times even dipping lower. Sales in Australia, Singapore, and Malaysia occasionally overtake sales in the United States. It seems that in the United States the fan community is not as accepting as the rest of the word is yet. I have sold books in countries I had never even heard of and had to pull out a map and look up, such as Mauritius, and places like the Isle of Man that I didn't even know were considered to be independent states. This, I feel, just helps to illustrate how manga—regardless of the country in which it was created—has permeated the world's cultures.

But I think the biggest interest in manga from outside Japan is now coming from the academic community. Academics, particularly in the field of cultural studies, seem to have taken notice that there is a group of artistic people out there in the world that are creating manga, but are not Japanese, nor do they reside in Japan. They seem to be curious about what makes these artists tick, why are they doing this style of art that does not originate from their home country, and what effect will it have on their economies and local cultures. I don't know what will come of these studies or what they are striving to achieve, necessarily. I just hope that the interest generated by them will filter down to the fans and that fans will be more inclined to look into manga created outside Japan and help build an international manga industry. As the business of manga goes, these works tend not to sell as well as their Japanese counterparts, but that alone has never stopped an artist from creating.

The business side is an important side, and all manga artists will have to learn how to carve out their own place in it. I am far from the best-known or bestselling artist, but after almost a decade and a half of hard work, passion, and drive I have carved out a niche for myself and continue to dig deeper. I started out as an amateur with the dream of creating manga, and through trial and error and outright failure, learning the ins and outs of the art style and art business, I have created my own studio. The books I have published sell internationally. My studio and I have continued to grow over the years to the point that I am now able to offer opportunities to other artists seeking a chance to have their work out into the world. I was frustrated many, many times, but I have learned from setbacks and was lucky enough to avoid getting ensnared in any major pitfalls. The way I was able to enter the manga world and business was definitely a road less traveled. Or perhaps it would be more appropriate to say "a road less drawn." Nevertheless, I feel that my art and I are better for it. I have had a wealth of experiences that have taught me a lot. Some of them have shown me that how you think something should be done at the outset is not always the only way for something to be done.

When talking about manga made outside Japan I often like to use the example of Van Gogh being inspired by Japanese prints. I see this as a precursor to artists of the world being inspired by manga; the revolving door of culture pivots on its axis once again. The one thing I think a lot of people forget about is that this is supposed to be *fun*. Arguing over whether it's real or fake, or if the term manga denotes place of origin, lessens the enjoyment of the artwork and stories. No one gets inspired by art unless they're having fun, and as long as people continue to have fun I guarantee that there is and will be manga from beyond Japan.

References

Pennington, Gail. 2014. "'Sharknado 2' Smashes Ratings Records." *St. Louis Post-Dispatch*, July 31. http://www.stltoday.com/entertainment/television/gail-pennington/sharknado-smashes-ratings-records/article_11b24922-6a29-5ac2-859c-0b5e32237134.html.

Rife, Katie. 2014. "Sharknado 3 to Rain Sharks on Washington, D.C." *A.V. Club*, September 12. http://www.avclub.com/article/sharknado-3-rain-sharks-washington-dc-209192.

Chapter 8
Sporting the Gothic Look: Refashioning the Gothic Mode in German Manga Trends

Antonija Cavcic

The young women in Japan known as the *24 Nen Gumi* [Year 24 Group] behind the phenomenon of homoerotic manga started out much like contemporary manga artists in Germany: they were aspiring artists in a male-dominated industry but with enough creativity and audacity in terms of their approach to convention and content to cultivate and maintain an intercontinental force of female manga producers and consumers. While Germany was not the first country to take heed to and adopt manga as a potential means of self-expression, self-employment, or to an extent, self-empowerment, I would argue that one major thematic and stylistic aspect of manga narratives, mutually appreciated and appropriated by the two nations, is the Gothic mode. What was established with *Toma no Shinzou* [The Heart of Thomas] (1974–74) by Moto Hagio and *Kaze to Ki no Uta* [The Poem of Wind and Trees] (1976–84) by Keiko Takemiya, both shounen ai manga series depicting psychological and sexual accounts of repressed and angst-ridden young men in exotic, Gothic backdrops, has since become a national—and now global—cultural phenomenon.

Takemiya and Hagio's seminal works, which are set in France and Germany respectively and are therefore temporally and geographically exotic locations from a Japanese perspective, also feature ostracized protagonists, who, isolated in their social settings, engage in or are subject to the exploration of sexual taboos involving physical, sexual, and psychological abuse. This early appropriation and appreciation of the Gothic mode and motifs in manga have persevered to this day in Japanese popular culture, art, design, and fashion. Though most blatantly visible perhaps in the popularity of Gothic Lolita style among teens and adults alike, top-selling and globally recognized contemporary Japanese manga titles such as *Vampire Knight* (2006–) by Matsuri Hino or *Black Butler* (2006–) by Yana Toboso demonstrate that the Gothic mode and its relative exotic and/or erotic allure, is neither a passing trend nor just a niche market inherited from largely Victorian and German literary origins.

Whereas recent cultural research and publications regarding manga's growing presence in German popular culture has generally been concerned with the rise of manga in Germany and cross-cultural stylistic trends, such as Paul M. Malone's "Transcultural Hybridization in Home-Grown German Manga" (2011) and "From BRAVO to Animexx.de to Export: Capitalizing on German Boys' Love Fandom, Culturally, Socially and Economically" (2010), or comparative fan consumption trends among fans in *Nutzen und Gratifikation bei Boys' Love Manga: Fujoshi oder Verdorbene Mädchen in Japan und Deutschland* [Benefits and Gratuity at Boys' Love Manga: Fujoshi or Spoiled Girls in Japan and Germany] (Kamm 2010), this chapter explores the relatively young German manga scene's reception of Japanese Gothic-inspired manga, and the revival and reconstruction of the Gothic mode in German amateur, or "doujin," and original titles. By examining thematic and stylistic trends from the aforementioned mainstream manga titles and locally produced German doujin manga, as well as taking into account responses from online questionnaires and email correspondence with selected doujin illustrators, this chapter demonstrates that the supposed problematic nature of localized content and issues concerning authenticity of traditional Japanese manga aesthetics can arguably be bypassed through the appropriation of the Gothic mode and its relative practice of Othering—whereby ghouls, vampires, demons, and even marginalized individuals cross all borders.

German. Gothic. Manga.

Prior to considering the current context and content of German manga incorporating elements of the Gothic mode, an overview of the relevant concepts will clarify any ambiguous terms necessary for further discussion. Fundamental to this is to establish consistent definitions of what will be referred to as "Gothic," the "Gothic mode," manga (as well as German manga), and the definitive characteristics which distinguish professional illustrators from amateurs.

Starting sequentially with the discursively contentious terms "Gothic" and "Gothic mode," the introduction to *The Cambridge Companion to Gothic Fiction* (Hogle 2002) alone encapsulates the extent of the term's discursive ambiguity. As Jerrold E. Hogle argues, "Gothic fiction is hardly Gothic at all," adding that Gothic literature has a history of "counterfeit," of borrowing from other genres, and "scattering" its own "ingredients into various modes" (2002, 1). Maintaining that Gothic fiction is unstable, Hogle rather suggests that "Gothic" is best considered a "symbolic realm" rather than a distinct category or entity. Alluding somewhat to Hogle's symbolic realm in his criticism on the status quo of Gothic as a genre, Fred Botting's Gothic is as a phantom-like entity, spreading itself, mutating, and diffusing across boundaries of history, genres, and media (2001, 1). Given this instability and mutability of Gothic as distinct genre of fiction, then, for simplicity's sake, referring to a text being "Gothic" as a mode is arguably more flexible than the alternatives. However, what then is a "Gothic mode"? Although not meticulously outlined, Hogle suggests that a text characteristic of the Gothic mode involves

> the story taking place (at least some of the time) in antiquated or seemingly antiquated space; this space holds some manner of secret important to plot and character development ... haunted by the blurring boundaries between the natural and the supernatural; the genre emphasizes the repressed or unconscious; the genre has social and political functions. (Hogle 2002, 1–2)

While Hogle's definition does not entail certain elements of Gothic aesthetics, motifs, or tropes, it will suffice for the purpose of a consistent argument on manga which may be considered characteristic of the Gothic mode.

But what then is a globally recognized definition of manga, let alone manga characteristic of the Gothic mode? Although the term "manga" was used prior to woodblock artist Katsushika Hokusai's alleged coining of the term in the Edo period, in his overview of manga, Jean-Marie Bouissou argues that manga really came into fruition as a medium and cultural phenomenon when "prewar Japan appropriated the imported art of comics and melded it with its own culture's diversified tradition of graphic narration ... as both a media for political and social debate and a mass market for teenage entertainment" (2010, 24). What Bouissou's argument highlights is that it is not the origins of manga that are significant. Rather, it is the fact that these comics were "appropriated" and popularized, mass-produced, and globalized, that has made manga a household name. A name in itself signifies that manga differs from that which it appropriated—manga is not comics.

A simple yet semantically vague definition might consider manga as comics with a distinct Japanese visual aesthetic or cultural essence, including the global variations and appropriations of manga both as a term and medium. However, some scholars have suggested that a comic may qualify as manga if the left-to-right reading format is reversed and monochrome graphics are employed (Schodt 1996; Thompson and Okura, 2007). While this classification of texts is largely dependent on format rather than style or content, it is arguably less problematic. Yet it is nevertheless subject to criticism. For example, how does one classify Japanese manga printed in full color? And what of monochrome comics formatted for left-to-right reading? For this precise reason and for the sake of coherency in this discussion, I posit that a visual narrative enclosed in panels—in either digital or print format, and irrespective of style and content—meeting two of the three following criteria can be classified as manga:

1. The text is clearly labeled and/or marketed as manga or doujin manga.
2. The reading method is right to left.
3. The text is predominantly printed in monochrome. Full color texts are only acceptable in digital form.

Granted, this system of classification is also subject to criticism, especially as formats of both digital and printed texts constantly evolve, but for the purpose of further discussion, it will suffice.

Provided a text meets at least two of the three above criteria and is accordingly classified as manga, what then is *German* manga? In contrast to Malone's argument in "Transcultural Hybridization in Home-Grown German Manga" (2011), I would suggest that German manga do not necessarily or entirely combine "imported manga aesthetics and the German language" (Malone 2011, 51), but they do combine certain formal properties of Japanese manga with the German language, as well as the illustrators' particular "ethnic backgrounds and individual influences and interests" (51). In this light, texts which are classified as manga, and produced or released in German language and/or in Germany will be referred to as either German manga or German doujin manga.

Having said that, this also highlights the need to distinguish doujin manga from professional manga. In "Dōjinshi Research as a Site of Opportunity for Manga Studies" (Noppe 2010), Nele Noppe considers doujin produced creations as fanworks, which explicitly appropriate characters and/or settings from copyrighted material, and include manga (*doujinshi*), fanfic (*shousetsu*), fan art (*ichimai irasuto*), individual pictorial depictions, musical pieces (*doujin ongaku*), and many other media (2010, 123). Although relatively comprehensive, Noppe's definition fails to acknowledge those doujin creators who produce original works. In addition, as opposed to referring to manga alone, the term doujinshi may also refer to magazines produced collaboratively by amateur writers and/or illustrators. For this reason, and if doujin which are not necessarily created by fans or are products of original work, slight alterations to Noppe's definition are required. As an alternative to Noppe's definition, works produced by doujin creators will be referred to using doujin as an adjective in non-hyphenated compound words (such as doujin manga or doujin games). Professional manga, on the other hand, refer mostly to original works of manga published by or licensed to established publishing companies.

German Manga, Gothic Mode, Made by Pros

Even in the face of restrictions throughout history, whether legal, technological, due to illiteracy, or simply the stigma attached to women's cultural participation in the public sphere, women have found and developed means to express themselves and engage in the production and consumption of popular culture. From the proliferation of progressive female novelists and periodical journalists of the Victorian era to the explosion of Japanese doujin artists producing provocative homoerotic manga in post-World War II Japan, the pen has been seemingly mightier than Excalibur or the Eastern equivalent, the *katana*. So what of German women and the production of manga, let alone Germany's production of manga?

According to Malone, in spite of its history of visual storytelling and lively traditions of both children's literature (the Brothers Grimm, for example) and caricature for adults, German-speaking countries did not develop a comics industry, let alone a manga scene, until after World War II (2011, 49). Although Keiji Nakazawa's *Barfuß durch Hiroshima* [Barefoot through Hiroshima], better known in English as *Barefoot Gen*, was the first translated manga to appear in Germany in 1982 (Pannor 2012), it was not until the late 1990s, as Malone notes, that Japanese anime and manga captivated young German audiences and publishers alike. This, he suggests, was realized with the success of German television network RTL2's broadcasting of the famed and influential anime series *Sailor Moon* and *Dragon Ball* (2010, 23). Thus, with the success of anime came the subsequent interest in manga, and in turn, the gradual development of Germany's own network of original manga artists.

It was not an easy road to success for German manga artists. Christina Plaka, for example, who attempted to break into the professional market at Carlsen Comics—and later went on to publish her successful *Yonen Buzz* series at Tokyopop—was rejected by publishing giant Carlsen not because she was a woman or too young, but because "neither publishers nor readers were interested in comics by German artists" (Böckem 2006, 10). For others their initial breakthrough was much like it would have been in Japan, through manga competitions such as Connichi or Leipzig Book Fair's "Manga Talent" competition, which initially fostered young female manga artists such as Anike Hage and Christina Plaka. Some of these manga artists, including the likes of Hage, Olga Rogalski, and Detta Zimmermann, also had their art or manga published in manga anthologies, such as Tokyopop's *Manga Fieber* [Manga Fever], before moving on to their current publishers as professional manga artists.

With the success of these women and the rising currency of manga and Japanese culture in Germany, comics theorist Heike Jüngst has gone so far to suggest that becoming a manga artist "has become a job today's German children dream of," and further maintains that "Japan had partly replaced the USA as a source for popular culture" (2006, 249). If it is acknowledged that Jüngst's statement holds some degree of validity, how then to account for the success and proliferation of female manga artists in Germany? Needless to say, social, industrial, economic, cultural, and to some extent, historical factors have contributed to the phenomenon, but what cultural experience or background do Japanese and German female manga artists have in common which might begin to explain this simultaneous proliferation of female manga artists?

While as a critical approach, New Historicism tends to overlook creativity, among other influential factors involved in the creation of a text, I nonetheless argue that, as former WWII allies and highly industrialized societies, Japan and Germany both share a deeply repressed trauma which continues to reverberate through each generation and arguably manifests itself in culture. More relevant to this argument, however, is the silenced and marginalized role of Japanese and German women during WWII, whose roles in so-called "reproductive warfare" involved surrendering their autonomy, their dreams, their families, and their bodies for the greater good of nations swayed by highly influential male leaders of unquestioned symbolic status. What was a self-sacrificing "Good Wife, Wise Mother" ideal in Japan, was Hitler's 1933 "Law for the Encouragement of Marriage" or "Mutter und Kind" [Mother and Child] slogan. It was childbearing as patriotic duty. In any case, women's gender roles left very little room for individual pursuits or work, let alone self-expression. As historian Catherine Yoonah Bae (2008, 343) notes,

> Japanese society underwent significant social changes from the Pacific War to the end of the American Occupation. Although adult women had gained the right to full access to the political system through constitutional reform, the legacy of the "good wife, wise mother" ideal did not disappear overnight.

Under these circumstances, I argue that manga, as a silent medium which allows for both anonymity and self-publishing, served as a platform for social commentary and self-expression for Japanese women, and later, German women. Of all genres of manga to allow for such, I argue that manga incorporating the Gothic mode—in their exploration of the psychological, the repressed, their frequent Othering, and settings enshrouded in secrecy—serve as the ideal platform for deconstructing those deeply embedded myths attached to nationalism, gender, sexuality and subjectivity. As highlighted in the introduction, Japan's *24 Nen Gumi* of female manga artists depicted the psychological and sexual accounts of repressed and angst-ridden young men in exotic and often Gothic backdrops. That is, with both *Toma no Shinzou* and *Kaze to Ki no Uta* set in locations "exotic" to Japan (i.e boarding schools in Germany and France, respectively), as well as in the relatively distant past (i.e. the twentieth and nineteenth centuries respectively), they reinforce Hogle's characteristics of the Gothic mode. In terms of the "blurring boundaries between the natural and the supernatural," the recurring spectral visions of Thomas after his suicide in *Toma no Shinzou* and unexplained incidents of fainting in both texts by protagonists Juli (in *Toma no Shinzou*) and Gilbert (in *Kaze to Ki no Uta*) indicate elements of the uncanny (spectral visions) and the supernatural (the unexplained fainting). Furthermore, both manga tap into the repressed or unconscious in that they deal with issues of sexual abuse, abandonment, death, and non-normative sexuality among several of the boys. These issues, which trigger a fear of abandonment or intimacy, are sometimes unresolved or avoided through death but mostly resolved in confessions or the unveiling of deeply repressed secrets.

The dominant visual aesthetics in the texts are also, to a lesser degree, suggestive of the Gothic mode and arguably reflect aesthetics in contemporary pop-goth culture. Although adopting Macoto Takahashi's style of starry-eyed and unconventional panel layout in shoujo manga illustration, common motifs in Takemiya and Hagio's works, such as the pallid or frail characters contrasted with dark clothing or backgrounds; the use of bold lining and dark shading; the emphasis placed on uniforms or costumes; and the high frequency of page bleeding, have arguably set the standard for successive manga, which may not incorporate the Gothic mode per se, but at least intend to emulate a Western-influenced pop-goth aesthetic. Contemporary examples include *Black Butler*, *Blue Exorcist*, *Le Portrait de Petit Cossette*, and *Vampire Knight* from Japanese manga and *Gothic Sports*, *Losing Neverland*, and *Lilientod* from German manga. I will refer to this particular style of manga illustration as the "Gothic look," since I would argue that the word "look" may connote transience better than "style."

Granted, whether these texts truly bear characteristics of the Gothic mode, either thematically or in terms of narrative elements, is debatable, but I maintain that the only text which fails to appropriate some Gothic tropes yet still somewhat sports the Gothic look per se, is *Gothic Sports*. To elaborate, *Black Butler* concerns a traumatized orphan and earl in Victorian England, who sells his soul to a demonic butler to avenge his parents' death. Similarly, *Blue Exorcist* (Kato 2009), incidentally inspired by Germany's Brothers Grimm) follows the trials and tribulations of a demonic bastard child as he learns the craft of exorcism to defeat Satan. As another deeply traumatized child, Cossette in *Le Portrait de Petit Cossette*, (Katsura 2004) is the spirit of a murdered girl, trapped in an antique Venetian glass. Playing on the tropes of incest and a protagonist with a traumatic and mysterious past is *Vampire Knight* (Hino 2005). In trying to unravel the mystery of her past, the protagonist Yuki only recalls being attacked by a vampire and then rescued by another. As the series progresses, she discovers her royal lineage and that her secret crush is indeed a member of the family. Also on the subject of forbidden love, or complex romantic relations, is *Lilientod* (Delseit and Peters 2011). In the tradition of both the Gothic mode and boys' love manga, this three-part series concerns a nobleman who becomes romantically involved with a murderer from within his own castle. The last of the three German examples is *Losing Neverland* (Sindram 2008). Set in Victorian

England, the acclaimed series tells the bitter story of young Laurie, who is forced by his father into a life on the streets and earning his keep as a rentboy.

While these texts convey diverse characteristics of the Gothic mode, which of the aforementioned stylistic motifs are common in both German and Japanese manga? Firstly, there is the prevalence of pallid or frail protagonists such as *Black Butler*'s Ciel, *Blue Exorcist*'s Rin, Cossette, Yuki and her vampiric classmates, Laurie, and to some degree, the majority of female players on the soccer team in *Gothic Sports*. In addition, dark clothing, suits and uniforms are also heavily employed, e.g. school or sports uniforms and work attire, as well as emphasis on black and white color contrast and/or color highlighting, with red, pink, and blue dominating in these particular examples. Morbid, tortured, sinister, or playful, the transnational appropriation of the Gothic look not only reflects the semantic contrasts between darkness and light but also that which is repressed—and that which is revealed or released.

In any case, whether exemplary of the Gothic mode in content or merely adopting a superficially Gothic look, both Japanese and German manga demonstrate and reinforce the notion that dark is universal and darkness prevails. As Dunja Brill argues in *Goth Culture: Gender, Sexuality and Style*:

> It is difficult to overestimate the importance of black to goth subculture. In Germany (the current capital of goth worldwide), the entire phenomenon is sometimes called "schwarz kultur" … In any language, from German "schwarz" to Japanese "goshikku," black is the center of the fashion palette. (2008, 1–7)

Whether fashion, style, trend, or look, the varying manifestations of Gothic aesthetics point to its current popularity and global presence.

Nevertheless, it is worth interrogating what German manga artists had in mind when producing their works. Can the popularity of their manga be accounted for on the basis of the success of their Japanese contemporaries? Did the German Goths not predate the art, architecture, literature, and manga adopting the Gothic mode? Needless to say, one could argue that the phenomenon is symptomatic of the postmodern condition and the effects of globalization, but I argue that authorial intent, as well as context, should be considered. On this premise, I take into account press releases, interviews, and correspondence with *Gothic Sports*'s Anike Hage, *Losing Neverland*'s Fahr Sindram, and *Lilientod*'s Anne Delseit and Martina Peters.

In an interview with Tokyopop on February 13, 2009, Hage explained that *Gothic Sports* started as an idea for a story set at school but needed an angle which would allow for more sports action (Robofish 2009). In terms of how much of her own experience goes into her work, Hage replied, "[M]ost things are invented but some aspects I took from my friends and families experiences as well as from of my own" (Robofish 2009). More relevant, though, is her response to the succession of questions regarding pop-goth culture:

TOKYOPOP: What does Goth culture mean to you?

ANIKE HAGE: I like some of the clothes and in some cases I like the music but that's all.

TOKYOPOP: How did you get involved with Goth culture?

ANIKE HAGE: My brother and most of his friends belonged to this culture and so it was unavoidable to meet those people in bars or on parties etc.—in small towns you can't escape!

TOKYOPOP: Is Goth culture widespread in Germany?

ANIKE HAGE: I would say so.

...

TOKYOPOP: Does the fact that the Goths were an Eastern Germanic tribe who fought against the Romans in the first half of the first millennium [sic] A.D. have any effect on the perception of Goth culture in modern Germany?

ANIKE HAGE: I don't think so. I guess the most Goths does not even know about these historical facts [sic]! In Germany the people think of Victorian style, medieval inspired clothes, mystical aspects, metal etc. when they talk about Goths, I would say.

(Robofish 2009)

Although based on her own observations and experiences, Hage's responses arguably indicate not only that her interest in Gothic subculture is partial, but that Germans associate Gothic subculture with that which is exotic—namely a "Victorian style." In another piece with the major German newspaper *Süddeutsche Zeitung*, although manga is described as Hage's profession per se, Hage stresses, rather, that she illustrates comics. She then argues ironically that any doe-eyed comic or character, including Mickey Mouse, is manga and defends her own Western style of illustration and local settings by asking the readers why she should draw about life in Japan if Japanese know much better about the subject. The origin of Hage's inspiration, she maintains, is her hometown's grammar school in Wolfenbüttel and her experience there. *Gothic Sports* is neither about

Japanese school, nor about Japanese school life; it is about her experience as a teen inspired by Gothic fashion (Hampel 2006). What these two excerpts arguably indicate is that the influence of pop-goth trends and Japanese manga and culture on Hage's work are neither arbitrary, nor do they play a major role in informing her stories. It is, rather, the universality of psychologically complex or angst-ridden teens in an awkward stage of identity formation, I argue, which informs both German and Japanese manga, as well as Other-laden narratives characteristic of the Gothic mode.

Sindram, on the other hand, admits to her love of both comics and manga, as well as Disney and Ghibli films on the basis that her admiration is for a text's story and visuals, rather than its cultural origins, which are important (Bünte 2006). Interestingly, though, in spite of stressing that *Losing Neverland* was created as a statement against child pornography in shotacon, when asked whether she was interested erotic manga, Singram admitted to loving shounen ai (Bünte 2006). Do these statements imply that Sindram condemns depictions of minors involved in sexual activity, while minors romantically bound to older partners is legitimate if not sexual? Whatever the case, and regardless of artistic inspiration, Sindram's conflicting statements confirm that the element of "forbidden" love or unconventional romantic relations, as a characteristic of the Gothic mode, is a universal theme, crossing genres, media, and cultures. With regard to the style and nature of her work, Sindram explicitly defines it as "Gothik Manga," adding that the story was inspired by a song from Klaus Hoffman, that her style of illustration is Victorian, and that she adopted narrative patterns from shotacon manga (Bünte 2006). What this suggests is that Sindram consciously chose to adopt a Victorian style of illustration over manga style, albeit appropriating elements of the Gothic look, identifiable in both German and Japanese manga. Again, this postmodern mishmash of influences to produce a look that is essentially Gothic—in Sindram's case, German, Victorian, and Japanese—and reflects Hogle's observation that the Gothic scatters itself and adapts and evolves into new, accessible forms.

Contrasting both Hage and Sindram's individual inspirations and artistic choices is *Lilientod*. As a collaborative work by Martina Peters and Anne Delseit, *Lilientod* is based on a complex web of influential factors. In their interview with anime and manga magazine *AnimaniA* on March 4, 2009, Delseit and Peters both revealed that although their current mutual interest lies in the genre of boys' love manga, their initial interest in Japanese manga, anime, and culture began with the iconic *Sailor Moon* series (Rudert 2009). On a personal level, Peters explains that her style of illustration is based on various Japanese and Western artists' styles and traditions, but adds that she has no particular role models to whom she can attribute her style (Rudert 2009). This is reinforced in another interview with *AnimePRO*, as Peters argues that she has no "idol" in the way of either storytelling or illustration (Brox 2013). On the subject of

Delseit's artistic influences, she responds similarly to Peters in stressing that she has no individual role models but nonetheless adds that her favorite author is one of Germany's national icons, Michael Ende of the *NeverEnding Story* franchise. Other "classic" sources of inspiration, Delseit adds, are going for walks, people watching, listening to music, lightning, and personal experiences (Rudert 2009). Evidently, there are a variety of influences that both artists infuse into their collaborative work. In addition, neither party clearly stated they could attribute their work to one specific artist or one particular tradition of graphic storytelling, whether Western comics or Japanese manga. What this reflects and reinforces is the postmodern palette-like method of creative production—the dipping, dabbing, and blending of original forms into a unique piece.

So, while Hage's creative palette comprised of her experience as a German teen exposed to manga, comics, and pop-goth culture, Sindram's was a blend of German songs, Japanese manga, and Victorian illustration, and Peters and Delseit's collaborative palette was a plethora of individual experiences and taste preferences but quintessentially homoerotic and sporting the Gothic look. Based on these personal accounts, and omitting the authors' financial motives, it could be argued that rather than seizing pop-goth culture as a unique marketing angle, the artists' appropriation of the Gothic look and/or the Gothic mode were contextually and personally motivated. By centering their texts on psychologically complex representations of Othered, alienated, or troubled young adults, these young women have tapped into and harnessed something that is universal and transcultural—both the Gothic mode and the Gothic look.

Manga See, Doujin Do

In contrast to professional manga artists or illustrators, whose creativity is potentially constrained by financial imperatives, doujin manga artists have free rein on, and little or no financial gain to be had from their content. Although this free rein on content and style allows for texts to vary wildly from the standard fare of mainstream manga, in their textual poaching of popular manga and anime titles and characters, German doujin manga artists nevertheless replicate, as well as deviate from, mainstream manga. Given the enduring popularity of manga adopting the Gothic mode and/or the Gothic look, determining the extent to which doujin manga artists replicate and/or deviate from the mainstream is viable without even visiting a bookshop. This can be done by investigating doujin works online.

There are a number of web-based platforms for uploading manga, art, or other creative works. Some of the more popular ones include deviantART, Tumblr, or to some extent, YouTube. Specifically, however, the doujinshi pages of Animexx.de, as Malone has also observed, "have introduced to a wide readership many artists who have gone on to publish their works in Germany's manga market" (2011, 33). In my correspondence with six original doujin manga artists featured on Animexx.de, I attempted to determine their individual inspirations and motivations to publish their work without revenue and with little or no attention from major publishers. The correspondence involved a questionnaire of up to 30 questions, which was forwarded to the respondents through Animexx.de's internal mail system. Most of the questions were open-ended and covered subjects such as online fandom activities, convention activities, revenue, fan interaction, and most importantly, their investment in manga and their appropriation of the Gothic mode and/or the Gothic look. All respondents were female, ranged from the age of 18 to 30, and initially showed interest in manga from as early as elementary school to as late as high school. Only one of the respondents was from Switzerland; the rest were based in Germany. However, prior to examining the responses in greater detail, excerpts from the following six German doujin manga, *Infected Romance* (KleinKonan 2013), *Neuschnee* (Hintara 2010), *Fourth Instance* (HasiAnn 2013), *My Neighbour Dracula* (ryodita 2011), *Bound by Chains* (RiNkO22 2013), and *Life after Death* (violeta 2013), will be examined for their style and content.

In spite of including both full-color and monochrome pages, the dark-on-light color schemes and prevalence of dark or bold shading found in these particular titles illustrate the stylistic parallels in both professional and doujin Gothic look-inspired manga. Moreover, while frail subjects are not consistently featured, the dark attire and pallid, vampiric complexions of the majority of subjects reinforce the notion that such motifs are not exclusive to the Gothic look characteristic of professional manga. In any case, the postmodern macabre mélange of the Gothic look and doe-eyed shoujo aesthetics produces what I refer to as the "*kimokawaii* effect"—the uncanny blend of the repulsively sweet or the disgustingly cute in order to evoke feelings of utter disgust yet inexplicable compassion or adoration. And this effect, I argue, serves as an ideal defense mechanism for one to grow accustomed to pain, trauma, or that which may be unpleasant or deeply repressed in an endearing light.

However, is the implicit Gothic look of such manga simply a case of style over substance? Or, put differently, does the content also reproduce elements of the Gothic mode? Though not entirely indicative of such, a brief synopsis of each manga nevertheless illustrates to some extent whether the content embodies elements of the Gothic mode. *Infected Romance* (KleinKonan 2013) could be considered a Gothic romance in the sense that the story is quintessentially a romance against all odds—a couple enduring the daily grind in the wake of a zombie epidemic. Along with the almost viral proliferation of zombie narratives in popular culture, the infectious nature of the subject has also infiltrated the direction of academic discourse. The main point of contention has been whether and, if so, to what extent zombies are "Gothic." To address the matter, Botting (2013) argues,

> Overdetermined in their cultural and political significance, yet resolutely not human, zombies provide another blank screen for otherness and enjoyment, a return to the all-too human/ utterly inhuman oscillation underlying humanism, another degree z zero of otherness against which a degree zero of humanity can be reinvoked.

Given Botting's implicit Othering of zombies, their uncanny nature in defying laws of non-contradiction, and, in part, their dread-inducing effect as the living dead whether considered as the Other, the monster, or the immigrant, I would suggest that *Infected Romance* at least appropriates the element of Othering in the Gothic mode. In a similar vein, the prevalence of Othering—such as the vampires in *My Neighbour Dracula* and *Bound by Chains*, the demons exploiting abused children in *Fourth Instance*, the presence of both demons and vampires in *Neuschnee*, and the ill-fated living dead protagonist in *Life after Death*—indicates that these texts, at least in their deployment of Other figures in supernatural or uncanny circumstances, also embody certain elements of the Gothic mode. The consistent Othering in both the mainstream and doujin manga featured in this chapter reflects, I would argue, Germany and Japan's lingering concern with immigration in a postwar and post-nationalist context. In any case, although formalists might assert that style *is* substance, or that form *is* content (accepting that the alienating effect of Gothic literature is invoked by the segmented and temporally disjointed nature of manga paneling and use of gutters), content is nevertheless a critical site of semantic significance.

Having said that, authorial intent, as demonstrated by the Hage, Sindram, and Peters and Delseit interviews discussed previously, does provide additional insight into the overall nature of any given text. On this note, it is worth turning now to my correspondence with Animexx.de's budding young manga artists and their responses to my survey.[1] In response to questions concerning the origin of their interest in "gothic-themed comics or manga," the appealing aspects of such manga, and why, in general, they enjoy such texts, Respondent A expressed her interest not in Gothic fiction necessarily, but in "[s]tories of people who are not necessarily evil, but have some kind of problem or are tossed into a situation where they are driven into doing horrifying things that haunt them, making them spiral into madness." In addition, her attitude towards depictions

---

1 Editor's Note: In the interest of fidelity, all extracted quotes throughout this chapter from Cavcic's survey respondents preserve as much as possible the spelling and text formatting as originally presented.

of death, either violent or otherwise, was largely related to the concept of closure and relief:

> I am way more worried about the characters when I know that they might die for good. That's the reason I'm sometimes thankful for gruesome depictions, not because I like violence or something, but because I then know that a character is dead. (Respondent A)

Respondent A listed an eclectic and culturally diverse range of creators as her major creative influences, including the likes of HP Lovecraft, Jhonen Vasquez, Toei Animation, Kaori Yuki, Hitoshi Okuda, and "a whole bunch of video games." On the other hand, Respondents B and C highlighted the importance of clothing. Respondent B expressed her preference for the "look" of characters based on their clothing, hair, and other factors, while Respondent C considered Japanese Gothic Lolita fashion, as well as the clothing, scenery, and décor of the Victorian era, e.g. as depicted in Toboso's *Black Butler*, as some of her major influences. Although individual responses varied, most respondents mentioned at least one Japanese anime, manga, or game title, indicating the overriding influence of Japanese culture not only in the production of German manga, but within Hogle's symbolic realm of the "Gothic." In this sense, the mutability and perhaps viral nature of both Botting's "Gothic" and Japanese manga style combined makes for a powerful transcultural and arguably universal formula that transcends all genres, media, and delivery platforms.

On the subject of the global expansion of manga, when asked to account for popularity of doujin manga among women in both Japan and Germany, Respondent D stated,

> For me, it's love for characters and story. Maybe for others it is the same. Also the manga market is bigger than the years before that changes a lot. Someday we will have mangas for every kind of person like in japan!

In a similar vein, Respondent A suggested that writing doujin manga is fun in the sense that it is possible to create "new and/or alternate stories to something we love," but she could not account for the large amount of women who write slash fiction or doujin manga. On the other hand, Respondent B suggested that the doujin phenomenon could be due to the fact that publishing doujin manga allows women to depict certain aspects of characters "which many female readers would like to see in the original Manga or in professional Manga series but which aren't dealt with in these." In terms of manga's appeal to women, she argued,

> I think that Manga, in comparison to western comics or more naturalistic drawings, have very soft drawn characters (especially the female ones) and also often very emotional storylines, which are probably more appealing to female readers than western comics. (Respondent B)

In a more self-aware, reflexive fashion than the other respondents, Respondent F argued,

> I don't think we are different from any other nation. Women here also like to be creative. But sadly I have the presumption that comics are not taken very serious in our country. I can't prove it, but considering that a lot of published german authors obviously feel the need to still produce doujinshi besides their paid work, gives me the impression, that the industry here might not be the most tolerant one, when it comes to new ideas (besides: not only comics, also movies and tv-series) … Like german movies everything has to be educational, serious, tame and lets face it: BORING. (Respondent F)

What these responses generally indicate is that the manga industry in Germany is still developing, and that publishing doujin manga allows women to both create and consume a sort of manga that the mainstream market has failed to provide. This is highlighted, in particular, in Respondent B's comments about "soft drawn characters" and "emotional storylines," as well as Respondent F's comment concerning the intolerance of the German industry. According to these responses, one could argue that while the German manga industry has come a long way, it still has a long way to go. In this light, publishing doujin manga provides a space for women to address the needs of those dissatisfied with the content available from major German publishers.

However, are there any other incentives for the doujin manga artist? Why publish online via Animexx.de, deviantART, Tumblr or other platforms for free file exchange? Unsurprisingly, given that Animexx.de is a platform for free file exchange (though occasionally leading to contracts with major manga publishers), all of the respondents admitted that they have neither sold any items nor made any money from their creative work on Animexx.de. Half considered their online publishing a hobby. In justifying their rationale, Respondent F revealed that she was currently working on new stories and added, "If I can manage to bring them online and the people will like it, I might try to sell it." Respondent E initially considered her activities on Animexx.de a hobby, or, at most, a part-time job, and added that she did not know if manga would be the right career move for her. Only Respondent C explicitly expressed plans to sell her manga and merchandise online and at conventions, considering her activities as "a way to get into the manga industry."

On the subject of fans and the extent to which being a part of the manga scene is in any way empowering, all of the respondents agreed that their fans are important, while only half admitted to feeling empowered as members of the doujin community. Respondent A suggested her fans were "infinitely important. They motivate me more than anyone else ever could." In terms of her attitude towards being part of the doujin community, she revealed,

> I feel like I've made a tiny name for myself, I have very loyal readers, some of them even making cosplay from my comics, and I've achieved more than I deserve. I feel great in this community ... I think this community opens up many opportunities for artists who want people to read their work. (Respondent A)

Further positive responses included Respondent C's comment that fans motivated her to keep illustrating and Respondent F's comment that "[w]hat is a story good for, if there is nobody who wants to read it? It makes me happy when they are entertained and I love to hear constructive critique to improve myself." Taken together, these reinforce the utility and significance of Animexx. de's feedback system as a source of external motivation for self-improvement. Those respondents who suggested they did not feel "empowered" per se, as members of the doujin community, justified their reasons for participating in it in terms their statuses as fans. Respondent B noted,

> I think of myself mostly as a fan like everyone else ... I don't feel empowered, because in the end, I'm just one of the fans standing in line of some exceptional doujinshi artist like everybody else.

In contrast, Respondent F admitted she was working as an illustrator "so the borders between [her] work and [her] doujinshis might be a bit blurred," adding, "[s]ure, work is work and hobby is hobby, but it is not that I desperately need the manga-subculture to be creative."

Whether as artists or fans of Gothic-inspired manga, Germany's doujin enthusiasts have employed Animexx.de as meaningful platform for self-expression, interaction, motivation, and self-promotion. While further longitudinal research is needed to determine the extent to which Animexx.de has empowered or assisted doujin manga artists, one thing is certain—with 8578 registered doujin manga artists and 17,960 freely accessible titles in the doujinshi category (*Animexx.de* 2013), the site is not, by definition, a platform for financial gain. Even so, its popularity and accessibility have provided a space for thousands of manga artists and fans alike to engage in creative and cultural activities which otherwise might not have been viable without the expansion of new digital technologies and increased connectivity.

Conclusion

As either singular or compound nouns, Gothic, manga, or Gothic manga are discursively contentious among academics, fans, and artists alike. While I have tailored my own definitions of the various terms for the purpose of discussion, I must stress that they are by no means definitive. They are, rather, based on one particular freeze-frame moment in the very transient and transcultural nature of the phenomena "Gothic" and "manga." When married, I have argued that the two combined terms make for an ideal transcultural formula for popular texts. That is, the mutability and viral nature of both Botting's "Gothic" and Japanese manga style combined transcend all genres, media, and delivery platforms. I have observed that, by centering their texts on psychologically-complex representations of Othered, alienated, or troubled young adults, German manga enthusiasts have tapped into a mode and market that is universal in terms of content, and transcultural in terms of style—harnessing both the Gothic mode and the Gothic look. And their motivations for doing so? As the published interviews and my survey of doujin manga artists have revealed, there are various contributing factors. Nevertheless, I have attempted to at least partially account for the overwhelming amount of German women producing manga appropriating the Gothic mode and/or the Gothic look. I posit that the "woman as Other"—defined only by her dualistic relation to "man" (de Beauvoir 1989, xxii)—is the likely underlying ideological force at play here. Having been Othered, both socially and ideologically, women have challenged or indirectly addressed the issue of their Otherness in the guise of fiction. As I have suggested in this chapter, manga, as a silent and often anonymous means of self-publishing, has served as an ideal platform for social commentary and/or self-expression for both Japanese and German women. However, perhaps it is the Gothic mode (rather than the Gothic look), in its exploration of the repressed, its frequent Othering, and settings enshrouded in secrecy, which sets it apart as an ideal platform to deconstruct those deeply embedded myths attached to nationalism, race, gender, sexuality and subjectivity. Be it *your* neighbor, Dracula, an evil resident, a demonic black butler, or Yukito Ayatsuji and Hiro Kiyohara's *Another* (2013), there will always be an Other to be deconstructed by another Other.

References

Ayatsuji, Yukito and Hiro Kiyohara. 2013. *Another*. New York: Yen Press.
Bae, Catherine Yoonah. 2008. "Girl Meets Boy Meets Girl: Heterosocial Relations, Wholesome Youth, and Democracy in Postwar Japan." *Asian Studies Review* 32 (3): 341–60.

Beauvoir, Simone de. 1989. *The Second Sex*. New York: Vintage Books.
Böckem, Jörg. 2006. "Sind die süüüß! [Are the Sweeeeeet!]." *KulturSpiegel*, September 9.
Botting, Fred. 2001. *The Gothic*. Woodbridge, Suffolk: D.S. Brewer.
Botting, Fred. 2013. "Globalzombie: From *White Zombie* to *World War Z*." In *Globalgothic*, edited by Glennis Byron, 188–201. Manchester: Manchester University Press.
Bouissou, Jean-Marie. 2010. "Manga: A Historical Overview." In *Manga: An Anthology of Global and Cultural Perspectives*, edited by Toni Johnson-Woods, 17–34. New York: Continuum.
Brill, Dunja. 2008. *Goth Culture: Gender, Sexuality and Style*. Oxford: Berg.
Brox, Jennifer. 2013. "Interview mit Martina Peters [Interview with Martina Peters]." *AnimePRO*, September 5. http://www.animepro.de/action/interviews/7238_interview-mit-martina-peters-.
Bünte, Christopher. 2006. "Interview mit Fahr Sindram [Interview with Fahr Sindram]." *Comicgate*, 17 July. http://www.comicgate.de/content/view/420/76.
Delseit, Anne and Martina Peters. 2011. *Lilientod*. Volume 3. Hamburg: Carlsen.
Hage, Anike. 2008. *Gothic Sports*. Volume 4. Los Angeles: Tokyopop.
Hagio, Moto. 2013. *The Heart of Thomas*. Translated by Matt Thorn. Portland, OR: Fantagraphics.
Hampel, Lea. 2006. "Comic-Heldin aus Wolfenbüttel [Comics Heroine from Wolfenbüttel]." *Süddeutsche Zeitung*, August 6. http://jetzt.sueddeutsche.de/texte/anzeigen/328419/Comic-Heldin-aus-Wolfenbuettel.
HasiAnn. 2013. *Fourth Instance*. http://animexx.onlinewelten.com/doujinshi/zeichner/69676/55083/.
Hino, Matsuri. 2005. *Vampire Knight*. Volume 1. Tokyo: Hakusensha.
Hintara. 2010. *Neuschnee*. http://animexx.onlinewelten.com/doujinshi/46493/.
Hogle, Jerrold E. 2002. *The Cambridge Companion to Gothic Fiction*. Cambridge: Cambridge University Press.
Jüngst, Heike. 2006. "Manga in Germany: From Translation to Simulacrum." *Perspectives* 14 (4): 248–59.
Kamm, Björn-Ole. 2010. *Nutzen und Gratifikation bei Boys' Love Manga: Fujoshi oder verdorbene Mädchen in Japan und Deutschland* [Benefits and Gratuity at Boys' Love Manga: Fujoshi or Spoiled Girls in Japan and Germany]. Hamburg: Kovač.
Kato, Kazue. 2009. *Blue Exorcist*. Volume 1. Tokyo: Shueisha.
Katsura, Asuka. 2004. *Le Portrait de Petit Cossette*. Volume 1. Tokyo: Kodansha.
KleinKonan. 2013. *Infected Romance*. http://animexx.onlinewelten.com/doujinshi/zeichner/299808/54496/.
Malone, Paul M. 2009. "Home-grown Shōjo Manga and the Rise of Boys' Love among Germany's 'Forty-Niners.'" *Intersections: Gender and Sexuality in Asia and the Pacific* 20. http://intersections.anu.edu.au/issue20/malone.htm.

Malone, Paul M. 2010. "From BRAVO to Animexx.de to Export: Capitalizing on German Boys' Love Fandom, Culturally, Socially and Economically." In *Boys' Love Manga: Essays on the Sexual Ambiguity and Cross-Cultural Fandom of the Genre*, edited by Antonia Levi, Mark McHarry, and Dru Pagliassotti, 23–43. Jefferson, NC: McFarland & Co.

Malone, Paul M. 2011. "Transcultural Hybridization in Home-Grown German Manga," *Global Manga Studies* 2: 49–60.

Malone, Paul M. 2013. "Transplanted Boys' Love Conventions and Anti-'Shota' Polemics in German Manga: Fahr Sindram's 'Losing Neverland.'" *Transformative Works and Cultures 12*. http://journal.transformativeworks.org/index.php/twc/article/view/434/395.

Nakazawa, Keiji. 1982. *Barfuss durch Hiroshima: eine Bildergeschichte gegen den Krieg* [Barefoot through Hiroshima: A Picture Story against the War]. Reinbek bei Hamburg: Rowohlt.

Noppe, Nele. 2010. "Dōjinshi Research as a Site of Opportunity for Manga Studies." *Global Manga Studies* 1: 123–42.

Pannor, Stefan. 2012. "Zum Tode Keiji Nakazawas: Zeichnen, um zu überleben." *Spiegel*, December 27. http://www.spiegel.de/kultur/literatur/nachruf-zum-tod-des-manga-zeichners-keiji-nakazawa-a-874872.html.

RiNkO22. 2013. *Bound by Chains*. http://animexx.onlinewelten.com/doujinshi/zeichner/555206/53448/.

Robofish. 2009. "Gothic Sports Interview: Global Volks-Manga!" *Tokyopop*, February 13. http://web.archive.org/web/20090213024756/http://www.tokyopop.com/Robofish/tp_article/688425.html.

Rudert, Sabine. 2009. "Interview mit Anne Delseit und Martina Peters Mit Zeichen- und Schreibfeder [Interview with Anne Delseit and Martina Peters: With Drawing and Writing Pen]." *AnimaniA*, March 4. http://www.animania.de/home/animania-aktuelle-news/article/interview-mit-anne-delseit-und-martina-peters.html.

Ryodita. 2011. *My Neighbour Dracula*. http://animexx.onlinewelten.com/doujinshi/zeichner/38616/34541/.

Schodt, Frederik L. 1996. *Dreamland Japan: Writings on Modern Manga*. Berkeley: Stone Bridge Press.

Sindram, Fahr. 2008. *Losing Neverland*. Volume 2. Germany: Cookies and Cream.

Takemiya, Keiko. 1976. *Kaze to Ki no Uta* [Poem of Wind and Trees]. Volume 1. Tokyo: Shogakukan.

Thompson, Jason, and Atsuhisa Okura. 2007. "How Manga Conquered the U.S.: A Graphic Guide to Japan's Coolest Export." *Wired*, October 10. http://www.wired.com/special_multimedia/2007/1511_ff_manga.

Toboso, Yana. 2007. *Black Butler*. Volume 3. Tokyo: Square Enix.

Toboso, Yana. 2009. *Black Butler*. Volume 6. Tokyo: Square Enix.

Tokyopop. 2013. "Manga Fieber [Manga Fever]." http://www.tokyopop.de/manga-shop/index.php?cPath=873_68.

violeta. 2013. *Life after Death*. http://animexx.onlinewelten.com/doujinshi/zeichner/374676/56773/.

Chapter 9
Constructing the Mangaverse: Narrative Patterns in Marvel's Appropriation of Manga Products

Manuel Hernández-Pérez

Even though American and Japanese publishers dominate comic book sales globally, their respective contexts and products could not be any more different. In the case of American comics, the best-known and most celebrated genre—often criticized for being considered mainstream—is that of superheroes. However, the relationship between genre, theme and audience in the history of manga presents a different pattern. Japanese comics, particularly diverse with regard to demographic and generic segmentation, show a greater homogeneity in the use of stylistic codes which have come to be known as Japanese Visual Language (Cohn 2010). The American publishing market has mobilized several strategies in order to benefit from the international success of manga, coupled with the parallel success of anime at the beginning of the twenty-first century. The most common strategies have been the introduction of Japanese cultural elements and the adoption and hybridization of Japanese Visual Language, through the publication of products of Japanese and international authorship. The publishing imprint Mangaverse (2000–03; 2005–06), a relative failure in terms of its reception, represents a good example for the analysis of these trends and appropriative strategies. Through this case, aspects of the story, the deconstruction/appropriation of characters, different forms of transcultural adaptation, and the hybridization of media and genres are all analyzed.

Comics in Japan and the United States

Few countries can claim to have brought so much to the world of comics as Japan and the United States. Both can be considered authentic historical "powers": main producers of contents in the sequential medium, unrivaled even by the influential contributions of the Franco-Belgian world to the *bande dessinée*. I will not pause here to enumerate the long list of authors who have contributed to the development of this means of expression in these two countries. It would be an unfair and unnecessary error to highlight some names while neglecting others who may be not as influential but may nevertheless be part of the tradition of these cultural industries. Instead, I shall adopt the strategy, in spite of its limitations, of describing the importance of the American and Japanese comics industries by means of a brief summary of the history of the development of their respective markets.

In both the United States and Japan, comics have a similar source; they are products of mass culture linked to the emergence of the mass media, especially the printing press. The first comics to appear in the US were an accompaniment of other contents offered by newspapers. Following this common model in Western countries, in Japan, comics also emerged in connection with the printing press. Charles Wirgman and George Bigot, directors of *The Japan Punch* (1878) and *Tobaè* (1887) respectively, would bring about as a consequence of their publishing activities the importation of aesthetic and narrative codes from this recently developed comics medium to Japan. The connection to the printing press also brought about the appearance of two quite different market niches in Japan and in the Western world. The first one was an adult audience through the natural evolution of the political caricature of the nineteenth century. Examples of this trend in the Japanese press have been studied in relation to the subsequent Russo-Japanese War (Mikhailova 2008, 980–86; Duus 2001); there are also numerous examples in the emerging American comic strips of the era (Hess and Northrop 2011). The second was the progressive development of the language of comics, in the case of comic strips and children magazines and, with the emergence of those genres—practically indistinguishable in their beginnings—an irreversible link of the comics medium to child and youth audiences.

By the end of the Second World War, the American market for comics was now strongly established and aimed at a young audience in the form of comic books. Just as with pulp literature, the first approximations of the American comic book dealt with a great range of themes such as the western, detective stories, adventure stories, romances, and science fiction, among others. However, as has been pointed out on occasion, the adoption of a multi-genre strategy was soon abandoned in favor of a single genre one. This was firstly centered on the success of detective fiction (*Detective Comics*, 1937) which would lead, after the success of *Superman* (*Action Comics*, 1938), to the later market dominance of the superhero comic (Lopes 2009, 19–20).

Parallel to the appearance of the comic book, the Japan of the 1930s adopted the youth magazine as a standard, taking as its model the *Shounen Gorakubu* [Boys' Club], which included, among other contents, collections of stories in much bigger volumes of up to 150 pages. Although the publication of these youth stories ceased during the war, manga narratives re-emerged strongly during the mid-1950s, absorbing influences from other media based on the graphic narrative, such as the *kamishibai* [paper drama performances] or the *e-monogatari* [illustrated stories] (Kinsella 2000; Holmberg 2011).

From then onward, the industries appear to have developed in very different ways, particularly with regards to the segmentation of their audiences, as well as in the co-existence of national products with other cultural products coming from the international market. In the comic book, for example, the predominant genre is near-exclusively associated with the theme of superheroes, which has frequently led to the erroneous genre-medium conflation in the American context (Eisner, Miller, and Brownstein 2005, 14). This tendency would be interrupted temporarily with the emergence of other genres, such as that of horror and science fiction. Also of great importance would be the appearance of other minor genres such as the comic strip, children's cartoon strips (aka "Funny Animals"), or romantic stories, which left the door open to the regeneration of the medium through new audiences.

However, despite the competitors, the superhero comic book has survived for more than 60 years. A look at distributors' figures, under the label of "Graphic Novel," might correspond to not only the contributions of independent authors, situated outside the mainstream, but also to the American editions of foreign authors, mainly of manga and European *bande dessinée*. This means that for the industry and the majority of the public, the American market is effectively equivalent to the comic book format and the superhero genre.

In the history of the Japanese market, on the other hand, it is not so easy to establish a simple and functionalist relationship between genre, theme, and audience. In Japanese comic book production, the considerable diversification of the market is not based on different publication formats or cultural tradition. The predominant genre, shounen, is defined by its audience (young boys), while other genres attend to different demographic segmentations. Therefore, the shoujo (young girls), the seinen (adult men), the ladies and josei (adult women) and the kodomo (children) genres exist as a natural evolution linked to that of the life courses of their respective audiences. These genres can be considered to be relatively isolated, while the themes in manga are a constant example of hybridization. Nevertheless, it is necessary to clarify that there are certain historical links, which include the predominance of the themes of sports[1] or of action[2] in shounen, as well as romance in shoujo.[3]

After numerous moments of crisis during the 1950s, '60s and '70s, the comic book market in the US has stabilized and experienced considerable growth starting around the year 2000 (Beaty 2010). One of the reasons for this might be the growing traffic of contents between the superhero comic books

---

1 *Slam Dunk* (1990–96); *The Prince of Tennis* (*Tenisu no Ōjisama*, 1999–2008).
2 *Bleach* (2001–); *Naruto* (1999–).
3 *Nana* (2000–09); *Nodame Cantabile* (2001–09).

and other cultural industries such as the cinema, video games, and animation. For example, the success of cross-media products based on the cinematic relaunching of characters may have stimulated the sale of comics related to those characters. Famous examples of this trend in integrated marketing of diverse industries would be the cinematographic sagas of *Batman* (1989–97; 2005–12), *X-Men* (2001–11), and *Spider-Man* (2002–07; 2012–14).

Other reasons for this upturn in sales of the comic market can be found in the increased penetration of Japanese products into the American market. Therefore, as in other Western countries, the success of anime in the 1990s caused a growing interest in the original manga upon which the popular anime series were based, which began to be distributed in an adapted form. Subsequently, with the creation of specific audiences for the medium of manga, publishers adopt a similar format to the common collection of serialized novels, known as tankoubon (sometimes also called just "tanks"), while also increasingly respecting the Japanese right-to-left orientation of manga. By the middle of the decade, around 2005, manga already represented over 40 percent of sales and was, along with other formats considered to be graphic novels, the largest contribution to sales of the publishing market in the US (*Publishers Weekly* 2007). By around 2011, however, there had been a drop in international sales of manga; the fall may be attributed to the increase in digital piracy and a decrease in demand. After this considerable fall, the sales of manga in North America have stabilized; the boom which began in the previous decade has evidently given rise to a "smaller and more sustainable" market (Alverson 2013).

The years 2000–02 were, therefore, a decisive moment in the recent history of the two industries. The fever for manga, which dominated the international markets, led to a proliferation of local authors who incorporated Japanese narrative codes and aesthetics into their productions. Such internationalization is increasingly evident in the markets of East Asia, with examples such as the adaptations of *manhwa* (South Korea) and *manhua* (China). However, in countries with a longer tradition in the medium of comics, such as the US, the introduction of elements derived from manga cannot be defined as a mere transnational adaptation. As will be seen throughout this chapter, the adoption of Japanese elements into the narrative of the American comic is dependent on the conventions of the superhero genre, which is idiosyncratic. To illustrate this trend, the example of Mangaverse, an imprint launched by the Marvel publishing house through different miniseries published between 2002 and 2006, has been chosen. Enjoying little commercial or critical success within this period, Mangaverse is remembered by fan audiences as one of the most controversial products among those created by this prestigious publisher.

Manga and the American Comic Book as Media

Before proceeding, it is necessary to clarify my own view that manga is not just an example of the medium of comics, known as sequential art. It is, on the contrary, a completely different medium. Note that terminology is of great importance here. The language of comics is ordinary, in spite of its diverse variations; it is common to all its manifestations. Using the terminology of narrative theory (Ryan 2004, 21), this language is defined by the use of two linguistic and iconic spatial channels which form a single semiotic system. This double channel system can be reproduced in different products like the American market's comic book, the graphic novel, or *bandé dessinée*. However, those cultural markets are not only defined by the use of a language and physical medium—the format—but they are also the consequence of a particular system of production and, in many cases, of a specific cultural framework.

On the other hand, even though both media share the same semiotic code, it is undeniable that they possess significant aesthetic and narrative differences. For some, these differences are so predetermined that they regard manga a separate language in itself. The so-called Japanese Visual Language (Cohn 2010) is characterized by the adoption of a particular style which is clear in the design of their characters, as well as a distinctive visual grammar of its own. The latter incorporates the use of non-conventional visual symbols and metaphors which require a basic cultural proficiency to properly decode (Cohn 2010, 187–90). Characteristic elements of this style are the use of kinetic lines and the emphasis on the visual value of typographies. Other authors, however, have pointed out how the visual grammar of Japanese manga represents significant differences in comparison with the American comics in terms of the reading experience it provides. This is determined by the relationship between the panels, which does not seek only to develop the action quickly but, on occasion, intends to look more deeply into the psychological consequences of the events being depicted (McCloud 1993, 77–8).

However, it is difficult to believe that in the long history of contact between the two media, beginning with the creation of the first comic strips in Japanese newspapers, no other episodes of mutual influence have occurred. Especially when for some the medium of comics is defined by its "transnational" nature (Stein 2013). In this sense, numerous figures of the American comic book have been influenced by modern manga, incorporating themes and many references to the visual style of manga, or introducing iconic elements of Japanese culture into their work. Such is the case of, among many others, Frank Miller (*Daredevil*, 1979–83; *Ronin*, 1983–84), Scott McCloud (*Zot*, 1984–90), or Stan Sakai (*Usagi Yojimbo*, 1984–).

The Figure of the Superhero as a Recurring Feature of Internationalization

Both the cultural products of the manga industry and the American comic book industry possess meanings that do not only appeal to their national or local publics, i.e. the natural audiences for whom a product is originally created. Both markets also have an international appeal. Shounen manga, for example, although originally aimed at a specifically young male demographic profile, is consumed by audiences of a variety of different ages and genders both in Japan and abroad. Because of the size of this audience segment, it should be considered a key part of the expansion of manga and anime culture in the West. On the other hand, the target audience for superhero comic books appears to have undergone more drastic changes, not only as a consequence of the international dissemination of its contents but also due to the natural aging of its primary public. Currently, the average reader is an adult, and the majority of the publishers' revenue does not come from the sales of comics but from the licensing of derivative products such as films, video games, and other branded merchandise (Wright 2003, 292–3).

Another consequence of the global dissemination of the American and Japanese comic is the contribution of new elements to the collective imaginary. In the case of manga and related industries, Japanese culture plays an important role in supplying narratives with original elements from history, literature, and national folklore. In a historic sense, the development of the gekiga genre during the 1960 and 1970s decidedly contributed to the reproduction of those national and cultural elements. Many of the authors from that era chose to introduce historical themes, in particular from the Tokugawa Shogunate (1600–1868), as a way of reinterpreting narratives from folklore and the historical novel from a modern social perspective. As a consequence, tales of samurai, ninja, and mythological creatures, which have always played an important part in manga,[4] became even darker, and the medium evolved, incorporating more adult narratives in line with its maturing audience. However, it is arguable that those elements of national narrative are also present in other media with a greater reach, impact, and international dissemination. Stories of samurai and ninja, for example, are also common on Japanese television and cinema. In the case of the American comic book, the most widespread narrative figure is the superhero, inevitably linked to its own genre. The superhero has been defined as one of the constants of the American comic book, a mono myth and a constant of the medium (Lang and Trimble 2004). So, in spite of its numerous episodes of crisis, regeneration, and transformation, the superhero genre has

---

4 These elements are also present in other graphic and sequential media and precursors of manga, like the *kamishibai* and the *e-monogatari* (Nash 2009; Holmberg 2011).

always enjoyed great social importance in its own market. As with the characters and themes of manga, their popularity could be due to the propagation and coexistence of thematic elements in other related media. In this sense, it has been repeatedly highlighted that the success of superheroes is due in part to the support and competition from serialized fiction, particularly radio and television series (Lopes 2009, 14; Gabilliet 2010).

The superhero, along with the samurai, the ninja, and other figures of Japanese narrative, has reached beyond the borders of their respective national narratives to form part of a wider set of meanings shared by international audiences. However, it could be argued that the influence and permanence of the American superhero is greater than that of other elements of Japanese culture. Their contribution can be framed within what, in the context of cultural studies, has been termed, "The Global Popular," a phenomenon which is indistinguishable from other aspects of globalization such as the internationalization of capital, financial systems, and cultural markets (During 1997, 808–12). One piece of evidence of the international nature of the superhero figure can be found in its historical connection with Japanese media and narratives. Characters similar to the American superhero are already present in *kamishibai*, as it reflects the influences of other American serial products, especially television series and pulp novels (Nash 2009, 101). Particularly significant is the work *Ougon Bat* [Golden Bat] (1931) by Suzuki Ichiro and Nagamatsu Takeo, which combines elements of Western adventure novels and serialized cinema, especially *The Mark of Zorro* (1920–), with Asian mythology and the supernatural.

Yet apart from the obvious similarities between Japanese action heroes and primitive American superheroes (as both are influenced by the same things) the growing presence of superheroes would continue without making any significant impression on manga in Japan. In 1966, the magazine *Shounen King* purchased the rights to the characters of Batman and Robin for the Japanese market, developing them for a year through the work of the artist Jiro Kuwata. Another iconic character from the American comic book universe, Spider-Man, would be reinterpreted by different manga artists for the magazine *Monthly Shounen Magazine* some years later (1970–71). Near-completely forgotten, their interest can be related to their striking *vintage* look and the boom generated by the stories of superheroes all around the world. In contrast to these transcultural experiments of limited commercial success, it is in other media, like the TV series, where the figure of the hero with superpowers has developed a more thriving tradition in Japan. In 1966, TBS started to broadcast *Ultraman*. Here the Japanese and American views of the superhero differ significantly. While the American hero, especially the prototypical figure of Superman, is linked to his humanity, Ultraman is an avatar of sorts, an anthropomorphic representation of a kind of force of nature. He is a "kamikaze" whose only noteworthy ability is that of fighting against giant monsters (Gill 1998, 35).

Finally, with the producers of American content becoming increasingly aware of the potential of growing international audiences, there have been many attempts to reinterpret the figure of the superhero from a different cultural framework. Following the first incursions of Batman and Spider-Man, there were other, more recent attempts. In the case of DC, the one that stands out is *Batman: Child of Dreams* (2000–01), published in the Kodansha's *Magazine Z* and produced by the manga artist Kia Asamiya. This would be followed, several years later, by *Batman: Death Mask* (2008) by Yoshinori Natsume, an internationally recognized figure in the industry. With regards to the international adaptations from the 1960s and 1970s—and even the end of the 1990s with works such the *X-Men* manga (1998–99)—there are significant differences in the relationship between the narratives of the characters and the hybridization of cultural elements. Firstly, there is greater interest in safeguarding the coherence of the saga's macro story world. The editorial line and the continuity of the characters' storylines are ensured by presenting stories which cohere with other tales about the characters in the Western market. This aspect of coherence is evident within the works of Natsume, edited by CMX. This is a publishing house belonging to Wildstorm Productions and therefore part of the Time Warner-owned DC Comics, which holds the rights to the original character. Additionally, an attempt at hybridization in a stylistic sense, or of visual code, does not appear to exist: in both cases it is shounen manga, and as such they are adjusted to the usual visual linguistic codes of the manga medium and the genre. It does not try to emulate the style of the Western authors, something which, although with varied results, at least formed part of the original aims of the work of Kuwata on *Batman* (Kidd, Spear, and Ferris 2008). Lastly, it is significant that Japan plays a decisive role in the storyline of both products, not just as a geographical location but also through several elements derived from its culture (e.g. ritual masks, martial arts, mythology). Through this symbolic resource, the relationship with the audience to not only amateur manga style but also the subtext of Japanese art and culture itself is deepened. The story of the character is reinforced by going into more detail about aspects of his past. For example, the *Batman* series was relaunched by the authors Frank Miller and David Mazzucchelli in 1987 (*Batman: Year One*), and since then it has been implied that the character has a deep relationship with Japan, as Bruce Wayne spent some years there in his youth. In later series, for example, readers discover that it is during this period that the future Batman learns *ninjutsu* with the *sensei* Kirigi (*Batman* #431, 1989).

In recent years, other attempts have been made to reinvent superhero characters by introducing elements of hybridization and transposition into the plots of their stories and those of other narrative worlds. Therefore, internationalization does not seem very different from other recent transpositions of contents by the publisher, such as the imprint *Marvel Fairy*

Tales (2006), *Marvel Apes* (2008), or miniseries such as *1602* (2003) and *Marvel Zombies* (2005–06). All these products incorporate, in one way or another, elements of transculturalization and internationalization, although it is as a secondary consequence of the alteration of the original framework of their respective stories. So, for some academics, internationalization is part of "some of the strategies by which authors seek to negotiate between the standardization implicit in comics continuity and the diversification desired by contemporary readers" (Jenkins 2009, 18). Among the cases recently studied would include *Spider-Man India* (Davé 2013; O'Rourke and Rodrigues 2007) and the different versions of *Spider-Man* manga (Stein 2013). But the case of defunct imprint Mangaverse (2000–03; 2005–06), which will be analyzed below, is particularly interesting in this regard. Firstly, it represents a test (on a large scale) of the horizon of possibilities that transculturalization and internationalization offers the figure of the superhero, not only in the context of a miniseries or character, but also in a completely new alternative version of the Marvel universe. Secondly, it is an authentic hybridization of visual linguistic codes which cannot be completely classified as belonging exclusively to the tradition of manga or that of the American comic book.

Case Study: Narrative Patterns in Marvel's Appropriation of Manga Products

In 2002, coinciding with the very start of the early twenty-first century manga boom in the United States that began with Tokyopop's 100% Authentic Manga campaign (Brienza 2009), Marvel decided to create a new imprint in order to appeal to these new audiences who couldn't seem to get enough manga. The product was launched as a miniseries in two issues with the titles *Marvel Mangaverse: New Dawn* and *Marvel Mangaverse: Eternity Twilight* in March 2002. Along with this miniseries, manga issues of *Punisher* (2002), *Fantastic Four* (2002), *X-Men* (2002), *Ghost Rider* (2002) and *Spider-Man* (2002) were also published. These were limited to a single issue of 40 pages each, with independent stories of previously presented characters. The sole exception was *Avengers Assemble!* (2002), which was connected to the central story and served as both an introduction to the climax and subsequent resolution of the events in *Eternity Twilight*. In June of the same year, the publication of a miniseries of six issues was launched with the name *Marvel Mangaverse*. In contrast with the first miniseries, the goal on this occasion was to create a regular series based on two very different story arcs. Later on, both series were rereleased as two volumes of trade compilations. In 2003, another series was added to the new imprint, with the main protagonists being Wolverine (*X-Men: Ronin*) and Spider-Man (*Legend of Spider-Clan*). There were no further new products during the subsequent period until, in 2005, *New*

Marvel Mangaverse: The Rings of Fate, was published. This miniseries, which ran for five issues, signaled the end of the imprint.

From a formal point of view, Mangaverse products cannot be classified as manga. In comparison with other products, such as those published by Tokyopop or CMX, they do not fulfill the traditional requirements of the manga format. Their difference lies in aspects such as the use of color, the number of pages, and size. As comic books, however, they have a distinctive visual style which tries to reflect the essence of manga/anime design and employs the use of the Japanese Visual Language. Therefore, it seems a logical solution to classify these products by labels belonging to other international products of transnational character. Terms such as "Amerimanga" and "Amerime" have been previously used as a way of expressing this influence. Although valid, it must be qualified that the term "Amerimanga" may be too inclusive. Originally, it was used to designate productions with Western capital (American) adopting an anime aesthetic (e.g. *Thundercats*, 1985–89; *Transformers: Generation 1*, 1984–93), and has subsequently been used in recent years to describe those American authors who have included features of manga narrative in their own works. As has been argued previously, the relationships between the Western and Japanese media have a long history of hybridization, and this has affected a much larger group of artists than is typically acknowledged. Indeed, the influence of manga in the American comic book is a fairly general characteristic that can be observed in greater abundance in products than those that would ever be labeled manga, even in the most liberal of senses. In terms of genres, however, Mangaverse can be considered as an interesting case of hybridization between the two classic traditions of the superhero genre from the American comic book and the shounen genre from Japanese manga, respectively.

Entering into the details of the respective storylines is beyond the aims of this chapter. However, I will comment on the most important aspects of the story with the aim of illustrating the theoretical matters most relevant to my argument. So, for this study on the narrative patterns of Mangaverse, closely related aspects shall be considered: the deconstruction/appropriation of characters and strategies of adaptation/transculturalization.

Deconstruction/Appropriation of Characters

The story of Mangaverse depicts alternative versions of some of the main characters from the Marvel universe. These Marvel staples are visibly altered, their identities reduced to a minimal semiotic relationship between the name (signifier) and their main attributed power (signified), which allows them to still be recognized. However, the identity of a character cannot be constructed solely with these elements. In the superhero genre, in order to be able to recognize a character through different storylines in a series, which might extend over decades in many cases, something else is needed. The most important parts of the personality of a character are their memories and their biographical histories, which are reconstructed by means of the recreation of the relationships of meaning which they maintain with other characters. Dr Banner, for example, it not only a scientist with an extravagant double personality but is actually also characterized by the relationships he establishes. These include his engagement and later marriage to Betty Ross as well as his antagonism with General Thadeus E. "Thunderbolt" Ross, his fiancée's father.[5] These and many more stories are represented in the form of semiotic relationships between various secondary actors, independent of the author-scriptwriter and of the period in which the comic was written. When these relationships are altered, the character cannot be recognized easily, due to the loss of their original identity. In the Mangaverse version, The Hulk is a totally independent entity from Banner—a monster whose physical aspect is similar to the well-known *Godzilla* (1954), one of the major icons of Japanese pop culture (see Figure 9.1).

Another of the main characters from Marvel, Iron Man, is transformed into Iron Maiden, whose alter ego is the sister of the original Tony Stark, Antoinette (Toni) Stark, who is in turn in a romantic relationship with Banner. Other elements are added from Japanese popular culture, widening the spectrum of influences from the manga-anime dyad. As an example, the manga version of Iron Man capitalizes on the natural association between the character's armor and the mecha that are frequently found in shounen manga. However, the Mangaverse version takes this further by reinterpreting the armor-man association into another classic icon, that of the super robot, which belongs to the Japanese *supersentai* [super group] genre. When the vehicles of the different members of the Avengers are joined together they form the "Ultimate Iron Man," a clear nod in the direction to their famous catchphrase, "Avengers, assemble!"[6]

Therefore, it can be stated that the first of the main features of the narrative of Mangaverse lies both in the appropriation of iconic elements of Japanese pop culture and in the reinterpretation (or deconstruction) of the identities of their most important characters. In this way, it fulfills one of the rules of serialized narrative, irrespective of the medium—the existence and maintenance of a social network. Understood as the set of personal relationships working as a

---

5 Establishing concrete references for the stories of any classic character is complicated because over the years many changes may take place; hence, many details of their biography are true only for a certain time. Even so, classic publishers such as Marvel and DC have published different guides to their stories and characters over the years. The information given here on The Hulk can be found in *The Official Handbook of the Marvel Universe* (1985a, 62–4).

6 In Mangaverse: *Avengers Assemble!* (2002) and *Marvel Mangaverse: Infinite Twilight* (2002).

Figure 9.1 The Hulk's transcreation in Mangaverse makes an explicit reference to *tokusatsu* cinema products such as the film *Godzilla* (1954). From *Mangaverse: Eternity Twilight* (2002) © Marvel

background for all the characters' motivations and attitudes, the social network, ultimately, causes the extension of the narrative. However, this social network and, therefore, the rest of the narrative are united around a small group of characters.

Forms of Adaptation/Transculturalization

In the American comic book, where the series are a product of collaborations between different groups of scriptwriters, cartoonists, colorists, and letterers, each team of professionals undertakes a task of adaptation each time a new installment of the series is made. The existence of different teams working on the same story (often even on the same story arc) explains the constant pace of publication and the increasingly elaborate finish on the product. So, the debut of a new artist or a new scriptwriter during some installments of the series allows time to be given to the professionals to work properly on subsequent episodes. These replacements are usually more obvious in the visual treatment of the series than in other aspects of the narrative, which is why it is normal for radically different aesthetic treatments coexist in the same story, albeit in different episodes.

Understanding these replacements as ways of adapting makes it possible to learn more about the complexity and the heterogeneous nature of the medium of comics. As often occurs with other serialized media such as television series, soap operas, or radio series, each new professional who is incorporated into the series can carry out important changes to the narrative. This creative process must respect the presence of elements recognized by the audience, because as with other genres, the public experiences pleasure in anticipating the result (Altman and British Film Institute 1999, 151). These changes are combined with other more innovative elements, differentiating a series from other similar products. These constant processes of copying and modification require the work of a manager (e.g. chief editor), who safeguards the overarching continuity and coherence of the story. Therefore, adaptation, understood as an exercise in intertextuality, would be the basic principle of all serialized narratives.

In the case of the Marvel products of the Mangaverse imprint, the processes of adaptation occur on different levels. In this sense, although there is a process of continuity between the first series of two issues and the rest of the imprint's comic books, it is their relationship with the regular Marvel series which attracts the most attention. Some authors have previously described Mangaverse using the term "transcreation" (Jenkins 2009; Stein 2013). This concept in fact comes from the creators of *Spider-Man India* who introduce the reinvention of the character by combining meanings shared by both Hindu and Hindu-American audiences (Saffell 2007, 265). Nevertheless, simply assuming that the underlying processes in the creation of both products are similar may be a slightly superficial assessment. For example, one of the problems that the transcreation of Spider-Man faces is the search for elements which can be more strictly identified as Hindu, a problem which is normally resolved by resorting to stereotypes (Davé 2013). In the case of Mangaverse, however, it is not difficult to find signifiers which can be understood as Japanese and/or belonging to the visual culture of manga and anime.

The difference between both products lies in the fact that, in the case of anime, the mechanics of identification with the audience are not based on a national identity but rather on the use of a cultural capital formed by the most famous products of manga and anime in the American market. A process of adaptation by colonization could therefore be spoken about in which the interest of the producers for particular sorts of foreign material has motivated the appropriation and reinterpretation of their main narrative elements (Leitch 2007, 110). Therefore, the various authors of the imprint—particularly Ben Dunn, creator of the first two miniseries—establish multiple references to

Figure 9.2 Hank Pym's transcreation in Mangaverse resembles the most iconic of Akira Toriyama's characters Goku, from *Dragon Ball* (1984–95). From *Mangaverse: Eternity Twilight* (2002) © Marvel

Japanese popular culture by means of the mechanisms of allusion. These are recognizable in the narrative but also, more obviously, in the visual design of the characters themselves.

The reinterpretation of Namor, Prince of Atlantis in *Mangaverse: Eternity Twilight* (2002), could be seen to be an example of this form of allusion. Namor had always been an ambiguous character, due to his proud and independent personality. This has allowed him to take on the roles of both the villain and the temporary ally (Marvel Comics Group 1985b). It was not surprising that the character had the function of antagonist in this story arc, even in the way in which the character was reinterpreted. It was obvious that the design of Ben Dunn in this issue made numerous references to *Dragon Ball Z* (1989–96), based on the manga of Akira Toriyama, which has become one of the most successful anime series in the world, including within the American market.

Namor, for example, was redesigned following the character of Vegeta, one of the most charismatic antagonists in the history of anime. Both possess a similar temperament and they perform the same functions of antagonist and occasional ally in their respective narrative worlds. The similarity with the anime character is reinforced through the adaptation of Baron Strucker, one of the classic bad guys, who was repositioned as Namor's henchman and has a very similar physical appearance to Nappa, Vegeta's bodyguard. Other anime characters could be clearly seen in the pages of Mangaverse. However, it is of more interest to clarify the sense and way in which this appropriation was executed. The inclusion of these characters was carried out arbitrarily, transferred from different products to a new text. Nevertheless, in doing so, they did not lose their ability to evoke meanings for a certain audience. With regard to the relationships of intertextuality established between *Mangaverse: Eternity Twilight* (2002) and *Dragon Ball Z* (1989–96), the aim of the author seems to be that of appealing to the audience's memory through the usual formulae of shounen manga, most particularly in the elaborate scenes of fighting and martial arts. Ultimately, the adopted aesthetic seems exaggerated and has a sense of parody. This serves as a reminder that both "parody and pastiche" are closely related forms of "adaptation" (Leitch 2007, 110).

Conclusion

As has been demonstrated throughout this chapter, the medium of comics can be a good example for the study of internationalization—understood as international production and distribution—and transcultural hybridization. A brief summary of the history of the medium in Japan and the US, two of the most important producers and markets in the medium of comics, illustrates the global circulation and hybrid quality of much of contemporary comic book culture. The imprint Mangaverse (2002–06) in particular illustrates these trends in two ways: firstly, via the deconstruction of its own collective imagination, particularly of the characters of the Marvel franchise, and secondly, by examining the appropriation of elements of manga and anime culture through different processes of adaptation from elements of Japanese pop culture, including colonization, pastiche, and parody. In essence, Mangaverse uses the classic formula of *What If?*, a collection started by Marvel in the 1970s that introduced new versions of their characters by altering their story. This formula added interest by appealing to new audiences of manga fans through the evocation of shared meanings, superhero background stories. These processes of alteration and rewriting are widely shared by other recent products from the franchise that have been referred as "transcreations" (Jenkins 2009, 11; Davé 2013).

Marvel's unceasing quest to cash in on manga and anime audiences has also been echoed in other products such as the imprint Tsunami (2003), a project that was launched between the two versions of Mangaverse. This project was no more successful than its predecessor, though some of their most successful collections (*New Mutants*, *Runaways*) were reintroduced into the publisher's other regular imprints. Furthermore, Marvel, which since the 1990s has also been a multimedia group, has developed other international products such as anime versions of their most successful characters in collaboration with the Japanese producer Madhouse. These include the *Iron Man* (2010), *Wolverine* (2011), *X-Men* (2011) and *Blade* (2011) series. Such productions are themselves worthy of another case study and strongly suggest that future collaborations of this kind will continue to exist between the US and Japan.

References

Altman, Rick, and British Film Institute. 1999. *Film/Genre*. London: BFI Publishing.

Alverson, Brigid. 2013. "Manga 2013: A Smaller, More Sustainable Market." *Publishers Weekly*, April 5.

Beaty, Bart. 2010. "The Recession and the American Comic Book Industry: From Inelastic Cultural Good to Economic Integration." *Popular Communication: The International Journal of Media and Culture, Theory and Critique* 8 (3): 203–7. doi: 10.1080/15405702.2010.493421.

Brienza, Casey. 2009. "Paratexts in Translation: Reinterpreting 'Manga' for the United States." *The International Journal of the Book* 6 (2): 13–20.

Cohn, Neil. 2010. "Japanese Visual Language: The Structure of Manga." In *Manga: An Anthology of Global and Cultural Perspectives*, edited by Toni Johnson-Woods, 187–203. New York: Continuum.

Davé, Shilpa. 2013. "Spider-Man India: Comic Books and the Translating/Transcreating of American Cultural Narratives." In *Transnational Perspectives on Graphic Narrative: Comics at the Crossroads*, edited by Shane Denson, Christina Meyer and Daniel Stein, 127–44. London: Bloomsbury.

During, Simon. 1997. "Popular Culture on a Global Scale: A Challenge for Cultural Studies?" *Critical Inquiry* 23 (4): 808–33.

Duus, Peter. 2001. "Presidential Address: Weapons of the Weak, Weapons of the Strong—The Development of the Japanese Political Cartoon." *The Journal of Asian Studies* 60 (4): 965–97.

Eisner, Will, Frank Miller, and Charles Brownstein. 2005. *Eisner/Miller: A One-on-One Interview Conducted by Charles Brownstein*. Milwaukie, OR: Dark Horse Books.

Gabilliet, Jean-Paul. 2010. *Of Comics and Men: A Cultural History of American Comic Books*. Translated by Beaty Beaty and Nick Nguyen. Jackson, MI: University Press of Mississippi.

Gill, Tom. 1998. "Transformational Magic: Some Japanese Superheroes and Monsters." In *The Worlds of Japanese Popular Culture: Gender, Shifting Boundaries and Global Cultures*, edited by Dolores P. Martinez, 33–55. Cambridge: Cambridge University Press.

Hess, Stephen, and Sandy Northrop. 2011. *American Political Cartoons. The Evolution of a National Identity, 1754–2010*. 2nd edition. Piscataway, NJ: Transaction Publishers.

Holmberg, Ryan. 2011. "Emonogatari in the Age of Comics, 1948–1957." *The Comics Journal*. http://www.tcj.com/emonogatari-in-the-age-of-comics-1948-1957.

Jenkins, Henry. 2009. "'Just Men in Tights': Rewriting Silver Age Comics in an Era of Multiplicity." In *The Contemporary Comic Book Superhero*, edited by Angela Ndalianis, 16–43. London: Routledge.

Kidd, Chip, Geoff Spear, and Saul Ferris. 2008. *Bat-Manga! The Secret History of Batman in Japan*. New York: Pantheon.

Kinsella, Sharon. 2000. *Adult Manga: Culture and Power in Contemporary Japanese Society*. Honolulu: University of Hawai'i Press.

Lang, Jeffrey S. and Patrick Trimble. 2004. "Whatever Happened to the Man of Tomorrow? An Examination of the American Monomyth and the Comic Book Superhero." *The Journal of Popular Culture* 22 (3): 157–73.

Leitch, Thomas. 2007. *Film Adaptation & Its Discontents: From Gone with the Wind to The Passion of the Christ*. Baltimore: The Johns Hopkins University Press.

Lopes, Paul. 2009. *Demanding Respect: The Evolution of the American Comic Book*. Philadelphia: Temple University Press.

Marvel Comics Group. 1985a. "Gardener to the Hulk (The Hulk)." *The Official Handbook of the Marvel Universe (Deluxe Edition)* 2 (5): 62–4.

Marvel Comics Group. 1985b. "Sif to Sunspot (Sub-Mariner)." *The Official Handbook of the Marvel Universe (Deluxe Edition)* 2 (12): 55–7.

McCloud, Scott. 1993. *Understanding Comics: The Invisible Art*. New York: HarperCollins.

Mikhailova, Yulia. 2008. "Intellectuals, Cartoons, and Nationalism during the Russo-Japanese War." In *Japanese Visual Culture: Explorations in the World of Manga and Anime*, edited by Mark W. MacWilliams, 155–76. Armonk, NY: M.E. Sharpe.

Nash, Eric Peter. 2009. *Manga Kamishibai: The Art of Japanese Paper Theater*. New York: Abrams Comicarts.

O'Rourke, Dan, and Pravin A. Rodrigues. 2007. "The 'Transcreation' of a Mediated Myth: Spider-Man in India." In *The Amazing Transforming Superhero!: Essays on the Revision of Characters in Comic Books, Film and Television*, edited by Terrence R. Wandtke, 112–28. Jefferson, NC: McFarland & Co.

Publishers Weekly. 2007. "Graphic Novels By the Numbers," March 5. http://www.publishersweekly.com/pw/print/20070305/4192-graphic-novels-by-the-numbers.html.

Ryan, Marie-Laure. 2004. "Introduction." In *Narrative across Media: The Languages of Storytelling*, edited by Marie-Laure Ryan, 1–40. Lincoln: University of Nebraska Press.

Saffell, Steve. 2007. *Spider-Man the Icon: The Life and Times of a Pop Culture Phenomenon*. London: Titan.

Stein, Daniel. 2013. "Of Transcreations and Transpacific Adaptations: Investigating Manga Versions of Spider-Man." In *Transnational Perspectives on Graphic Narrative: Comics at the Crossroads*, edited by Shane Denson, Christina Meyer and Daniel Stein, 145–62. London: Bloomsbury.

Wright, Bradford W. 2003. *Comic Book Nation: The Transformation of Youth Culture in America*. 2nd edition. Baltimore: The John Hopkins University Press.

Chapter 10
Pinoy Manga in Philippine *Komiks*

Karl Ian Uy Cheng Chua and Kristine Michelle Santos

Philippine *komiks* (comics) have been around since the 1920s and have entertained generations of Filipinos with epic stories of heroes defeating their adversaries and heartwarming tales of local life. The visual styles of *komiks* also vary. Tony Velasquez's iconic Filipino man, *Kenkoy*, had a cartoon-like flair akin to *Blondie*, while the local superman, *Captain Barbell* by Mars Ravelo, had hyperrealist visuals mimicking the style of Jack Kirby.

To a degree, Philippine *komiks* have always been highly associated with American culture, since they date back to the American occupation of the Philippines. There is an inherent understanding that *komiks* are a byproduct of American colonial life. The ease in which *komiks* became an integral form of entertainment during the Philippines of the post-World War II period reflects the willingness of local society to accept and absorb American culture. In fact, cultural historians consider the immediate postwar success of local *komiks* to be the Golden Age of Philippine *komiks*. This eagerness to learn and succeed in all things American takes its roots in Philippine society's drive to be considered equals by their former colonizers. This too is seen in the locally noted successes of particular *komiks* artists in the American comics industry, such as Alfredo P. Alcala, who illustrated *Conan the Barbarian* (1982–89); Whilce Portacio, who became a co-founder of Image Comics in 1992; and Gerry Alanguilan, who has worked as an inker for Marvel comics since 1996.

In recent years, anime (Japanese animation) and manga (Japanese comics) have become so popular with young people that various local *komiks* publishers have considered shifting gears from the once hyperrealist visuals seen during the Golden Age of Philippine *komiks* to the more wide-eyed, tone-heavy aesthetics seen in Japanese manga. These works are called Pinoy[1] manga.

The growing popularity of this visual style has shifted the aesthetics of local comics, and it has raised debates about the identity of Philippine *komiks*—can

---

1 Editor's Note: The word "Pinoy" is an informal demonym referring to people of Filipino descent living both within the Philippines and abroad. Though sometimes still regarded as derogatory, the term has gained a measure of mainstream acceptance and is most commonly used in the context of popular entertainment to signal cultural and/or national identity.

one even consider Pinoy manga as Filipino? What space does Pinoy manga occupy in Philippine culture? When their works are heavily associated with Japan, a country with a fractured history with the Philippines, especially after World War II, will Pinoy manga ever be accepted or become as successful as *komiks* did? In this chapter, we examine the development of Pinoy manga as a *komiks* aesthetic in the Philippines; the challenges this comics movement has faced within the local *komiks* community; the space it is trying to generate for fans whose tastes and interests are shifting; and, finally, how Pinoy manga reflects the comic culture of the Philippines.

A Brief History of Philippine *Komiks*

Several scholars have written histories of the Philippine *komiks* industry, with the earliest being *A History of Komiks of the Philippines and Other Countries* (Marcelino 1985a). Comics scholar John A. Lent has since built upon this work in *The First One Hundred Years of Philippine Komiks and Cartoons* (Lent 2009) and more recently in *Southeast Asian Cartoon Art: History, Trends and Problems* (Lent 2014). These three texts have all defined *komiks* as comics made in the Philippines by local artists.

These works would also narrate a distinctive history of Philippine *komiks*, firstly by identifying its origins with the national hero, Dr Jose P. Rizal. His first work was *Ang Buhay ni Pagong at Matsing* [The Lives of the Monkey and the Turtle], an illustrated Spanish translation of a popular folk tale. Rizal's works manifest a variety of styles, from picture stories, which combine an illustration on top and dialogue at the bottom, to a proto-comic which combines the two, but within a panel. But as these were meant as personal gifts for friends, his work did not have the large reach or influence necessary inspire an entire comics industry. That said, historians still consider his proto-comics work essential in associating Filipino *komiks* with the Philippine identity, by associating the act of comics making to taking part of the nationalist movement.

All of these histories would agree, however, that the title of "Father of Filipino *Komiks*" should be bestowed upon Antonio "Tony" S. Velasquez. Velasquez was working as an illustrator for *Liwayway*, a Tagalog language weekly magazine. *Liwayway*'s editor-in-chief, Chino Roces, approached Velasquez to work with Romualdo Reyes on a comic to be published in the pages of *Liwayway*. The two men created the first serialized and commercially published *komik* entitled *Mga Kabalbalan ni Kenkoy* [The Misadventures of Kenkoy]. This two-page *komik* was created during the American Occupation (1899–1946), a time where there was an influx of Western, particularly American, culture to the Philippines.

Kenkoy, the main character, was a man who lived with the modern times and dressed in the most fashionable Western-style suit, setting his hair with pomade like Americans did. Kenkoy was the man who "walked the talk," the representation of a Filipino who adapted to this new culture and embraced the English language despite his inability to pronounce things correctly. *Kenkoy* was an enormous success and became the first long running *komik* in the Philippines.

However, Velasquez is not deemed the "Father of Filipino *Komiks*" because of *Kenkoy* alone. Velasquez also helped fellow *komiks* artists find a space to publish their works in the succeeding *komiks* magazines he managed (Marcelino 1985, 11–12). After the war, on November 15, 1946, the magazine *Halakhak Komiks* was published under the leadership of Velasquez. It was a 40-page weekly and, unlike *Liwayway*, it became the first magazine dedicated solely to *komiks*. It contained one-page *komiks* and four-page serialized *komiks* drawn in the American style. Unfortunately, this *komiks* magazine was short-lived, lasting just ten issues.

Afterwards, Velasquez was offered management of a company that would specialize in publishing *komiks* magazines, continuing the legacy of *Halakhak Komiks*. Thus was the largest *komik* book publisher in the Philippines established in 1947 as Ace Publications. Its first serialized title, launched on June 14, 1947, was named *Pilipino Komiks* and had an initial print run of 10,000 copies. At its peak, ten years after its launch, the new issues would be released in print runs of up to 120,000 copies. This success encouraged Velasquez to publish five more titles for the company, which included *Tagalog Klasiks*, begun in 1949, *Hiwaga Komiks* in 1950, *Espesyal Komiks* in 1952, *Kenkoy Komiks* in 1959, and finally *Education Klasiks Komiks* in 1962. Ace Publications would follow the format of its predecessor *Halakhak* by compiling several *komiks* strips and *komiks* serials in the same 38–42 page American style comic book. But even with the success of its titles, the company was eventually forced to close in 1962 (Villegas 2005).

Despite the closure of Ace Publications, investors did not want to leave this profitable market. Velasquez was once again contacted, this time to manage the Graphic Arts Services Incorporated (GASI), on August 1, 1962. The titles released by GASI include *Kislap Komiks* in September 1962, *Pioneer Komiks* in October 1962, *Aliwan Komiks* in January 1963, *Pinoy Klasiks* in August 1963, *Holiday Komiks* in September 1963, and *Teens Weekly Komiks* in 1968. The company would suffer a stumbling block with the declaration of Martial Law in 1972 and the imposition of censorship laws. Nonetheless, it was able to survive and release new titles in 1982 such as *Nobela Klasiks, Kuwento Komiks* and *Damdam Komiks*. However, their success would ultimately be short-lived as these GASI titles would be canceled one by one, until the company would close shop in 1998 (Villegas 2007).

Several reasons have been attributed to the eventual collapse of *komiks* consumption. One was the advent of television; access to TV sets had become prevalent since the 1970s. Not only were movies available to a larger viewing public via the television, Japanese animation had begun to creep into Philippine television too, due to their cheap broadcasting costs. Lent (2009, 97–9) further adds that television has changed the habits of these consumers by creating a desire for immediate gratification from entertainment media. Thus, *komiks* consumers were no longer willing to wait for the next installment of a four-page serial *komik* which only came out once a month. To address this new demand, *komiks* were published biweekly. Yet this would prove to be counterproductive for the industry, as the speed of production necessitated by this new publishing schedule became more important than the quality of the works. As a consequence, artists quickly burned out, and consumers became ever more disillusioned with the medium.

In spite of the cancellation of popular titles and the closure of large publishing firms, there were still a number of popular titles in print after the Golden Age had undoubtedly ended. One was *Pilipino Funny Komiks*. This was first published in 1978 by Islas Filipinas Publishing Co., Inc., a subsidiary of Atlas Publishing, which was owned by the Roces family, the same group that owned the *Liwayway* magazine, *Halakhak Komiks*, Ace Publications, and GASI. Unlike its predecessors, which were primarily aimed at adults (although self-censorship by Philippine *komiks* artists allowed their works to be read by all ages), this title was published primarily for children. The last time this title was in print was for its 1405th issue in 2005 (Alanguilan 2008).

The "Death" of Filipino *Komiks*

The Golden Age of *komiks* did not last long, and *komiks* began to have a decreasing presence in the market. Indeed, a number of Filipinos have proclaimed the official "death" of Filipino *komiks* to have been in 1972 in various newspaper articles and online blogs (Barcelona 2009; Alanguilan 2010; Robles 2012). Marcelino credited the downfall of Filipino *komiks* to the influx of American comic book titles and the advent of new media, such as radio, television, movies (Marcelino 1985, 4–46). Lent (2004) would also include the advent of the internet as further competition to the *komiks* industry. Due to the measures implemented by the *komiks* publishing industry to survive, production costs were cut, leading to low wages for artists and the continued use of cheap materials (Lent 2004, 94–5).

Alanguilan (2010) has noted low quality paper and inks resulted in the publishing industry's low regard for, and investment in, *komiks* in general, and vendors, instead of selling their copies of *komiks*, would increase their profits by renting them at a cheaper price for three hours, which did not translate into income for the publishing companies (Flores 2008). National institutions, such as the National Library, moreover, found no value in preserving *komiks* for future generations.

An essay by Lawrence Mijares suggests a different underlying cause of the "death" of the industry, blaming the *komiks* publishing monopoly held by the Roces (Valiente and Salvador 2007, 52–6). Mijares states that the Roces family used their affiliates to corner the *komiks* market in terms of capacity to distribute throughout the Philippines. Hence, competitors had to match this burgeoning giant's distribution networks if they wanted to infiltrate the industry. So it came not as a surprise that the industry would seem to have died with the Roces' cancellation of their *komiks* publishing activities (Mijares 2004).

But did the industry really die? Marcelino (1985) and Lent (2004; 2009), as well as *komiks* artists themselves, focus on the "Golden Age" of the post-World War II period until 1972. This "Golden Age" was a period when *komiks* could sell between 20,000 to 120,000 copies per issue, and it was characterized by the market dominance of titles using American visual styles. It also coincides with the rise and fall of Ace and GASI. With the loss of these companies, there was no immediate rush of smaller companies attempting to fill the niche and continue their publications. Nonetheless, it could be said that the Roces-owned Ace and GASI paved the way for future iterations of *komiks* in the Philippines.

The Beginnings of Pinoy Manga

With *komiks* disappearing from bookstores and newsstands, and new media such as television becoming a staple in Philippine homes, many potential readers of *komiks* would sooner watch the next cartoon on the television than purchase or rent the latest comic. In the late 1970s, there was an influx of Japanese anime on Philippine television. Shows such as *Choudenji Mashiin Borutesu V* [Super Electromagnetic Machine Voltes Five] (1977–78), known as *Voltes V*, and *Mazinger Z* (1972–73) became increasingly popular with Philippine youth. When these shows were shown on local television, they were localized and dubbed in English, erasing the Japanese nature of these shows. Hence, many children were unaware of the cultural origins of these shows.

There were also growing concerns over the violent content in children's media. Television cartoons, and to a degree, *komiks*, were often viewed as entertainment for children. The action-filled stories of these mecha anime left an such indelible mark on children's memories that when President Ferdinand Marcos issued a presidential decree that banned them, even children felt adversely affected by the Martial Law of the 1970s (Fondevilla 2007, 445).

However, not all Japanese anime were banned from television. The likes of *Candy Candy* and *Sekai Meisaku Gekijou* [World Masterpiece Theater] were regularly broadcast. Similar to the earlier mecha anime, these were also dubbed either in English or Tagalog. After Marcos was ousted during the EDSA Revolution, which began in 1983 and culminated in 1986, many of the once banned shows, along with others were reintroduced on local television. A new generation of children was increasingly exposed to the visual aesthetics of Japanese anime. Meanwhile, the children who had once been robbed of their mecha anime became passionate in researching more about the origins of *Voltes V* and in this manner became some of the earliest Japanese pop culture enthusiasts. These people were crucial in the education of the younger generation of fans on the Japanese context of these shows and the world of Japanese culture.

Hence, by the time a local comedy show decided to use the opening theme of *Voltes V* in 1998 as part of a sketch that mimicked a local religious television show, there was a generation of fans who were able to understand the cultural connections between *Voltes V* and Japan. The nostalgia created a demand for the show, which encouraged a local television channel to repackage *Voltes V* not just as a cartoon but a *Japanese* cartoon, an anime. This generated attention from a new, younger generation of fans who were soon demanding more anime from local television stations and branded merchandise related to these shows. Various Japan-oriented university clubs were integral in proliferating information on these shows as well as introducing related goods such as Japanese manga (both in their original and in translated Chinese editions) to other people.

It is from these university clubs that some of the earliest Pinoy manga artists were inspired to create short zines which they sold at school fairs. The manga format opened up a world of artistic and thematic possibilities beyond the popular American comics format that demanded hyperealistic visuals, spandexed superheroes, and colored pages. Also, it was easier to produce because it was drawn mostly in black and white and was far cheaper to reproduce for consumption because it could be easily photocopied by a school copier.

A particular group of college friends were integral in steering the direction of *komiks* towards a more manga style. In 2000, Jescie Palabay and his college friends decided to publish *Culture Crash*, a bi-monthly comic magazine that integrated Filipino, Japanese, and American visual styles and themes. As Palabay noted in his editorial message in the first issue, "[T]his comic is a direct result of the crash of cultures that we have been exposed to. We've based our work standard on those already established by publishers in the U.S., Europe, and Japan, but still produce them in a very Filipino way. We try to retain that Filipino character at the very heart" (Palabay 2000).

Despite its cultural attempt to be an amalgamation of every comics culture that had influenced Filipinos, *Culture Crash* had very Japanese aesthetics and motifs. *Cat's Trail* had similarities to magical shounen manga adventures; *One Day Isang Diwa* [One Day, One Spirit] took inspiration from shoujo manga set in a school. *Pasig* had its similarities to Masamune Shirow's post-apocalyptic world, and *Solstice Butterfly* took inspiration from robot-themed stories. The only thing that *Culture Crash* did that took after American comics was that fact that every page was fully colored.

Culture Crash couldn't have come at a better time, as there was an increasing public demand for all things anime and manga. Initial success as a magazine eventually led to the production of three public conventions attended by

Figure 10.1 Elmer Damaso, "One Day Isang Diwa," *Culture Crash*, Volume 1, Issue #6 (2001)

thousands of fans of not only the magazine but of the cultures it tried to represent; clearly, manga as a visual style had become something that Filipinos could appreciate. It also pointed to the shifting tastes of youth people, increasingly divorced from the once revered *komiks* and American comics. Finally, *Culture Crash* paved the way for similar comics magazines such as *Questor* and *Mangaholix*, which followed the same format as *Culture Crash*. These magazines were the beginnings of Pinoy manga.

Pinoy Manga in *Komiks*

The popularity of both *Culture Crash* and *Mangaholix* raised controversial questions about the place of locally produced manga in Philippine *komiks*. One of Pinoy manga's strongest critics was local comics artist Gerry Alanguilan, who felt that manga had such a specific artistic style that it was heavily tied to Japanese identity. As such, he felt that it was "inappropriate" for Filipino artists to use a manga style for their comics; Filipino artists ought to be creating comics which are uniquely Filipino. Alanguilan saw Pinoy manga as unoriginal. He then added that, if anything, the Pinoy manga experience should jumpstart a quest to seek the identity of Philippine *komiks* (Alanguilan 2007). In Michael Turda's assessment of manga and its place in Philippine comics, he felt that Philippine *komiks* was immersed in realism, and the cartoonish and wide-eyed aesthetic of Pinoy manga did not capture that realism (Turda 2007).

Alanguilan and Turda's arguments against manga may reflect differing levels of cultural exposure among local readers. American comics are highly available in the Philippines, and most local comic readers are more knowledgeable about the American comics scene than they are about Japanese comics. These two artists also identify specific aesthetics of manga that are accurate for only a small portion of all manga. If anything, this reflects their lack of familiarity with the medium, particularly with how diverse manga is. Scott McCloud's *Understanding Comics* shows the diversity of comics by illustrating the pictorial vocabulary of comics. In this vocabulary, McCloud demonstrates how comics artists can represent reality or concepts, and in both cases, manga artists move freely in between realistic and conceptual art styles and are just as diverse as American and European artists (McCloud 1994, 52–3). Rather than understanding manga as a medium or a format in which comics are published in Japan, most local artists perceive manga as a visual artistic style, or a "group style" as Alanguilan (2007) would call it.

Perhaps one could say that Alanguilan and Turda's generalizations also reflected the access Filipinos have to manga. Compared to other countries in Southeast Asia (e.g. Indonesia and Thailand), the Philippines does not have a well-developed local publishing industry for translated manga. Instead, most consumers rely on imported English-translated manga. Those who are able to read Japanese can just import manga directly from Japan.

The arguments of these local artists against manga also inspired Pinoy manga artists to speak out about their craft and to contribute to the discussion on Pinoy manga and their deliberate choice to use manga aesthetics. Melvin Calingo is one of *Culture Crash*'s artists, the creator of *Pasig*. Calingo tries to define a Filipino *komik* as a comic written for Filipino audiences, regardless of the style in which an artist chooses to write his comic or even the nationality of the comics creator. He cites the importance of capturing the vernacular language in recognizing the identity of a Filipino *komik* (Calingo 2007). Also opposed to Alanguilan's opinion of manga as a threat to Filipino creativity and comics, Emil Flores believes that Pinoy manga reflects the hybridity of Filipino culture, highlighting the ability of locals to incorporate and adapt to particular cultures and fusing it with their own (Flores 2004, 52). Elbert Or spoke of how a manga style's simplicity also made it easier to conceptualize a character, as it allowed him to generate characters without having to worry about particular racial features. In contrast to realistic illustrations used in comics, "manga style" as interpreted by local artists gave them freedom to explore various aesthetics outside of styles that were already prevalent in the local scene (Fondevilla 2007, 448).

The arguments and disagreements surrounding Pinoy manga and its place within Philippine *komiks* could be viewed as a microcosm of the debates that surround Philippine identity. Given the long history of the Philippines as a country colonized or occupied by countries such as Spain, the United States, and Japan, local individuals, communities, and institutions sometimes feel a great need to identify things as concretely Filipino.

In the case of Philippine *komiks*, scholars have long identified the *komiks* published during the Golden Age of *komiks* as concretely and inherently Filipino in nature, glossing over *komiks*' debt to American culture. To a degree, one could think of this as an overlooked matter, but at the same time one could interpret this as the capacity of scholars to represent an inherent, almost "organic nature," to Philippine culture, as though it is within the innate, natural capacity of Filipinos to produce something of equal greatness to the Americans. That is why there was a need to attribute comic art to the Philippine national hero, Jose Rizal. Moreover, there was a need to remind people that comics flourished during the American occupation and that *komiks* are a legacy of that time. Hence, there is a strong impetus within some parts of the local comics community to protect the perceived greatness the *komiks* industry had by retaining the American connection to *komiks*.

The coming of manga to the local comics scene poses a threat to this American connection. Japan, of course, did not make the best first impression with the local community. The Japanese occupation of the Philippines during

World War II has still left its scars. Japanese popular culture has also become notorious for its violence, as seen in the earlier presidential ban of Japanese mecha anime. There are also various social issues linked with Japan which suggest a looming negativity associated with the country. Thus, to some, incorporating manga within Philippine *komiks* culture was like rubbing salt on an open wound. It seemed to reflect the ignorance and neglectful attitude of the younger generation, who have little care for the history and identity of Philippine *komiks*. Given this situation, it is interesting to note how scholars such as Flores (2004; 2008) have used the term "Pinoy manga" to distinguish it as a completely different medium from Philippine *komiks*.

The Future of Pinoy Manga in Philippine *Komiks*

By 2000 onwards, interest in anime and manga had grown immensely, giving birth to an anime boom in the Philippines. Not only was there an influx of anime and manga goods into the market but there were also a growth of various communities and events that celebrated these media. This boom continued for the next few years and was beneficial to the growth of magazines such as *Culture Crash*, *Questor*, *Mango Jam*, and *Mangaholix*.

In her study of Pinoy manga, Kahori Sakasai noted that to a degree this was a byproduct of the globalization of manga and anime and that the appropriation of these works locally served as a step toward bringing these Japanese media closer to home (Sakasai 2006, 17–19). One could look at it as the Filipinization of manga as the medium reached Philippine shores. However, unlike other countries where manga finds its way to the market as a localized translated text, Pinoy manga is the next best thing that locals have to seeing something similar to manga in the vernacular.

That said, as with every fad, even interest in these local magazines faded. The decision to end the publication of *Culture Crash* due to financial reasons was the beginning of the end of commercially published Pinoy manga magazines (Lent 2014). The reach these magazines had been mostly within the Manila metropolitan area. Local bookstores did not have any system to facilitate wider distribution for comics, and it was left to the publishers to find a way to distribute their magazines in various bookstores. Thus, it was difficult for publishers to reach provinces that were outside of the Luzon area—and even more so to expand their audience well outside of the orbit of the capital. Bookstores had always had difficulty in categorizing local *komiks*; Pinoy manga were an even worse situation. These works were dispersed between the graphic novel sections, Filipiniana, manga, children's literature, and so on. The miscategorization of many Philippine *komiks* and manga made it difficult for fans to find these works and to easily identify them for possible purchase in those stores which did carry them.

Apart from distribution, another issue behind the crash of Pinoy manga magazines was the competition it had with other forms of media, particularly the internet, which provided fans access (both legally and illegally) to English-translated Japanese anime and manga. This access also meant that local fans began to finally distinguish the difference between locally produced manga and manga from Japan. The aforementioned discussions on nationalistic issues surrounding Pinoy manga and Philippine *komiks* did not help strengthen the interest in these magazines, either. There were also economic factors that weakened the purchasing power of their audiences. Given all of this trouble, the manga magazines started to fold.

However, this did not mean the end of Pinoy manga. Instead, artists turned to other formats. The graphic novel is considered by Lent (2014) to be the saving grace of Philippine *komiks*. Rather than releasing weekly or monthly serials in stores, many artists such as Carlo Vergara (*Ang Kagilagilalas na Pakikipagsapalaran ni Zsazsa Zaturnnah* [The Amazing Adventures of Zshazsha Zaturnnah]), Budjette Tan (*Trese: Murder on Balete Drive*), and Gerry Alanguilan (*Wasted* and *Elmer*) prefer to publish their works as completed graphic novels. This trend is also seen in Pinoy manga titles such as *Love Is in a Bag* and *Angel Crush* by Ace Vitangcol.

Despite this growing trend, the publication of local graphic novels can be a little tricky. Most artists rely on connections with *komiks* publishers such as Visprint, Inc. When these are inaccessible, many turn to self-publishing. A great number of *komiks*, particularly Pinoy manga, are sold in various comics events and conventions. Many artists who sell their manga in these events often group together with their friends to either publish an anthology or illustration of their work as a studio. These smaller conventions have been helpful for smaller independent anthologies such as *Oh No! Manga* and *Ice Cream Studio*, as they became a reliable source not only for an audience but for a community which can support their craft. In the case of *Ice Cream Studio*, which is based outside of the capital, they take the opportunity to connect with their readers in person through these events. That said, manga still has a fairly limited reach in these events, as they are often based in Manila and have an attendance not exceeding 20,000 people.

Alternatively, some Pinoy manga artists have chosen to look towards American publishers to get jobs related to manga. Artists such as Elmer Damaso (*Cat's Trail, One Day Isang Diwa*) has also published manga titles such as *Ninja Diaries, Unearthly*, and—especially notable—a remake of Tatsuo Yoshida's *Mach GoGoGo* (or *Speed Racer* in the West) for Seven Seas. Kriss Sison, known for his *Mangaholix* work, *Ninja Girl Ko*, also followed after Elmer Damaso and worked with Seven Seas to illustrate *Amazing Agent Jennifer* and *Last Hope*. Tintin Pantoja,

Figure 10.2 Enjelicious, "Looking for a Better Boyfriend," *Oh No! Manga* (April 2012)

a Filipino artist, has also actively published works such as *Hamlet: The Manga Edition*, *Manga Math Mysteries*, and more recently, *Who Is AC?* with Hope Larson. While one would think that this presence of Filipino manga artists in American manga publishing would merit some of the same accolades that Filipino comics artists routinely get for working with DC or Marvel, these published manga artists get little acclaim for their *manga* work overseas because, unlike American comics, their works are mostly unavailable in local bookstores.

While many Pinoy manga artists aspire to get their works in print, to be read and consumed by locals in hard copy, other artists turn online. Webcomics have been an interesting development in comics publishing in recent years. For local artists who have little upfront personal funding to publish their works, let alone the connections to get a publisher to look their way, the webcomic has become a platform for creativity that allows them to actively create comics without being bound by editorial demands and deadlines. To a degree, putting up a webcomic online allows an artist to have a larger global reach. As such, artists such as Kevin Libranda, who publishes his manga *Novus Karma* via comic portals such as Ink Blazers, has a loyal set of readers from all over the globe. Artists such as CinnamonRub, who specialize in BL and yaoi-themed comics, also prefer publishing online as the internet is usually more liberal in its collective handling of, and response to, sexual themes and topics. Michael David, creator of *Kubori Kikiam*, also looked to online bookstores such as Amazon as a place to distribute his comics. Not only does he have a fervent following locally for his work; now he has been gaining a following in Germany and France, too.

Webcomics are an interesting new space for Pinoy manga artists to exercise creative freedom. The online medium has also given these artists a larger global audience. That said, unlike earlier works, many of these artists do not make an effort to fully promote their work at local conventions. Hence, they hardly have any presence within the local fan community and continue to be divorced from the *komiks* scene.

Conclusion

The story of Pinoy manga in the Philippine *komiks* scene is a story of difference—the kind that diversifies aesthetics, generates new artistic spaces, and expands the world of Philippine *komiks*, proving that the industry is not yet "dead." However, this very difference also creates a divide, and rather than embracing Pinoy manga as part of the local *komiks* scene, it has isolated a local community whose tastes in comics have departed from the substance and styles popular during the Golden Age of *komiks*.

Furthermore, Pinoy manga is a reflection of the country's postcolonial struggle as it tries to continue to shape its own distinctive identity as a nation.

As more cultures continue to affect and influence artists and their patrons, as was the case with Pinoy manga, the bastions of Philippine *komiks* raise their defenses to protect what they feel truly counts as Filipino *komiks*. As such, the Philippine comics industry is a case of an artistic medium in limbo, similar to how, to a degree, the national identity has always been in limbo. Perhaps someday Pinoy manga as a category of comics of lesser status will cease to exist, and it will be fully incorporated into and recognized by the Philippine comics community. When that day comes, perhaps Philippine *komiks* supporters will finally recognize that the shape and identity of Philippine comics has always relied upon a hybrid culture and aesthetic.

References

Alanguilan, Gerry. 2007. "Filipino Comic Artist and Manga." In *Komiks Sa Paningin Ng Mga Tagakomiks* [Komiks in the View of Komik Creators], edited by Randy Valiente and Fermin Salvador, 98–105. Manila: Central Book Supply, Inc.

Alanguilan, Gerry. 2008. "Funny Komiks Returns!" *Komikero Dot Com*, August 15. http://gerry.alanguilan.com/archives/640.

Alanguilan, Gerry. 2010. "Philippine Comics: Struggling or Not?" *Komikero Dot Com*, November 3. http://gerry.alanguilan.com/archives/2888.

Barcelona, Noel Sales. 2009. "The Comics Wars." *Bulatlat*, May 9. http://bulatlat.com/main/2009/05/09/the-comics-wars/.

Calingo, Melvin. 2007. "Filipino Komiks and Everything in Between." In *Komiks Sa Paningin Ng Mga Tagakomiks* [Komiks in the View of Komik Creators], edited by Randy Valiente and Fermin Salvador, 107–12. Manila: Central Book Supply, Inc.

Damaso, Elmer. 2001. "One Day, Isang Diwa [One Day, One Spirit]." *Culture Crash Comics*, September.

Enjelicious. 2012. "Looking for a Better Boyfriend." *Oh No! Manga*, April.

Flores, Emil M. 2004. "Comics Crash: Filipino Komiks and the Quest for Cultural Legitimacy." *Journal of English Studies and Comparative Culture* 7 (1): 46–58.

Flores, Emil M. 2008. "The Death and Life of the Komiks." *Azrael's Merryland*, February 11. http://azraelsmerryland.blogspot.jp/2008/02/death-and-life-of-komiks.html.

Fondevilla, Herbeth. 2007. "Contemplating the Identity of Manga in the Philippines." *International Journal of Comic Art* 9 (2): 441–53.

Lent, John A. 2004. "From 1928 to 1993: The First 75 Years of Philippine Komiks." *Comic Book Artist* 2 (4): 74–95.

Lent, John A. 2009. *The First One Hundred Years of Philippine Komiks and Cartoons*. Tagaytay City: Yonzon Associates.

Lent, John A., ed. 2014. *Southeast Asian Cartoon Art: History, Trends and Problems*. Kindle edition. Jefferson, NC: McFarland & Co.

Marcelino, Ramon R., ed. 1985. *A History of Komiks of the Philippines and Other Countries*. Manila: Islas Filipinas.

McCloud, Scott. 1994. *Understanding Comics: The Invisible Art*. Reprint edition. New York: HarperCollins.

Mijares, Lawrence M. 2004. "What Really Killed the Filipino Komiks Industry." *Siklab*, May.

Palabay, Jescie James. 2000. "Culture Crash Comics ... Messages from the Editor." *Culture Crash Comics*, August.

Robles, Joms. 2012. "Rise and Fall of Komiks." *Panel Magazine*, March 20. http://panelmag.wordpress.com/2012/03/20/rise-and-fall-of-komiks.

Sakasai, Kahori. 2006. "Manga and Pinoy Komiks: Repeated Adaptations of Globalization." Tokyo University.

Turda, Michael. 2007. "To Draw or Not to Draw Manga." In *Komiks Sa Paningin Ng Mga Tagakomiks* [Komiks in the View of Komik Creators], edited by Randy Valiente and Fermin Salvador, 113–14. Manila: Central Book Supply, Inc.

Villegas, Dennis. 2007. "PilipinoKomiks: GASI: The Rise and Fall of a Komiks Giant." *Pilipino Komiks*, August 19. http://pilipinokomiks.blogspot.jp/2007/08/gasithe-rise-and-fall-of-komiks-giant.html.

Index

Page numbers referring to illustrations are marked in **bold**.

24 Nen Gumi [Year 24 Group] 147, 152–3

Abrademi, *see* Associação Brasileira de Desenhistas de Mangá e Ilustrações [Brazilian Association of Manga and Illustration Artists]
Ace Publications 187–8, 189
Acme (publishing house) 49
adaptation 3, 33–4, 97, 100, 140–43, 174–5, 178–82, 195
ADV 1
Afternoon (magazine) 122
Ahmed, Maaheen 12
Alanguilan, Gerry 188, 192, 195
Alexander, Jeffrey C. 96–7
Amazing Agent Jennifer 195
Amazon Kindle 1, 39
AnimaniA 85, 156
Anime Expo 109
Anime News Network 98, 103–8
Animexx.de 85
AniWay 80
Antarctic Press 35, 97
Aoi House 98
Appadurai, Arjun 78
Arnold, Adam 98, 104, 106
Associação Brasileira de Desenhistas de Mangá e Ilustrações [Brazilian Association of Manga and Illustration Artists] 48
Astley, Jill 41, 99

Aurita, Aurelia 117, 125
Aurora Publishing 1, 37
avant-garde 12, 119, 128–9
Aventuras de Tupãzinho, As [Adventures of Tupãzinho, the] 46–7, 53
Azuma, Hiroki 78, 107

Bae, Catherine Yoonah 152
Bainbridge, Jason 11
Bakuman 101
Bandai 1
bande dessinée/BD 13, 116, 168–9, 171
Barbucci, Alessandro 80
Barefoot Gen 84, 97, 151
Barfuß durch Hiroshima [Barefoot through Hiroshima], *see Barefoot Gen*
Bari, Valéria 51
Batman 36, 170, 173–4
Beaty, Bart 115, 120, 169
Beauvoir, Simone de 163
Beedee (publishing house) 80
Berndt, Jaqueline 4
Bizenghast 36, 98
Black Butler 147, 153–4, 160
Blue Exorcist 153–4
Botting, Fred 159
Bouissou, Jean-Marie 4, 11, 149
Bourdieu, Pierre 108
boys' love/BL (genre) 1, 7, 9, 10, 12, 15, 26, 35, 37–8, 85–6, 98, 148, 197; *see also* gloBL; shounen ai; yaoi

Braga, Amaro 52
Brill, Dunja 154
Broccoli 1
Buffy the Vampire Slayer 57, 59

Calingo, Melvin 193
Canepa, Barbara 80
Carlsen Comics/Verlag 84–5, 151
Cat's Trail 190, 195
Cathedral Child 35
Certeau, Michel de 121
Chan, Queenie 2, 11, 98
Chao, Tien-yi 9
Chen, Yi-ching 9
Chico Bento Moço [Young Chico Bento] 53
Chin, Bertha 78
Chine: Régards Croisés [China: Viewpoints] 129
Choo, Kukhee 9
Choudenji Mashiin Borutesu V [Super Electromagnetic Machine Voltes Five] 189–90
Chromatic Press 11, 27, 40–43, **42**, 99
CLAMP 15, 34, 79, 81
Cloonan, Becky 36, 41–2, 98
CMX 1, 37, 97, 174, 176
Cohn, Neil 14, 167, 171, 176
Combo Rangers 49–50
 Combo Rangers – Somos Heróis [Combo Rangers – We Are Heroes] 50
Comiket 79
Comixology 39
Conrad (publishing house), *see* Acme (publishing house)
Cool Japan 5, 75–6
Corée: La Corée Vue par 12 Auteurs [Korea: Korea Viewed by 12 Authors] 129
cosplay 84, 110, 162
crowdfunding 38–9
Culture Crash 190–92, **191**, 194
Cwiertka, Katarzyna 75

Damaso, Elmer **191**, 195
Dark Horse 34, 55, 97
Davé, Shilpa 175, 179, 182
DC Comics 1, 26, 36, 37, 174
DeAngelis, Jason 98
Death: At Death's Door 55
Del Rey Manga 2, 11, 98
Delbressine, Marissa 81–3, **82**, 89
Delseit, Anne 86, **88**, 89, 153, 154, 156–7
Demonology 101 38
Denison, Rayna 76
deviantART 85, 157, 161
Diaz-Przybyl, Lillian 25, 40, 99
Digital Manga Publishing (DMP) 1, 35, 39
Dirty Pair 35, 97
Disney 76, 78, 109, 156
Distant Soil, a 97, 99
DJ Milky, *see* Levy, Stu
domestication, theory of 3–4
Doran, Colleen 66, 97
doujinshi 11, 31–3, 35, 77, 79–81, 86, 90, 135–8, **136**, 150, 151, 157–62
Dragon Ball 34, 84, 151, **180**, 181
DramaQueen 9
Dreaming, the 11, 98
Dungeons & Dragons 24, 51
Dunn, Ben 35, 55, 179, 181
During, Simon 173
Duus, Peter 168
dz-manga 13

East Coast Rising 36, 98
Eclipse Comics 35
Eco, Umberto 121
Editora JBC 50
Edrel 45, 47
Egmont Ehapa 85
Eisner Awards 2, 36, 38
Elfquest 97, 99
Estórias Adultas – Gibi Moderno [Adult Stories – Modern Comic Book] 47

INDEX

L'Événement Nouvelle Manga [The Nouvelle Manga Event] 117–19

fan art 80–81, 150; *see also* doujinshi
fandom 31–4, 36, 83, 85–6, 148
    politics of 108–12
    transcultural 77–8
Fanfare (publishing house) 119, 124
fanfiction 31–4, 43; *see also* doujinshi
fansubs 115
fantasyscape 78–9, 84–9, 90
female gaze 14, 25–7, 28, 30, 32, 34–6, 38, 40–43
Fireangels 85–9
Flores, Emil M. 188, 193, 194
Fondevilla, Herbeth 189, 193
Foucault, Michel 128
Four Immigrants Manga, the 70
Franco-Belgian comics, *see bande dessinée/BD*
Fruits Basket 1, 26, 34–5
fujoshi 48
Fukue, Mario 47
Fukue, Paulo 47

Gabilliet, Jean-Paul 173
Galbraith, Patrick W. 76
gekiga 9, 172
Gill, Tom 173
Gillain, Anne 126
Gillan, Jennifer 77, 78
Gladir, George 122–3
gloBL (genre) 10; *see also* boys' love/ BL (genre); shounen ai; yaoi
Go! Comi 1
Godzilla 177, **178**
Goffman, Erving 96
Gold Ring 12–13
Goong 9
Gothic Lolita 84, 147, 160
Grafipar Publishing 48
Graphic Arts Services Incorporated (GASI) 187–9
Gravett, Paul 115, 121, 122, 123

Groensteen, Thierry 115, 121, 122
Gueydan-Turek, Alexandra 13, 14
Guy Jeans 122–3

Hage, Anike 151, 154–6, 159
Hagio, Moto 34, 147
Halakhak Komiks 187–8
Hayles, N. Katherine 77
Hayley, Emma 11
Hernandez, Lea 35, 41–3
Hess, Stephen 168
Hicks, Faith Erin 38
Highmore, Ben 127
Hills, Matt 76, 78
Hitchcock Morimoto, Lori 78
Hitokiri 135–8, **136**
Hogle, Jerrold E. 148–9
Hokusai, Katsushika 149
Hollow Fields 11
Holy Avenger 49, 51–2
Hsu, Stacy 9
hybridity 55–6, 59, 83–4, 89, 111–12, 150, 169, 174–5, 176, 193, 198

ICv2 1, 42, 100
Ikoma, Fernando 47
Image Comics 138, 186
Ink Blazers 197
International Manga Award 10, 138
Iser, Wolfgang 121
Ito, Mizuko 76, 77
Ivy, Marilyn 75
Iwabuchi, Koichi 8

Japanese Visual Language (JVL) 14, 167, 171, 176
Japon: Le Japon Vu par 17 Auteurs [Japan: Japan Viewed by 17 Authors] 129
Jauss, Hans Robert 129
Jenkins, Henry 76, 77–8, 175, 179, 182
josei (genre) 7, 28, 34, 37
Jüngst, Heike 76, 151

Kabalbalan ni Kenkoy, mga [Misadventures of Kenkoy, the] 186
kaiju 55, 66, 69
Kamm, Björn-Ole 148
Kaulfersch, Ron 98
Kaze to Ki no Uta [The Poem of Wind and Trees] 147, 152–3
Keizi, Minami 44, 45–6
Kickstarter 38–9
Kinokuniya 12
Kinsella, Sharon 7, 79, 169
Kiyama, Henry Yoshitaka 69–70
Knights of the Zodiac, see *Saint Seiya*
Kobo 138
Kodansha 97, 98, 106, 122, 174
 Kodansha Comics 1, 99
kodomo (genre) 7, 169
komiks 10, 186–9
Kuroko's Basketball 129

ladies (genre) 7, 28, 169
Lang, Jeffrey S. 172
Last Hope 195
Le.Gardenie 10
LeGrow, M. Alice 98
Leitch, Thomas 179, 181
Lemon Law 86–9, **87**, **88**
Lent, John A. 9, 10, 186, 187, 188, 189, 194, 195
Leong, Sonia 11
Levy, Stu 6, 33–4, 98
licensing 140–43
Lie, John 103
light novels 23, 104
Lijewski, Christy 43
Lilientod 153, 154, 156
Liwayway 186–7, 188
Lopes, João H. 49
Lopes, Paul 168, 173
Losing Neverland 153, 154, 156
Luyten, Sonia B. 49, 122
Lyga, Scott 56, 66–9

Mach GoGoGo, see *Speed Racer*
Magazine Z 174

magical girls 24, 28; see also *Sailor Moon*
Malone, Paul M. 85, 86, 148, 150, 151, 157–8
Manga Fellowship Program 122–3
Manga Fieber [Manga Fever] 151
Manga Nouvelle Vague, see Nouvelle Manga
Manga Shakespeare 11
Manga Tropical 49, 52
Mangaholix 192, 194, 195
Mangaverse: Eternity Twilight 175, **178**, **180**, 181
manhua 9–10, 104, 170
manhwa 5–6, 15, 98, 104, 170
Marcelino, Ramon R. 186, 187, 188, 189
Marie, Michel 125–6
Marvel 10, 14, 26, 35, 36, 41, 55, 99, 129, 175–81
Massee, André 80, 81, 83
Matsumoto, Taiyo 123
Mazinger Z 189
MBQ 4, 5, 98
McDonaldization 84
McCloud, Scott 77, 122, 171, 192
McGray, Douglas 5, 75–6
McLelland, Mark 76, 86
mecha 55, 66, 135, 177, 189–90, 194
Media Blasters 34
Megatokyo 38, 97
Mikhailova, Yulia 168
Miller, Ann 115, 121
Miller, Frank 55, 169, 171, 174
Minzpyjama **87**, 89
Mixx Entertainment, see Tokyopop
Miyazaki, Hayao 76
Moé 7
Moliné, Alfons 115, 121, 122
Monte, Sandra 48–9
Morning (magazine) 122
Ms. 13-Dot 9
Müller, Ego 78

Nagado, Alexandre 46, 49
Nakayoshi 24

INDEX

Nakazawa, Keiji 97
Nananan, Kiriko 117
Napier, Susan J. 75, 78
Naruto 1, 129, 169
Neaud, Fabrice 117–19
New Historicism 152
Ng, Wai-ming 9, 10
Ngai, Sianne 84
Ninja Diaries 195
Ninja High School 35
No Man's Land 98
Noh, Sueen 9
Noppe, Nele 91, 150
Norris, Craig 11
Northrop, Sandy 168
Nouvelle Manga
   manifestos 117, 121–5
Nouvelle Vague [New Wave] cinema
   115–16, 125–7
Nye, Joseph S. 76

Off*Beat 38, 43
Oh No! Manga 195, **196**
Okura, Atsuhisa 149
O'Malley, Bryan Lee 14, 56, 57–65, **62**
One Day Isang Diwa [One Day, One Spirit] 190, **191**, 195
One Piece 129
Oni Press 56
Oost West [East West] 81–4, **82**
Orientalism 75
Original English Language (OEL)
   manga 2, 4, 10, 11, 13, 16, 35, 55, 95, 97–9, 134
   origin of terminology 97
O'Rourke, Dan 175
Otakon 109
Otaku 63, 76, 107
Otmazgin, Nissim Kadosh 5
Ozaki, Minami 79

PageFlip Publishing 12–13
Pagliassotti, Dru 10
Palabay, Jescie 190

Pan Juvenil Company 47
Panini (publishing house) 50
Pantoja, Tintin 195–7
paratexts 14, 56, 58, 64–5, 69
Park, Judith 12
Pattillo, Lissa 41
Peepo Choo 4, 5
Pellitteri, Marco 11
Perfect Commando Productions
   140–43
Peters, Martina 153, 154, 156–7, 169
Pini, Wendy 97, 99
Plaka, Christina 12, 151
Poincelet, Frédéric 117
Pokémon 34, 83, 84
politique des auteurs [policy of authors]
   126–7
Ponent Mon 119, 123, 124
Power Rangers 49
Pretty Guardian Sailor Moon, see *Sailor Moon*
Princess Ai 6
Project A-Ko 29
Prough, Jennifer S. 4

Quelques Jours en France [A Few Days in France] 129
Questor 192
Quick, Jenn Lee 38, 43

Ranma ½ 34, 69–70, 99
Ranz, Olalla Hernández 116
Read, Herbert 128
Reeder, Amy 36
rem 36, **42**
Rising Stars of Manga Contest 34, 35, 98
Ritzer, George 84
Rizal, Jose P. 186, 193
Rodrigues, Pravin A. 175
Rogalski, Olga 151
Rosca, Madeline 11
Ross, Sharon Marie 77
Ryan, Marie-Laure 171

Saffell, Steve 179
Said, Edward, W. 75
Sailor Moon 15, 24–34, 48, 81, 85, 106, 151, 156
Saint Seiya 45
Sampa 49
Sandman 55, 99
Santos, Carlo 97, 103
Sato, Francisco N. 48
scanlation 2, 39, 115
scenario-dispositif [scenario-device] 126–7
Schneider, Greice 115, 121
Schodt, Frederik L. 6, 109, 149
Schwark, Mike 98
Schwarzer Turm 85
Scoble, Rebecca 41, 99
seinen (genre) 7, 34, 169; *see also* gekiga
SelfMadeHero 11, 98
Seto, Claudio 45, 46, 47–8
Seven Seas 11, 98, 104, 195–7
Sharknado 140–43
Sheringham, Michael 121
Shimamoto, Julio 46, 48
Shimizu, Isao 6
Shinshokan 6, 9
shotacon 12, 86, 156
Shogakukan 1, 5, 98
Shotarou Complex, *see* shotacon
shounen ai 147, 156; *see also* boys' love; gloBL; yaoi
Shounen Jump 101
Shounen King 173
Shounen Magazine 173
Shueisha 1, 98
Sindram, Fahr 153, 154, 155–7, 159
Sison, Kriss 195
Sky Doll 79–80
    Space Ship Collection 80
Smile (magazine) 97
Smith, Felipe 4, 5, 10, 98, 103, 106
Smits, Ivo 75
Sousa, Mauricio de 14, 52–3
Sparkler Monthly **42**, 43

Speed Racer 195
Spider-Man 35, 57, 170, 173–4, 175
Stein, Daniel 171, 175, 179
story manga 7
Studio Kôsen 43
Studio Proteus 35
Sugiura, Tsutomu 5
Sushi Girl 97–8
Sweatdrop Studios 11
SyFy Channel 141–3

Takahama, Kan 117
Takahashi, Rumiko 69–70
Takemiya, Keiko 147, 153
Tan, Budjette 195
Taniguchi, Jirô 117
Tankoubon 86, 170
Tavicat 98
Tezuka, Osamu 6, 52–3, 63, 76, 109
Thompson, Jason 149
Thompson, Jill 55
Thompson, John B. 8, 11
Thorn, Matthew 86
Tokyopop 1, 2, 5, 6, 11, 16, 25, 33, 34–6, 37, 38, 39, 41, 43, 95, 97–9, 104–6, 151, 154–5, 175, 176
Toma no Shinzou [The Heart of Thomas] 147
Toronto Comic Arts Festival 43
Tsai, Chin Chia 9
Tseng, Chi-Shoung 9
transcreation **178**, 178–81, **180**, 182
transculturalism 75, 76, 77–9, 82–3, 90, 122–3, 148, 150, 157, 160, 163, 167, 172–5, 178–81
transmedia 76, 77–9, 83
Trifonova, Temenuga 116, 120, 125
Trimble, Patrick 172
Truffaut, François 126
Tumblr 157, 161
Turda, Michael 192
Turma da Mônica Jovem [Monica Teen] 52
Twilight 8, 26, 31, 36, 99

INDEX

Ultraman 173
Unearthly 195

Valaskivi, Katja 5
Vampire Knight 147, 153
Vampire Princess Miyu 101
Van Von Hunter 98
Velasquez, Tony 185, 186–7
Vergara, Carlo 195
Vieceli, Emma 11
Vitangcol, Ace 195
Viz Media 1, 16, 34–5, 37, 98
Vollmar, Rob 12, 116
Voltes V, see *Choudenji Mashiin Borutesu V* [Super Electromagnetic Machine Voltes Five]

Warren, Adam 35
webcomics 37–40, 49–50, 99, 138, 197
Whiting, Robert, *see* Guy Jeans
Who Is AC? 197
Wolferen, K.G. van 75
Wong, Benny 10
Wong, Wendy Siuyi 9

Wright, Bradford W. 172

X-Men 57, 129, 170, 174, 175, 182
Xu, Yanrui 9

Y Square 12
Yabu, Fábio 49
Yamanaka, Chie 9
Yang, Ling 9
yaoi 77, 81, 84–9, 197; *see also* boys' love/BL (genre); gloBL; shounen ai
Yaoi Press 98
Yonen Buzz 12
Yonkoma 80
Yoo, Soo-Kyung 9
Yoon, Yeowon 9
Yoshihara, Mari 14
young adult (YA) fiction 26, 29
Yukiko no Hourensou [Yukiko's Spinach] 116, 125
yuri 77, 81, 86, 89

Zetsuai 1989 79
Zimmermann, Detta 151